Business Intelligence For Dummies

W9-CCH-715

Business Intelligence Insights

Business intelligence insights may come in a variety of forms:

- Query responses: raw data produced by the BI system, allowing the user to draw immediate conclusions.

- Reports: structured and formatted data, built as part of a scheduled event, or on the fly as an ad hoc report.

- Derived Analysis: Insights produced by interpretation of a front-end system's output, after that application has applied rules, heuristics, other business information, and context to it, such as in a dashboard or scorecard.

Key Steps of KPI Cycle

Business intelligence is a process that allows businesses to create clarity around their strategic approach by determining key performance indicators (KPIs). Level of success in any business endeavor can be measured or quantified in some way:

Step 1: Build or define the core business strategy or objectives.

Step 2: Specify progress metrics (KPIs), and define thresholds that indicate degrees of success.

Step 3: Measure performance over time as a baseline.

Step 4: Adjust tactics and gauge correlative changes in success metrics.

Step 5: Apply lessons to subsequent strategy definition.

But business intelligence is very much a cultural phenomenon; moving away from gut-feel strategic choices, and moving toward an evidence-driven rational approach to business.

Vendor Web Sites

Microsoft: http://www.microsoft.com/sql/solutions/bi/default.mspx

Oracle: http://www.oracle.com/solutions/business_intelligence/index.html

SAP: http://www.sap.com/platform/netweaver/components/bi/index.epx

IBM: http://www-306.ibm.com/software/data/db2bi/data-warehousing

Business Objects: http://www.businessobjects.com

Cognos: http://www.cognos.com

Pentaho: http://www.pentaho.org

Microstrategy: http://www.microstrategy.com

Netezza: http://www.netezza.com

Teradata: http://www.teradata.com

SPSS: http://www.spss.com

Information Builders: http://informationbuilders.com

SAS: http://www.sas.com/technologies/bi

Common Operational Data Sources

Mainframe legacy systems: large central computing and storage environments known for their ability to process and harbor enormous quantities of data. Mainframes still form the foundation of many companies' data centers. Their data is notoriously difficult to get to as many of the legacy applications are obsolete, proprietary, or pre-standards software.

- Enterprise Resource Planning (ERP): often implemented throughout the organization in modules that map to specific business domains such as supply-chain, human resources, finance, accounts payable, and so on, ERP systems store a lot of transactional data used in today's BI environments.

- Customer Relationship Management: a common data source for business intelligence, CRM systems do just what they say: they process and store customer profile and behavior information, like purchase activity.

- E-Commerce: Web applications can act as source data systems for business intelligence platforms by feeding real-time sales activity.

Business Intelligence For Dummies®

Common BI Applications

Vendor	Source Data	ETL, Data Integration, Warehousing	Query and Analysis	Reporting, Information	Other Front-End Tools	Specialty Apps
Microsoft	SQL Server, Access	Integration Services aka SSIS (formerly known as DTS)	SQL Server Analysis Services, Access, Excel	SQL Server Reporting Services, Access	Excel Pivot Tables, Performance Point 2007 (enterprise scorecarding)	MS Sharepoint Server 2007 (report distribution)
Oracle	Oracle 11g	Warehouse Builder	Warehouse Builder, Oracle Hyperion Essbase Discover 10g	BI Suite Enterprise & Standard Editions: query, analysis, reporting, Siebel Answers, Interactive Dashboards Discover 10g	Oracle Data Mining	Business domain operational analytics applications, Hyperion System 9 Financial Management, Financial Planning
SAP		SAP BW	Netweaver BI	Netweaver BI	Netweaver BI	ERP Software, Financial Analytics (formerly Outlooksoft)
IBM	DB2	DB2 Data Warehouse, Warehouse Manager WebSphere DataStage (ETL) IBM Information Server	Various	BIRT, Design Studio, Alphablox	IBM Intelligent Miner (data mining)	Websphere Content Discovery (unstructured search)
Business Objects		Business Objects XI R2: Data Integrator (ETL) Data Federator (virtualization) Rapid Marts (standard platform data marts)	Business Objects XI R2: Web Intelligence (query tool) Voyager (OLAP) Desktop Intelligence (query tool)	Crystal Reports	Crystal Xcelsius (visualization tools), Crystal Vision (dashboard), InfoView (BI portal)	Information OnDemand (hosted BI solutions), Performance Management (Formerly Cartesis)

For Dummies: Bestselling Book Series for Beginners

Business Intelligence

FOR

DUMMIES®

Business Intelligence FOR DUMMIES®

by Swain Scheps

Wiley Publishing, Inc.

Business Intelligence For Dummies®

Published by
Wiley Publishing, Inc.
111 River Street
Hoboken, NJ 07030-5774
www.wiley.com

WILEY

About the Author

Swain Scheps is Manager of Business Analysis at Brierley + Partners, Inc. and a technology veteran making his first foray into the world of book authoring. He wrote the masterpiece resting in your hands with a great deal of input and inspiration from BI guru and fellow *For Dummies* author Alan R. Simon.

In the late 1990's Swain, along with most people reading this book, had his dot-com boom-to-bust experience with a company called. . .well, that's not really important now is it. (Anyone interested in buying some slightly under-water stock options should contact the publisher immediately.) After that there were consulting stints at Compaq, Hewlett-Packard, and Best Crossmark developing sales support applications and reporting tools. As of this writing, Swain basks under the fluorescent lights of Brierley, a technology company whose specialty is building customer relationship and loyalty management systems for retailers. The author has had the opportunity to learn from the very best as Brierley also provides unparalleled business intelligence and analytics services for its clients.

Swain lives in Dallas, Texas with wife Nancy and a mere four dogs. He writes about more than just technology; his work has appeared in Fodor's travel guide books, military history magazines, and even another *For Dummies* book.

Dedications

For Nancy and Marion M. "Turk" Turner and the rest of the crew of the submarine USS *Perch* (SS-176)

Author's Acknowledgments

BI belongs to the world, but this book, its concepts and arrangement, belong in spirit to technology author and BI guru Alan R. Simon. His ideas form *Business Intelligence For Dummies*' foundation, and his initiative led ultimately to its creation and publication. I was fortunate enough to have Mr. Simon's input and guidance throughout the writing process.

As is the case with any book, the creation of this one was an extended collaborative effort. It's a collection of ideas, definitions, anecdotes, examples, and practices from various points in the technology field. To write a book on BI requires putting a lot of thumbtacks into the virtual map; I cover a lot of ground in a number of subjects. Aiding that journey were Meg Dussault at Cognos and Steve Robinson at Autotrader.com.

I also owe a debt of gratitude for the BI team at Brierley + Partners, Inc that contributed advice and material for this book: Dominick Burley, Craig Nelson, Tim Lepple, and Jason Canada offered guidance on a number of topics. Others who helped and supported along the way were Jennifer Jaynes, Robert Owen, Pete Davies, and Bill Swift.

My friends and family have encouraged me throughout the process, offering inspiration, guidance, and support as I assembled this book. Mad props also go to Christopher Shope who donated his laptop, among other things, to this cause.

My agent Matthew Wagner has been a rock of stability in this occasionally tumultuous process. And I would be remiss if I did not mention my friend, mentor, and fellow *For Dummies* author Kevin Blackwood. He's helped in innumerable ways to get my writing habit pointed in the right direction. The extraordinarily patient team at Wiley also deserves a shout-out: Greg Croy, Pat O'Brien, Leah Cameron, Barry Childs-Helton, and others who toil behind the scenes to ensure there's plenty of black-on-yellow on everybody's bookshelf.

And finally a thank you goes to my beloved wife Nancy, who endured the better part of a year listening to the click-clicking of the keyboard and fielding my complaints and worries. Without her, this book — and all wonderful things in my life — would not exist.

Publisher's Acknowledgments

We're proud of this book; please send us your comments through our online registration form located at www.dummies.com/register/.

Some of the people who helped bring this book to market include the following:

Acquisitions, Editorial, and Media Development

Project Editor: Pat O'Brien

Acquisitions Editor: Greg Croy

Senior Copy Editor: Barry Childs-Helton

Technical Editor: Rick Sherman

Editorial Manager: Kevin Kirschner

Media Development Manager: Laura VanWinkle

Editorial Assistant: Amanda Foxworth

Sr. Editorial Assistant: Cherie Case

Cartoons: Rich Tennant (www.the5thwave.com)

Composition Services

Project Coordinator: Erin Smith

Layout and Graphics: Reuben W. Davis, Alissa D. Ellet, Melissa K. Jester, Shane Johnson

Proofreaders: Joni Heredia, Jessica Kramer

Indexer: Galen Schroeder

Publishing and Editorial for Technology Dummies

    Richard Swadley, Vice President and Executive Group Publisher

    Andy Cummings, Vice President and Publisher

  Mary Bednarek, Executive Acquisitions Director

    Mary C. Corder, Editorial Director

Publishing for Consumer Dummies

    Diane Graves Steele, Vice President and Publisher

    Joyce Pepple, Acquisitions Director

Composition Services

    Gerry Fahey, Vice President of Production Services

    Debbie Stailey, Director of Composition Services

Contents at a Glance

Table of Contents

Introduction

· ·

*L*et's get this joke out of the way right now. Business intelligence is indeed an oxymoron at many companies.

You've worked for that company before, or maybe you work there now. That company is a boat on top of an ocean of data that they're unable to dip their cups into and drink. And because they're so out of tune with the data flowing through their systems, they base their decisions on gut feel rather than facts and history. The most common analysis tool is a spreadsheet. They take wild stabs in the dark at what the long-term trends look like for sales, or profit, or some other measurement. And speaking of measurement, they often measure the wrong things entirely; they look at numbers that have little or no relationship to the long-term success of the business.

Welcome to *Business Intelligence For Dummies,* a book written for people in organizations that want to break the cycle of business stupidity. If you picked this book up off the shelf, you've probably heard of BI but aren't sure what it means. Sure, it's got the feel of another one of those techno-buzzwords that will fade out of fashion in a few years.

But BI is here to stay. And this book is for executives and managers dying to learn more about the technologies, tools, processes, and trends that make up business intelligence. It's for business people who need a way to derive business insights that are accurate, valuable, timely, and can be acted upon to positively influence the enterprise.

Maybe you've heard talk of BI in the hallways and want to learn more about it. Maybe you've come to the realization that more and more jobs require some knowledge of BI. Maybe somebody gave you this book for Christmas and you don't have the heart to ask for a gift receipt. No matter how you came by it, you'll learn a lot by reading it; there's a lot to know.

Be aware that if you're looking into how to spy on the company next door, if you want to talk into a shoe phone at the office, or you're looking for advice on how to dig through dumpsters to find clues about your competition, you'll want to move on down the shelf. We're not talking about *that* kind of business intelligence.

About This Book

This is a business book. Sure it's a book about technology, but it's not a highly technical book. It's not supposed to be. The whole idea is to make some fairly confusing topics accessible to the non pocket-protector set. If you're a Microsoft SQL Server administrator and you think this book is going to show you how to extend UDM with SSAS stored procedures, you're bound to be disappointed.

But that's what's so great about this book. It separates out the eye-crossing, head-scratching technical jargon and puts important technology concepts into terms most business people with a modicum of technical knowledge can understand.

How to Use This Book

If you don't know how to use a book, you're a long way from needing *business* intelligence, buddy. It's like other books; it's got a cover, chapters, pages, words, and an extraordinarily handsome and well-regarded author.

But I guess there are a few reading strategies that will suit you best depending on what you're looking to get out of *Business Intelligence For Dummies*. Consider these two pathways to BI enlightenment with this book:

- ✔ If you want to see a specific topic that's come up in conversation around the water cooler, or perhaps in a meeting, you can jump right to the chapter that covers it and start reading. For example, maybe there's been a lot of chatter about OLAP or Dashboards in the office and you've been nodding your head acting like you know what those words mean. I'd advise you to move quickly to the chapters covering those topics before someone learns your secret.

- ✔ If your agenda has more to do with getting the big picture, and you want to see BI's origins and context before moving through the topics, that works too. The chapters are self-contained vehicles of knowledge, but they are ordered in such a way that one BI topic blends nicely into the next. On the other hand, if you start reading about something that puts you to sleep or makes you mad, by all means write your Congressman a strongly-worded note, then skip ahead to the next chapter. Hey, you did it in high school when you had to read *A Tale of Two Cities*, so nothing's going to stop you from doing it here.

I would not, however, advise that you skip ahead to the last few chapters to see how the story turns out. Although the end of the book is riveting and ties up a few loose ends, it's not really that kind of book.

There are a few important related books that expand on some of the topics contained in this book. If you find the need for additional information, *Data Warehousing For Dummies,* (Wiley) is a few years old but provides a solid foundation of knowledge for data integration topics. Then there are the product specific books that touch on technical topics related to BI like Mark Robinson's *Microsoft SQL Server 2005 Reporting Services For Dummies.*

How This Book Is Organized

The information presented in this book is arranged into six self-contained parts, each of which comprises several self-contained chapters. It's like one of those Russian dolls, except painted yellow and black, and made out of paper instead of . . . well . . . whatever they make those dolls out of.

For most of the book, you'll be able to consume a chapter whole; I do my best to tell you everything you need to know inside each chapter without forcing you to save places throughout the book with various fingers and ad-hoc bookmarks. But I admit, on occasion I'll refer you to another area in the book because it's really important you understand where to get more information about a subject; but if you don't feel like being re-directed, just say no to cross-referencing.

Part I: Introduction and Basics

These early chapters are a primer on business intelligence. They lay the BI groundwork and will keep get you covered if you need a quick knowledge injection before you run to a meeting or an interview where the topic will come up. You'll see the one true definition of BI, at least according to me and a few thousand BI gurus. You'll also get to know BI's family tree, where it all began, and what related technologies you should get to know.

You'll be especially pleased at the easy-going language and tone of these chapters. Not much bits-and-bytes talk is necessary because, as you'll see in Part I, business intelligence is about business first, technology second.

Part II: Business Intelligence User Models

Unfortunately, you'll find out in Part II that a business intelligence environment doesn't just hum along quietly in the background like an air conditioner, spitting out business insights and cool air. BI joins powerful tools to the fingertips and eyeballs of people just like you, who go to work every day and need to make better business decisions, regardless of the scale or scope of those decisions.

Each of the main user application classes gets its own chapter here, from basic reporting and querying up to new-fangled technologies just now emerging into the market place.

Part III: The BI Lifecycle

More than anything, business intelligence is a process. It's about creating a culture that makes evidence-based rational decisions, that seeks out a clearer picture of its past and present. In this part we'll talk about what makes that process work well inside organizations, how a business intelligence culture gets planned, hatched, and how it grows and develops over time. You'll see what substrate works best for BI to take hold, and how to develop a sound business intelligence strategy. In the last chapter in this part, you'll get familiar with a BI roadmap, which sets you up nicely for the next part . . . read on!

Part IV: Implementing BI

This is how we do it. If you're a project manager or analyst of some kind, this part will warm the cockles of your heart. We're talking about building a sound project plan for your upcoming BI implementation and gathering — and managing — the functional and business requirements. If that sounds like any other IT project to you, you're half-right. BI projects share characteristics with other big technology efforts, but BI has its own special set of challenges for a project team to face down, and we'll talk about them here. Designing and building a BI environment is no easy task, but following up your initial success with ongoing victories is even harder.

Part V: BI and Technology

This is a special topics part, where we delve into areas that every budding BI guru should know about, but for the dabblers and dilettantes, they're on a need-to-know basis only. The BI universe tracks closely with that of data warehousing, and that topic gets covered in depth in this part of the book. It's also here that we start naming names, talking about who the big BI vendors are, what you should know about their products and services, and what they have to offer the market place.

Part VI: The Part of Tens

If you've never read a book in the *For Dummies* series, this will be a nice surprise. If you have read another book in the series, this part will be like seeing an old friend again . . . one who doesn't owe you money that is.

The Part of Tens, as always, is a collection of interesting BI topics, challenges, and warnings broken out into ten easy-to-digest chunks. There are ten keys to BI success, ten secrets to gathering good BI requirements and the like. These chapters are a good chance to test your knowledge after you've read the rest of the book, or a way to get a jolt of BI know-how if you haven't.

Icons Used in This Book

Look for those familiar *For Dummies* icons to offer visual clues about the kind of material you're about to read:

The best advice in the book is listed next to this icon. If you're thinking about a foray into BI, you're going to need it.

I can't quite recall what this icon means, but I think it has something to do with quickly revisiting an important BI concept. Don't forget to remember these things.

If BI was easy, every company out there would have implemented it long ago. This icon is the equivalent to a flashing red light on your dashboard. Ignore it at your own peril.

Every now and then I'm forced into some techie banter to add some color and background to a topic. You should try to read it one time, but don't get upset if it floats over your noggin at high altitude.

Time to Get Down to Business . . . Intelligence

If you feel the need for speed — getting up to speed on BI that is — you're off to a good start, so let's light this candle.

Now I'd like you to take a moment and go back and review the table of contents one more time. Just kidding! March onward. Start with the first page of Part I or flip to a random page and start reading to see if it makes the slightest bit of sense to you. I'll endorse whatever reading strategy you have in mind, just have fun. Oh what heights you'll hit, so on with the show, this is it. *Drumroll.* . . .

Part I
Introduction and Basics

The 5th Wave   By Rich Tennant

"Look—what if we just increase the size of the charts?"

In this part . . .

You've been running your lemonade stand for several years, and success has been an occasional visitor. This being the high-tech age, you've dutifully recorded business data of every kind since you started mixing sugar and water together; the daily sales, the employees who have come and gone, the customers who frequent your street corner, the supplies you buy once a week to mix your elixir.

So how can you put all that information to work for you? Some of the data's on your laptop, some of it's on your desktop at home, and a little bit of it is on your handheld. It would be nice to be able to look into the past and find meaningful insights about what's made your lemonade stand successful in the past, and what might make it more successful in the future. That might help make decisions easier.

You need a business intelligence solution. The chapters in this part will show you what BI is, how it's related to other technology areas, and how it can work for lemonade stands just like yours.

Chapter 1

Understanding Business Intelligence

From the CEO down to the lowest levels of any organization, every minute of the day someone is making a decision that has an impact on the company's performance. Sometimes a decision is at a very high strategic level that affects the fate of the entire organization, and other times a decision might be narrowly defined and tactical, affecting a single person or department for a very short window of time. When taken together, these decisions make up a significant portion of the "day in the life" at any given organization, be it a company, governmental agency, or nonprofit organization.

In spite of the dramatic advances in technology and tools that aid in the decision-making process, however, far too many people still make decisions the old-fashioned way: by blending a gumbo of tidbits of current information, best recollections of the past, advice from others, and a whole lot of "gut instinct," and then assessing which path is likely to give the best possible outcome for the decision at hand.

Decisions drive organizations. Making a good decision at a critical moment may lead to a more efficient operation, a more profitable enterprise, or perhaps a more satisfied customer. So it only makes sense that the companies that make better decisions are more successful in the long run.

That's where business intelligence comes in.

Business intelligence is defined in various ways (our chosen definition is in the next section). For the moment, though, think of BI as using data about yesterday and today to make better decisions about tomorrow. Whether it's selecting the right criteria to judge success, locating and transforming the appropriate data to draw conclusions, or arranging information in a manner that best shines a light on the way forward, business intelligence makes companies *smarter*. It allows managers to see things more clearly, and permits them a glimpse of how things will likely be in the future.

Limited Resources, Limitless Decisions

All organizations, whether business, government, charitable, or otherwise, have limited resources for performing their missions. Companies are forced to make do with what they have — all the time. You can't put a Nobel laureate in every position, and you can't pour unlimited dollars into an endless quest to make all your factories and offices more efficient.

The most precious resource is *time*. The marketplace is in constant motion, and companies must not only move correctly, they must move quickly. Otherwise competitors will fill any available vacuum in the market, resources will get used up, and your organization will inexorably wither away.

Business intelligence's entire *raison d'être* (that's French for "shade of lipstick" — just kidding) is as an ally at those inflection points throughout the life of a business where a decision is required. Business intelligence is a flexible resource that can work at various organizational levels and various times — these, for example:

- ✔ A sales manager is deliberating over which prospects the account executives should focus on in the final-quarter profitability push

- ✔ An automotive firm's research-and-development team is deciding which features to include in next year's sedan

The Name Game

Business intelligence is commonly known simply as BI. That's pronounced "Bee Eye," not "Buy." We'll go back and forth in this book between the full phrase and the abbreviated name. And if you're wondering why there aren't any periods in the acronym (as in, "B.I.") it's because of a custom in the technology world: Once a concept has gained widespread acceptance and becomes known by its initials alone, the punctuation disappears.

Extracting periods from techno-acronyms (CPU, GB, ICBM, whatever) is the mission of the International Punctuation Review Board, a group of Internet billionaires, former ambassadors, and high school football coaches who meet in Geneva every four years to review which new buzzwords qualify for punctuation-free status. (Just kidding. Everything about acronyms in the *previous* paragraph is true but the Board doesn't really exist. Yet.)

✔ The fraud department is deciding on changes to customer loyalty programs that will root out fraud without sacrificing customer satisfaction

The decisions can be strategic or tactical, grand or humble. But they represent two roads diverging in a yellow wood: Considered in the aggregate, the roads taken and those not taken represent the separation between successful and unsuccessful companies. Better decisions, with the help of business intelligence, can make all the difference.

Business Intelligence Defined: No CIA Experience Required

So what the heck *is* business intelligence, anyway? In essence, BI is any activity, tool, or process used to obtain the best information to support the process of making decisions.

Right now you're scratching your head and wondering, "Does he really mean *anything*?" And the answer is a qualified yes. Whether you're calling the Psychic Hotline, using an army of consultants, or have banks of computers churning your data; if it helps you get a better handle on your company's current situation, and provides insight into what to do in the future, it's BI.

But by popular demand (and so I don't have to write a chapter called "Using a Magic 8-Ball for Improved Portfolio Risk Management") we'll narrow the definition just a tad. For our purposes, BI revolves around putting computing power (highly specialized software in concert with other more common technology assets) to work, to help make the best choices for your organization. Okay, there's a little more to it than that. But before digging into specifics, it is (as the Magic 8-ball would say) decidedly so that you should understand some context about how BI is defined, and who's defining it.

The more you learn about BI, the more likely you are to encounter a wide swath of definitions for the term. Sometimes it seems as if nearly every new article on BI characterizes it in a new way. BI invariably gets unceremoniously tagged with an array of newfangled labels and connected with a whole catalog of different technologies that can leave your head spinning as you try to peg which elements are included in the definition and which ones aren't.

And it's no mystery why there is no single definition for business intelligence. Vendors and consultants define the phrase in a way that conveniently skews toward their particular specialty. Academics, authors, and consultants also have their own pet definitions of BI; one may barely resemble the next.

Don't get knocked off course. Regardless of who's saying it, when you put BI on a stove, turn the heat up, and boil it down to its constituent elements, you'll always find the same thing left in the pot: technology and tools to support decision-making.

For the purposes of this book, and for your needs beyond this book, you'll only need to know this one single definition (drum roll, please):

Business intelligence is essentially timely, accurate, high-value, and actionable business insights, and the work processes and technologies used to obtain them.

If you look up *actionable* in the dictionary, you see it actually means any deed that might cause you to get *sued;* here *action* refers to *legal* action. But feel free to use this specialized meaning of "actionable" with BI-savvy pros such as techies and finance folks. Just don't use it when you're talking to an attorney (unless, of course, you're a partner in the same law firm).

Contrary to what you may have been led to believe, there are no stone tablets with a single list of processes, protocols or hardware/software combinations that define BI once and for all. In technology, those things are always evolving. And they are often different from company to company, and different depending on the situation. Today's common definitions of the essential BI components are markedly different from the definitions bandied about in the 1990s. What remains constant, though, is that BI's purpose has always been to produce *timely*, *accurate*, *high-value*, and *actionable information*.

Pouring out the alphabet soup

If you think BI's definition sounds a little familiar, it's not just a case of *déjà vu* (that's French for "I've had this head cold before"). The concept of BI is not necessarily new; companies have been trying for years to press their systems into service to produce better strategic insights. You might have come across some of these acronyms in your past.

- **DSS**: Once upon a time, a company was in need of systems that would support the decision-making process. The IT crew got together and came up with Decision Support Systems. Pretty clever, eh? DSSs gained popularity by helping managers apply computing power and historical data to structured problems, such as production scheduling and other types of recurring planning decisions.

- **EIS:** The corner-office gang took notice of the success of DSS and decided that just like executive bathrooms, they deserved their own decision-management tools, and Executive Information Systems (EIS) technology was born.

> ✔ **MIS, MDS, AIS, and so on:** Plenty of other BI predecessors came and went — Management Information Systems, Management Decision Systems, Analysis Information Systems, and so on, and each one laid claim to some new style of supporting companies' decision-making processes.

Business intelligence has a big family tree. All of these technologies contributed to today's incarnation of BI, some more than others. And some of the disciplines and movements that warranted their own acronyms still exist today — in some cases calling themselves "next-generation BI" or, at the very least, "extenders" of BI.

There are several forces driving the multiple incarnations of what is basically the same idea. First, there is a motivation among vendors and IT consultants to mint a phrase that catches on in the technology world. Doing so helps set them apart from the competition (as if they've invented a better mousetrap).

Perhaps more important — and more cynical — is the tendency within the technology world to sheepishly leave behind heavily hyped initiatives that don't quite live up to the buzz in their initial go-around. For example, earlier generations of DSS and EIS often suffered from the same shortcomings that affected all types of technology implementations in that era. The unknowns of cutting-edge technology, the unpredictability of organizational politics, and other deficiencies sabotaged early implementations. The ideas were sound, but the failures gave the specific concept being adopted a bad reputation.

But the underlying concepts would always survive. After all, who could argue with the value of using high-power computing to support decisions? What executive wouldn't want to put IT resources to work delivering valuable information to the office every day? And so, as memories of past failures faded, new ways of thinking evolved — and more advanced technologies came along — those same vendors and consultants would leave behind the now-tainted label, coin a new term, and begin selling the "new and improved" solution.

A better definition is in sight

It might be useful to take a quick second look at the term *insight*. Insights are the ultimate destination for the many roads that all those authors, consultants, vendors, and various other nerds will send you down when you embark on a BI project. "Insight" does a good job of encompassing the deliverables that flow forth from a good BI project. Imagine those as the glowing light bulbs that appear over your head about some aspect of your business. Insights are a new way to look at things, a moment of clarity, a way forward. When BI delivers a business insight, you've divined some fact or hypothesis about some aspect of your organization that was previously hidden or unknowable.

Insights is actually a more intelligent word than . . . well . . . *intelligence.* After all, "intelligence" can mean so many different things, depending on the context. So the next time you think about BI and an instant of confusion obscures its definition from you, it helps to mentally substitute the word *insights* for *intelligence* and just attach BI to the phrase *business insights.*

But the good news is, with the kind of BI we're describing here, you don't *have* to play James Bond to improve your market position. With the real business intelligence, there are no double agents, no foreign sports cars, and the word "detonator" will never be relevant (unless your project goes *very* poorly.) BI is kind of like spying — but only if spying on *yourself* counts.

If your BI project goes well, you can ask your boss to start calling you "Q".

BI's Big Four

So what do we mean when we talk about insights that are accurate, valuable, timely, and (benignly) actionable? As you dig into BI's main characteristics, you'll see why each is so important to the process. In fact, if the knowledge gained from BI fails to meet any of the four criteria, the process has failed.

Accurate answers

When decisions are taken in your organization they are inevitably informed with conclusions drawn by a range of experts using important pieces of information about the enterprise's current state. For BI to be of any value in the decision making process, it must correctly reflect the objective reality of the organization, and adhere to rigid standards of correctness. As such, the first hallmark of insights produced from BI processes is their accuracy.

As with any technology-related tool or process, the GIGO rule is in full effect with BI — that's Garbage In, Garbage Out. GIGO says that if the BI insights are not accurate, the decisions made are less likely to be the correct ones for your enterprise. Imagine a sample BI report that shows one of the company's sales territories lagging woefully behind the others. When folded into the decision-making process, that piece of knowledge might well lead executives to adjust the sales process (or perhaps the personnel). But if the picture is wrong — say the offices and departments were incorrectly aligned to the various territories, so sales dollars weren't correctly allocated — then the conclusions (and the resulting actions taken) not only fail to help the company, they might actually make things worse.

Getting it right is important from a political perspective as well. For BI to have an impact, company *stakeholders* (those key employees whose business domains affect, and are affected by, BI) must trust it. Nothing's more frustrating in the world of business intelligence than a development team toiling for months to produce a report that an executive looks at and, within 30 seconds, dismisses it by saying, "Those numbers aren't correct."

But such things are common. After all, BI insights are often surprising, counterintuitive, and even sometimes *threatening* to groups within an organization. The sales manager who is shown numbers that indicate her team is lagging behind will be motivated to find ways to challenge the validity of the report. Any errors, no matter how small, will call into question the veracity of the conclusions drawn from the data.

BI must represent the absolute closest thing to the truth that's possible, not only to produce results, but to protect its reputation among the skeptics! Without accuracy, insights that are the product of BI are worse than worthless. They can be harmful to the company. And once that happens, nobody will ever trust BI again.

Valuable insights

Not all insights are created equal. Imagine, for example, that after a multimillion-dollar BI-driven probe of sales-history data, a grocery store chain finds that customers who bought peanut butter were also likely to buy jelly.

Duh.

BI insights like this are certainly accurate, but they are of limited value to the decision makers (who probably know that most supermarkets place those two items close together already). Part of what distinguishes BI is that its goal is not only to produce correct information, but to produce information that has *a material impact* on the organization — either in the form of significantly reduced costs, improved operations, enhanced sales, or some other positive factor. Further, high-value insights usually aren't easily deduced — even if data-driven analysis weren't readily available.

Every company has smart people working for it who can connect the obvious dots. BI insights aren't always obvious, but their impact can be huge.

On-time information

Have you ever had a heated discussion with someone and thought of the perfect retort to their witless argument exactly five minutes after you walk away from them?

The French call this phenomenon *"esprit d'escalier —"*(the spirit of the staircase). You never think of your best comeback until you've left a person's apartment or office and are walking down the stairs in defeat.

The lesson is simple: What makes people effective in a debate is that they can not only deliver sound information, they can do it at the precise time it's needed. Without timeliness, great verbal pugilists like Oscar Wilde or Cicero would have gone down in history as nothing more than good (but obscure) writers full of *esprit d'escalier*.

In business, information delays can make just as big a difference — and they can come in many forms:

- Sometimes it's a technology problem where the hardware or software can't compute fast enough to deliver information to users.

- Sometimes the problems relate strictly to workflow and logistics; the data isn't fed into the systems often enough.

- Logistics problems can pop up from time to time — for instance, what if a report has to be translated into a different language?

Every step in the process takes time, whether it involves microchips or humans. In the aggregate, those time intervals must be small enough to make the output of a BI process still relevant, useful, and valuable to a decision maker.

Timeliness is as important a quality in your business insight as any other. The best decision support processes involve up to the minute information and analysis made available to decision makers in plenty of time to consider all the courses of action. Stock traders at hedge funds use massive spreadsheets full of constantly updated data. The data streams in and is manipulated in a series of processes that makes it usable to the trader. He or she buys and sells stocks and bonds using the results of those calculations, making money for the firm and its clients. If the trader's applications were slower in producing translated data, they would miss opportunities to execute the most profitable trades and their portfolios would start to look like ones the rest of us have.

Actionable conclusions

Accurate is one thing, actionable is another. Imagine if the conclusions reached at the end of the BI cycle were that the company would be better off if a competitor would go out of business, or if one of its factories were 10 years old instead of 30 years old.

Those ideas might be accurate — and it's no stretch to believe that if either scenario came to pass, it would be valuable to the company. But what, exactly, are the bosses supposed to do about them? You can't wish a competing company out of business. You can't snap your fingers and de-age a factory. These are exaggerated examples but one of the biggest weaknesses of decision support tools is that they build conclusions that are not *actionable*. To be actionable, there has to be a feasible course that takes advantage of the situation. It has to be possible to move from conclusion to action.

Ideally, the BI team at your company would produce a report that would guide future actions. The executives would conclude that a price should be lowered, or perhaps that two items should be sold as a package. These are simple actions that can be taken — supported by BI — to improve the position of the company. In BI-speak, that means insights must be *actionable*.

The BI Value Proposition

BI links information with action inside an organization. But because of the confusion over defining BI, it's not always clear where the value of a BI solution lies. What exactly do businesses *get* from a BI implementation? If you're thinking about BI, you're naturally wondering "What's in it for me?"

The answer is that when companies utilize BI, they don't just have a swell new toy for the IT team to deploy, or a snazzy new report or data store. Sure, it can be all of those things, but more than anything, the BI value comes from promoting good decision-making habits.

Encompassing BI is a rational approach to a continuous improvement loop:

1. Gathering data

2. Making decisions and taking action based on that data

3. Measuring the results according to predetermined *metrics* (a fancy word for measurements) for success

4. Feeding the lessons from one decision into the next

By using a continuous cycle of evidence-based actions, organizations adopt a rational approach to their decision-making process — and BI can support that cycle. Figure 1-1 shows how this continuous loop can work. Through business intelligence concepts and tools, companies glean meaningful insights from their operational data. If the insights fit the four criteria of BI (remember: *timely, accurate, high-value,* and *actionable*) the company can apply them to its regular decision-making process. Those decisions, now informed with BI insights, lead to actions — and, if all goes well, improved operational results. (Don't lose sight of the fact that improved results are what this is all about). And so the cycle begins anew; the first round of results becomes part of the historical data record, and the related BI insights are refined even further.

The process of using data to make better decisions can involve just about any piece of an organization. If there are lessons to be learned from operational data, be it customer behavior, financial information, or another category, BI can play a part. By using BI practices to transform raw data into meaningful conclusions, a team makes better decisions. The actions taken as a result of those decisions produce a new round of results — which can be fed back into the system as new empirical evidence to draw the next round of conclusions.

BI can improve any decision by supplying it with (everybody, now!) *timely, accurate, valuable,* and *actionable* insights.

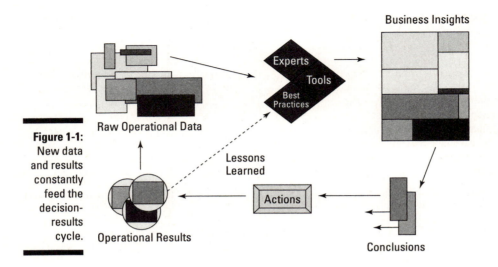

Figure 1-1:
New data and results constantly feed the decision-results cycle.

A Brief History of BI

Business intelligence is an approach to solving business problems. It's a framework for managing tactical and strategic operations performance. BI is only possible because of advances in a number of adjunct technologies, such as computing power, data storage, computational analytics, reporting, and even networking technologies. But its origins are definitely more humble. In this section we'll take a look at how BI evolved to where it is today.

Data collection from stone tablets to databases

From the beginning of history, organizations have always had a need to collect and store data. Several thousand years ago, there were armies and imperial bureaucracies, working out ways to collect taxes, feed people, wage wars, and so on.

The first recorded use of written language *was* data storage: Sumerian stone tablets that tracked shipments of wheat through the local granary.

Data storage started as a notion of faith, an act of foresight and planning by the world's earliest worry-warts and packrats. (It might not have seemed important to remember the names and hometowns of the soldiers in the Praetorian Guard of the Roman Empire, but somebody realized they'd get a lot better turnout at the 20-year reunion if they made an effort to collect and keep that information. That toga-wearing bureaucrat would have loved BI.)

Available research on BI

You can look up all kinds of research and white papers on the Internet to check out the impact of BI on business. But don't just skim through the study looking for the return-on-investment (ROI) number without understanding the context. Numerous important peer-reviewed studies show that BI projects have a positive ROI, provided they are done correctly, and with the proper goal in mind. When BI produces timely, accurate, high-value, actionable conclusions, and those conclusions are applied correctly, the ROI will be positive. But lots of things can go wrong along the way. For every BI success story, there are horror stories, just as you find with any other technology. So how do you do it *right?* How can you maximize ROI? Read on . . . .

Record-keeping really came into its own as better forms of paper were invented. It allowed for more information to be stored and accessed in a smaller space.

Reading a book written on stone tablets is a real pain in the neck.

From silicon in *stone* to silicon in *microchips,* that challenge continues to this day: storing more and more information in smaller and smaller space. The modern organization makes use of computer power for its data storage.

The growth of computing power and data storage

The first computers were tabulating machines, designed and built to perform one-off calculations. But scientists and inventors developed information-storage capability almost neck and neck with the growth of computing power. After the 1940s, both technologies exploded.

Mass storage began to take form when the properties of magnetic tape were used to store analog patterns of information. That turned to disk drives, a decades-old technology that is still in use today in a form that would be recognizable to its inventors, but on a scale that would blow their minds.

To manage the growing mountains of stored data, programmers developed Database Management Systems (DBMSs) of growing power and complexity. Relational database technology came about as a response to the increasing information-storage demands. This was a revolutionary way to maintain data that dramatically sped up transaction time by splitting data elements into their component pieces and storing those pieces separately.

Transactional systems

As computing systems became more powerful and ubiquitous, businesses began taking advantage of them to manage their daily transactions.

Point-of-sale (POS) systems are the classic example of a transactional system. A POS system has one main purpose: to allow sales reps to quickly enter sales transactions, collect payment, and issue a receipt to the customer for that purchase. Handily enough, if the POS is some kind of computer (rather than just a cash register that goes *cha-ching*) it can be connected with accounting systems that gather and organize sales information for later use.

Companies normally have many transactional systems, each one a source of its own unique kind of data, each one designed to perform one primary business role. Transactional systems help with the day-to-day operations of the company — for example, a system that tracks shipments between warehouses or handles customer billing.

The emergence of decision support

With so many disparate transactional systems, a company stores an enormous amount of data. It didn't take long before CEOs wanted to take a peek. After all, if they could see summaries of all that stored transactional data, they could gain insight on certain aspects of their business (say, how often shipments move between Warehouse A and Warehouse B, or what day of the week their customers are more likely to buy dessert). Examining transactional records in the aggregate seemed to offer a wellspring of good business insights. But no sooner did companies try it than a horde of problems sprang up — for example, these:

- The systems were often separated, not only physically, but perhaps also by separate storage protocols, naming conventions, or even political barriers within a company. That meant the analysis had to take place individually for each set of transactional records.

- Transactional systems such as the point-of-sale database were designed for speeding transactions along — not for doing research. Digging through the data to learn which products appealed enough to certain demographics to purchase at certain times of the year (or to unearth other such business insights) was undeniably useful, but a transactional system by itself was the wrong tool for that job. More powerful information systems were necessary to get the most out of the data.

In the late 1980s, companies began to recognize the potential value that the data represented. In response, they became motivated to build systems to extract the knowledge buried in their files. And so BI was born.

Business intelligence came to encompass the wide range of technologies, protocols, and practices that is required to produce valuable business insights. What BI actually means to one company may be different from what it means to another because every company represents a different situation, with different installed technology, and different needs. That's why business intelligence doesn't fit into a perfect definition you may have read on a vendor's website. BI means timely, accurate, high-value, and actionable insights . . . and whatever it takes to produce those insights.

BI in the by-and-by

As computing gets more powerful and software more useful, it seems BI — whether operating under its current name, or dressed up yet again as a "new" undertaking — will continue to increase in importance to large organizations. But look for it to take root in ever-smaller enterprises as well, as small businesses realize they can finally take advantage of the advancing technology.

The BI concept is a flexible organism that will undoubtedly grow and evolve in response to whatever direction the advancing technology may take it. Some near-term trends seem apparent:

✔ **Origins in various business units:** BI started as IT pet projects. After all, who else knew what was possible? But as executives and decision makers get used to thinking in terms of business intelligence, more (and bigger) BI initiatives will be driven by departments other than IT.

✔ **Analytics delivered to the desktop:** Vendors have created powerful add-ins to go with already-flexible and potent desktop tools (such as Microsoft Excel). Starting with MS Office 2003, continuing with Office 2007, advanced analytical tools will be available to just about everyone in the company who has a computer.

✔ **Following the data:** BI has traditionally been associated with data-warehousing technology (which we discuss in depth in the coming chapters). But future BI technology will be able, with increasing efficiency, to reach out into the source systems, grab data, and transform what it finds into what it needs to perform its analysis.

BI's Split Personality: Business and Technology

BI is built on the massive computing power available to today's enterprises. But it isn't just about bits and bytes. Business intelligence requires a company culture dedicated to the principles and practices that make high-quality, usable insights possible. Simply installing software and flipping a switch won't get a company to the promised land.

The commitment to BI has to come from both the business *and* technology sides of a business:

✔ Business managers must engender a rational, measurement-based approach to setting strategy and running operations.

✔ IT must be prepared to support the BI culture to the extent that business managers are prepared to push it into all levels of the company.

BI: The people perspective

Business intelligence is about giving people new tools and perspectives; it's designed to let decision makers ponder what-if questions. That only works if those decision makers are not only able to use the BI tools but are also prepared to ask the right questions.

That's where BI truly straddles the world between business and technology — it's both an art and a science. There is no set formula for determining the "right" reports and analytics for a particular company. No book explains every single possibility to consider in your analysis cycle.

What's required is putting the right kind of people in positions where BI is to play a role. Or the BI attitude must be spread by the company's leadership. BI is about a commitment to a rational approach to making decisions — and that approach must be supported at all levels of the organization, by IT executives and business executives.

So, Are You BI Curious?

Would your organization benefit from a business intelligence solution? There is no automatic answer to that question, but nearly every company can see improvement from adding some rigor to the decision-making processes. The following list of questions you might ask about your organization could indicate whether a BI approach makes sense:

✔ Can you view sales data in more than one view simultaneously? For example, if you wanted to see quarterly sales data by sales manager, product line, and customer type, how long would it take to produce the report?

✔ Is there data locked in transactional systems about your customers that you'd like to see but can't because the system just isn't designed to view the data the way you want?

✔ When your company makes strategic decisions, are you relying on hard data before you proceed or is it coin-toss time? Do you base your actions around evidence of the past and verifiable conclusions about the future? Do you consider statistical correlations between causes and effects? Or is it a seat-of-the-pants maneuver?

✔ You know what items your customers buy the most, but do you know what items your customers buy in *pairs*?

✔ Do you know what your company does best? How do you know it? Is it a gut feeling or do you have metrics to back up your conclusions?

Chapter 2

Fitting BI with Other Technology Disciplines

*I*n this section, we look at the most prominent technologies commonly associated with BI. Because these other classes of software are common in so many companies, it's important to understand how business intelligence is related to them. The associations — some casual, some arrangements of convenience — are of interest and importance to anyone considering a BI implementation.

These disciplines exist outside the immediate realm of BI — but in each case, business intelligence concepts and approaches have had a dramatic effect and helped the underlying technology round itself out into full form. The relationship between BI and each of these technologies is a two-way street. Each technology area has benefited from the BI process, and BI has grown and in response to the widespread adoption and evolution of these technologies — especially data warehousing, Customer Relationship Management, Point-of-Sale systems, and Enterprise Resource Planning.

Best Friends for Life: BI and Data Warehousing

Maybe you remember the old Reese's Peanut Butter Cup commercials featuring the inevitable collision between the person carrying peanut butter and the person carrying chocolate. "You got chocolate in my peanut butter!" the former would exclaim, followed by the other proclaiming "You got peanut butter on my chocolate!" After a moment of consternation they realized the wonder they had created by mixing those two essential substances of the universe together at last.

The collision of data-warehousing technologies with BI practices was a *Eureka!* moment for companies:

- ✔ Executives needed better access to the company's day-to-day data so they could evaluate conditions more accurately and make better decisions.
- ✔ The IT department was developing protocols and systems to bring widely dispersed and variable databases under one roof in order to run companywide statistical analysis and basic reporting.

When the two concurrent goals came together it was a chocolaty-peanut butter delight. (From a business perspective, anyway.)

Like Batman and Robin, BI and data warehousing are inextricably linked. The product of the two technology areas is more beneficial to companies than the sum of their parts. While each discipline is important in its own right, together they enable businesses to go beyond organizing operational data. BI and data warehousing make a transcendent combination — a powerful competitive weapon that can actually guide the business in ways previously considered impossible.

The data warehouse: no forklift required

The whole purpose of a BI implementation is to turn operational data into meaningful knowledge. That means BI must be connected with an organization's data to be effective. With data spilling out the doors and windows of any enterprise, the challenge is to put all the *necessary* data in one place, in one common format. Data warehouses are the perfect architecture to meet that challenge head on.

A *data warehouse* is a single logical (but not necessarily physical) repository for a company's transactional or operational data. The data warehouse itself does not create data; it's not a transactional system. Every byte of data inside the data warehouse has its origins elsewhere in the company.

So what data are we talking about then? Most enterprises produce data in a variety of different departments or domains; there might be transactional sales information coming directly in from a point-of-sale system (POS), customer data from a Customer Relationship Management System (CRM), and an endless variety of operational systems that help the run. The data dispersed throughout all these different applications is likely saved in a variety of formats, on a range of hardware — say, a dedicated storage network, a mainframe, a database server on the Web, or even on various desktops. It could be anywhere.

Data warehouses are different from standard transaction-based data-management systems. A data warehouse aggregates information about a single subject area — and management then uses that resource in one of two ways:

- ✔ to create focused reports on one aspect of the enterprise
- ✔ to query in order to gain insights on that subject

Both activities are read-only. That makes sense because typically no data is deleted from a data warehouse. Transactional systems, on the other hand, add, delete, and update the data they store.

Turning "apples-to-celery" into "apples-to-apples"

A data warehouse is a collection of data from different systems, focusing on one subject area. But because the data originates from a multitude of sources, it's going to be in different formats. Part of a data warehouse implementation involves manipulation — or transformation — of the data prior to storage so that it resides in a single common format.

Imagine you're merging phone lists from two different Excel spreadsheets. One lists names as "Smith, Jason E." and the other spreadsheet lists names in the format "Jason E. Smith". There are some names that appear on both lists, but some are unique to one list or the other.

After merging the two lists, you alphabetize them and look at a sample of the combined list:

Jacob Rogers	214-555-5406
Jacobs, Jeff Z.	972-555-9044
Jeff Z. Jacobs	972-555-9044
John A. Smith	214-743-0000
Johnson, Albert S.	817-342-4971

If you've merged the lists without transforming the data into a single format, the result is a unified — but confusing — list. First, how would you look someone up if you didn't know whether they are listed by their first or last name? Then there's the problems caused by duplicate entries. If one person is listed twice (once in each format), then you'll have problems if you need to update the person's information, to say nothing of the ambiguity in doing lookups. On top of that, you'll have trouble creating a simple summary report of this data; you know how many list entries there are, but how many unique *people* are there?

Data warehouses resolve differences

In the real world, data differences can go well beyond name-formatting on an Excel spreadsheet. Related data might be stored on completely different applications, in different storage media. Data might be missing or completely corrupted. Warehousing data can be an enormous task — you have to do three things to all that data from disparate sources:

- ✔ Put the information in a single format.
- ✔ Check for systemic data errors.
- ✔ Translate the data into useful units of knowledge.

In addition, your company may have organizational and geographical boundaries that separate information and prevent it from being used in concert with other key insights. So data warehousing technology must not only aggregate data of all flavors, it must also work with software and protocols that transform that data into common formats so information from one data source can be logically related to information from other data sources. Figure 2-1 shows a simple system where three different systems that collect similar data feed information into a data warehouse, which offers a single view of reality.

Say your company, Acme Lemonade Stands, keeps a central record of all customers who phone in delivery orders — including their full contact information and some basic data about their lemonade-buying habits. Out in the field at the sidewalk lemonade stands themselves, the cash register and the Point-of-Sale applications track each individual sales transaction at the counter. Then there's a billing system that handles invoicing to customers on account.

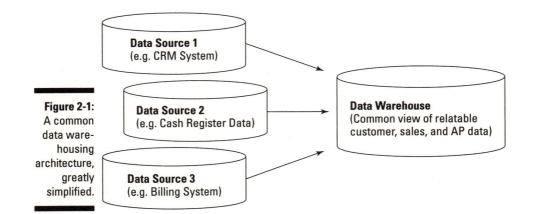

Figure 2-1: A common data warehousing architecture, greatly simplified.

Each of those databases is kept separate from the others in different parts of the company, on different platforms and systems, with different kinds of users and patterns of usage. What's more, those data storage systems are designed to fit their mission — to store transactional data quickly. That can cause a problem because those systems (and their attendant data structures) may not lend themselves to producing reports on performance metrics such as profitability by lemonade stand.

If your title starts with a capital letter C, you're probably going to want to view all that data together. After all, executives make strategic decisions about the direction of the company by getting an accurate picture of business performance in many areas. For example, the CEO of Acme Lemonade might like to know about the relationship between daily cash flow and invoicing, then tie it back to specific customers and customer types and adjust marketing strategy accordingly. Building a unified report like that would be difficult because the data resides in three different places. Without a data warehouse the CEO is out of luck.

If it sounds like we're edging closer to BI (*high-value, accurate* and *timely* business insights that we can use as the basis for an *action*), you're right, we are. Business intelligence and data warehousing are closely related because it is the single data store (the aggregation of disparate data sources) that allows BI processes to take place. When BI produces insights for a CEO about how the company is performing, it's because the technology under the hood has allowed all that different data to sit together in the same place and be *manipulable* (subject to being jiggered, tinkered with, and looked at).

All paths lead to the data warehouse

Companies store an incredible amount of operational data: sales transaction details, operational reports, personnel information, and accounting data, just to name a few. What used to involve rows of filing cabinets and enormous vaults of physical storage space can now be stored digitally. Just like that crazy great-aunt you have who hasn't come to terms with the fact that the Great Depression is over, companies are packrats about data, keeping everything they can think of.

For BI to work, it requires wide-open roads between the places where the data lives. There can't be barricades, checkpoints, or washed out bridges. When all of an organization's information is present, correct, and relatable to itself, BI can function at the highest level.

Data warehousing is a key technology for enabling BI. When you implement a data-warehousing solution, you've taken a significant step toward business intelligence. That's not to say you can't do data warehousing *without* BI —

many organizations do. For example, many companies utilize data- warehousing technologies and approaches to create Operational Data Stores — ODSs (okay, some purists argue that data warehouses and ODSs are very different — but we can let them argue). Where DW and BI are focused largely on management reporting for executives, the same aggregation of data can also be extremely useful for mid-level managers who keep track of operations.

Imagine a manager who wants to keep an eye on operations at the call center. The key to making this happen is data-warehousing technology that does its work in this sequence:

1. Brings in external data from different sources.

2. Transforms the data into a common format.

3. Cleans the data for any incorrect or missing data.

4. Correlates the calls and call durations with operational and transactional information from other parts of the company.

5. Produces regular daily reports that show the correlation.

 Data warehousing really pays off if it's a prelude to enabling a business intelligence solution. After the data is collected and the barriers between the islands of information are broken down, the next logical step is to build bridges between those islands that create meaningful corporate insights (yep — accurate, timely, material, and actionable).

ERP and BI: Taking the Enterprise to Warp Speed

From the advent of business computers, up through the late 1980s and early 1990s, the systems that drove and supported the enterprise were designed — and run — mostly independently of each other. Even systems that would naturally fit together — say, finance and accounting or supply chain and inventory — were built and operated as separate entities. In the early 1990s, companies began to see computing power as a way to integrate vast and diverse transactional systems. As a result, Enterprise Resource Planning (ERP) systems were born.

From mainframe to client/server

The computing power that originated most legacy software was centered on *mainframe computers* — gargantuan machines that existed in big rooms, or even took up entire floors of buildings. Their cousins, the minicomputers, had a similar role as centralized points for all of a company's processing. In those days, the IT staff consisted of as many electrical engineers as it did computer programmers — because the mainframes and minis were at least as much electromechanical machines as they were computers — and sometimes reprogramming meant rewiring.

By the late 1980s, *microcomputers* (which we know now as *personal* computers) were getting small and powerful enough to place on workers' desktops, bringing about the rise of the *client/server* model. That led to pulling tasks away from the legacy systems and pushing them to workers' desktops. It also meant great advances in networking protocols and practices, linking people and data together for the first time. This had some fantastic advantages in terms of individual productivity, flexibility, and scalability.

The term *legacy application* most commonly refers to older, mainframe-oriented data-processing software. IT managers who cut their teeth on the newer client/server architecture came to view older mainframe applications as dinosaurs, an inherited burden that had to be upgraded or replaced ASAP. But today, *legacy* has become a catchall pejorative that refers to *any* last-generation technology.

ERP came about as companies saw the need to integrate the core business computing systems to fit with their new client/server architecture. The battle cry arose: mainframe computing, with its magnetic tapes, punch cards, and outrageous electric bills, was dead. Why do data processing in one central place, they asked, when the work can be done on computers distributed throughout the business?

The great migration

The advantages of running ERP systems were clear. Workers could produce and consume data as never before. The old centralized data processing applications could now become more interactive, and customized to fit the company's needs. And yet the client/server architecture still provided centralized storage of information, which meant ERP applications could run and have everyone in a company looking at the same data.

SAP was first on the scene, but others quickly followed. PeopleSoft, Baan, Oracle, Lawson, and JD Edwards were all pioneers in client/server ERP. Salesmen from these companies fanned out across the country, into IT departments, all with the same promise on their lips: "You can do away with your big expensive mainframe computer systems." And the IT departments were listening.

SAP slurps up the ERP market

The company that is considered the founder of Enterprise Resource Planning software is the German firm SAP, founded in 1971. In 1973 they introduced R/1, an application that did something quite revolutionary for the day: It handled real-time processing of finance and accounting business functions. (In fact, the R stood for *real-time*). R/1 became R/2 in the early 1980s, which was the first true ERP suite. R/2 expanded its finance and accounting functions along with human resources and operations packages. For the first time, multiple departments (and physical locations) had a single view of company data. And SAP isn't just a pioneer from the old days. The company continues to be the market leader in ERP — having released R/3 in the early 1990s and building on the product from there — developing over 30,000 clients all around the world.

Like it's 1999: the Y2K catalyst

In the mid-1990s, computer nerds everywhere became aware of a problem brewing in the chips of companies everywhere around the world. No, the Master Control Program from *Tron* wasn't about to take over the world. It was much worse . . . .

The famous Y2K Bug

The *legacy systems* (old data-processing software that was still running on corporate mainframes and minicomputers) weren't designed to understand that the year after 1999 was 2000, not 1900. That's because these systems were only capable of tracking years in terms of two digits, so 1971 was represented as 71, 1999 as 99 — and when 99 turned to 00 in all those computers, would disastrous amounts of data disappear? Nobody knew.

When the legacy systems were developed in the 1960s (and 1970s in some cases), the new millennium seemed so far in the future that nobody thought the systems they were building would still be relevant and operating on December 31, 1999. Surprise: Much of the software written back then would become the basis for future generations of code. Programs would be reused, repurposed, and generally expanded upon with each successive release. There, lurking in the heart of every system that used that code — at the core of thousands of businesses across the world — was a simple and powerful bug that could bring factories, plants, and networks to a halt.

ERP saves the day

One solution to the Y2K problem was to have programmers dig through the old code and fix it. But this was time-consuming, expensive, and not guaranteed to work.

ERP companies offered a more complete solution to the problem: By completely replacing legacy systems with a unified set of ERP applications, companies could remove all doubt about Y2K. Not only that, but the new systems offered upgraded capabilities over the legacy systems.

The sales pitch (essentially "upgrade now or else") worked. The Y2K problem was a boon for ERP companies as organizations installed products from SAP, PeopleSoft, and the others at a record pace. Indeed, 1996 through 1998 proved record years for ERP vendors. (In case you're wondering, by 1999 sales had dropped off because companies had run out of time to begin new implementations.)

Cold war reporting

Legacy systems were designed for data processing — crunching numbers. As such, the reporting capabilities were minimal. Summoning information from data storage beyond the standard basic diagnostic and status reports produced after batch processes were complete required a Herculean effort by analysts and programmers.

In the early days of ERP, the focus was on merely replicating the core functionality of the legacy systems, so ERP software was relatively light on reporting capabilities. The systems may have been unified, but there usually was still a need to call in armies of programmers to hard-code custom reports against the transactional databases — just like before.

ERP leads to the foundations of BI

The weaknesses of hard-coding reports was apparent — as were the problems associated with trying to use data from live transactional and operational systems in queries and reports. These challenges led ERP companies to begin incorporating some basic data-warehousing approaches into the new unified suites of applications — in conjunction with some advanced reporting capabilities.

Now companies could truly have their cake and eat it too with their ERP systems:

✔ Their legacy systems all spoke the same language.

✔ The data warehouse aggregated the data.

✔ The new reporting tools made it easy to put the company's data under a microscope.

The foundation for BI was laid. Forward-thinking ERP vendors started adding powerful reporting and analytic packages to their application suites to add further value for their customers.

SAP was a trendsetter, introducing SAP BW in 1997. BW stands for *Business (Information) Warehouse,* a set of applications that offered customers advanced reporting and trend-spotting capabilities. And because BW was melded with the rest of the SAP application suite, clients could run the powerful BI tools against any set of data in the entire system — from manufacturing to sales. Business Warehouse was a sales success for SAP; other ERP vendors followed suit.

Customer's Always Right

Too bad the customer *data* isn't! (Well, at least some of the time.) And that challenge is why CRM was born.

CRM stands for *Customer Relationship Management.* It refers to software that handles all aspects of an organization's interactions with its customers. That may include the entire sales cycle, from winning new customers, to servicing and tracking existing customers, to providing post-sales services.

CRM joins ERP

CRM applications can touch lots of pieces of a business. Of course, the sales force itself relies heavily on robust CRM applications that can track leads, perform customer analysis, handle transactions and so forth. But beyond the sales force, CRM's tentacles reach into product management, inventory and procurement, accounting and finance, and others. Imagine using all that data about customer relationships to plan the use of enterprise resources. Some ERP vendors did. So, in the late 1990s, they began including CRM applications in their enterprise suites. PeopleSoft made its CRM play through acquisition when they acquired a CRM company called Vantive in 1999. Vantive was a *pure-play* CRM vendor; that's the only class of software they sold. Other ERP vendors, such as Oracle, built their application in-house.

Core CRM

Early CRM was always transactional in its approach, rather than analytical. The idea was to use technology to automate and facilitate the sales cycle as much as possible. So early incarnations of CRM would include features that tracked leads, scheduled sales operations, and recorded purchase history (along with other operational functions). But as CRM evolved, companies began to put greater demands on it to do more. Rather than just keep track of yesterday, CRM customers wanted the software to participate in the process — and help predict what customers were going to do.

Companies began to see the potential for expanding CRM's role as they looked at all their contact points with customers. Call centers were foremost among these contact points; there hundreds of customer-service representatives would work phone banks while sitting in front of the custom-built applications they used to perform order entry or trouble-ticket functions on behalf of customers.

Customer decisions

In the late 1990s, data-crunching capabilities were on the rise in other parts of the company, it was only natural that CRM systems would become more involved in decision-support processes.

E-commerce was also exploding in the late 1990s; the competitive fever required companies to wring every dollar they could from their online markets. That's when companies such as e.piphany came into being by merging traditional core CRM functions with BI-like analytical features and reporting capabilities.

Campaign management and more

Marketing was also transformed. Campaign management companies such as e.piphany guided their clients' marketing practices to make them more *customer-centric*. Yes, of course that's a silly tautological buzzword — customer-centric marketing . . . as if there's any other kind. But there is a germ of truth to it. Products from this new generation of CRM companies allowed analysis and integration of customer data in a way that companies had never done before.

That gave companies a new capability to create precision-guided campaigns, to tweak their sales cycles to fit perfectly with the kinds of customers they attracted. Companies could suddenly measure the effectiveness of their sales force in ways never before imagined, and it spawned entire new marketing practices like customer loyalty management, churn management (a.k.a. harassing existing customers to buy more), and customer reacquisition processes to help bring straying former customers back into the fold.

CRM with a scoop of BI on top

Now that CRM had gone beyond merely keeping track of what a sales force was doing — now that it was more than a fancy rolodex with customer names stored within — the applications sprouted wings and began delivering customer-focused analysis and reporting that created a new science of working with customers. Some of the new features included

---

Siebel comes full circle

In 1993, a former Oracle executive named Tom Siebel made a highly public (and sometimes acrimonious) break from Oracle to found Siebel Systems, which would go on to become the standard-bearer for CRM companies for years to come. After Siebel dominated that market for nearly a decade, other companies began to duplicate Siebel's CRM success — not only major industry players such as SAP and Microsoft, but also upstarts like e.piphany and Salesforce.com (a hosted CRM application). After several soap-operatic twists and turns, Oracle acquired Siebel for $5.8 billion. (Looks like you *can* go home again after all.)

- ✔ Campaign management
- ✔ E-mail marketing
- ✔ Real-time personalization
- ✔ Demand-chain and collaborative marketing

Of course, all was not perfect. Many of the new-generation CRM companies would die the same death as the most frivolous of dotcom companies. But even though the profits weren't always there, the value had been demonstrated. BI was here to stay in the realm of managing customer relationships.

BI-BUY! E-Commerce Takes BI Online

Like the early CRM software, the original e-commerce applications were simple. Their one-dimensional functionality was good for facilitating fairly rudimentary business transactions over the Internet — at that time, almost entirely business-to-consumer sales. But in the early 1990s, the general public was just getting used to the idea of the Internet's existence; buying goods online represented a great leap forward.

When the Internet first began popping up in homes, CRM software displayed little more than the same content you might find in sales brochures. There was little if any interaction with the company sites; it was strictly billboard ware.

E-commerce's early days (daze?)

A few visionary companies started to change all that by actually selling products and interacting with customers on their Web sites. One of the first was Cyberian Outpost, who sold computers and peripherals off their site.

As retailers stumbled through e-commerce's growing pains, they had several key tasks to accomplish: They had to develop the software itself (catalogs, shopping carts, credit card processing) plus develop data-capture and reporting systems to match the transaction processing. As was the case with CRM and ERP systems, these functions had to be built from scratch, hard-coded by a mix of Web and traditional developers. At first the back-end analysis systems added little intelligence to the e-commerce process itself, it was little more than ex post facto reporting and analysis.

E-commerce gets smart

Amazon founder Jeffrey Bezos and his apparent fascination with analytics were largely responsible for pushing BI into the e-commerce realm — and driving his company to billion-dollar heights in the process. Early on, Bezos operated a company that lived, ate, and breathed data. Managers pulled metrics and reporting data from every conceivable piece of the Amazon operation. It started with a motivation to make the fulfillment and inventory systems as lean and efficient as possible — something Bezos knew could only be achieved by using hard data to drive management decisions. Then Bezos applied the same analysis-heavy mindset to the storefront too, where he tracked every move customers made — and had the Web application respond to those moves.

The results of Amazon's BI culture manifest themselves today in the company's marketplace hegemony as well as in the user features you encounter when you shop online. When you log in, you see the last products you looked at, along with products judged to fit your tastes (according to your browsing and buying history). When you add books to your shopping cart, the system performs real-time analysis to recommend other books to you. BI actually helps shape customer behavior in real time.

Real-time business intelligence

Amazon's ability to influence customers is only possible because it collects a mountain of customer data. As you shop, sophisticated analytics are running in the background — comparing your habits and online activities with those of millions of customers who came before you. This customer-facing system can then react to you in real time (the industry calls it *shopping time*) and present you with options that make you more likely to spend more, return again and again, and be happy with the experience.

That instantaneous reaction — BI capabilities shaping a Web site's behavior on the fly — represents a level of complexity and utility that isn't commonly seen in the other technology disciplines we've discussed in this chapter. ERP, CRM, and planning systems are most useful for looking at *past* data and doing one-time analysis to guide decision-making. But e-commerce brought BI into the present tense.

The Finance Function and BI

One more area of software functionality has been touched by business intelligence: financial reporting and analysis. The finance departments of companies of all shapes and sizes go through the process of assembling budgets, corporate planning initiatives, and performance forecasts. BI can help out there in unprecedented ways.

The budgeting and planning process for organizations has always been intensely manual — low-level analysts and staff members would crunch numbers and create individual spreadsheets that then had to be merged and summarized before becoming part of the next level. Team budgets would roll up into departmental budgets, from there up into divisional budgets, and eventually up into the overall corporate budget.

This process left very little room for analysis. Any changes to the planning process would have to be cascaded up and down throughout the company to really understand its full effects — a process that's simply not feasible in most companies.

As with ERP, CRM, and e-commerce, business intelligence found fertile soil in the global finance functions. CFO's were desperate to move beyond the pencil-and-paper processes and Excel spreadsheets that had dominated the area for so long.

Business intelligence technology allows planners to perform what-if analyses, run budgets through predictive and profitability analyses, and create scorecards and dashboards to aid in corporate performance- management practices . . . for openers. BI not only speeds up these processes, it also gives the finance department far more confidence in the numbers themselves.

Chapter 3

Meeting the BI Challenge

*J*ust about everybody agrees that having timely, accurate, high-value, and actionable insights available before making critical business decisions would be extremely helpful. What marketing executive *wouldn't* want a report that clearly shows the optimum mix of products to send to the marketplace as a package? What V.P. of Sales *wouldn't* like reliable figures on which territories and accounts are the most profitable? But wanting something doesn't make it a reality.

While good business intelligence is within virtually any company's grasp, many obstacles can get in the way. There are technology landmines, project hurdles, and even political challenges. As you prepare for a BI implementation, you need to be ready to answer some tough questions about how your company operates. You have to make some decisions about what exactly you want out of your BI solution. And you should brush up on your diplomatic skills to lay the groundwork for unifying your team behind a common goal.

This chapter is about identifying all the things that can go wrong with BI. If you know in advance which problems lie in wait for you, they're much easier to solve (or avoid altogether). If you charge ahead without considering what can go wrong, you'll join the ranks of companies whose BI implementations either never got off the ground or foundered once they were launched.

What's Your Problem?

A typical business intelligence solution has many moving parts — including an array of software and hardware that must work together in concert. With BI's heavy reliance on IT, it's no surprise that many companies squander the bulk of their planning process on technology. This tech focus is a misconception that will get you into trouble.

Hardware and software selection is not actually the most difficult part of a BI implementation. A company that focuses on choosing server vendors, designing architectures, and the like is missing the real problem: identifying accurately what the business actually needs.

The real challenge of BI is coming up with a workable answer to the question "What's our problem?" For business intelligence solutions to go to work for you delivering important business insights, your organization must determine the purpose of the implementation. Okay, that may sound all pie-in-the-sky and a little bit *meta*, but you do need to ask some preliminary questions to identify the kinds of *business* questions you want BI to answer.

Some of these questions are obvious, some require in-depth research, some might bring a range of responses depending on whom you ask within your company, and some may have no single answer — just an educated guess will have to do. Here's a sampling of those questions:

- ✔ What data is currently available to be measured and analyzed?

- ✔ What measurements can we monitor that indicate success in one or more areas of the business?

    These are the *key performance indicators* (KPIs); we talk about them more in Chapter 6.

- ✔ When do we need the answers? Do we need them all at once?

- ✔ How will we take action if certain insights demand it?

- ✔ How prepared is the company culture to effect change once we get our answers?

And there are more of these — many more — to answer before you start thinking about technology. Some range from mundane project and logistics questions, but many are darn near philosophical questions that cut straight to the heart of the way your organization is run, and approaches change. Taken together, answering these questions shines light on the entire purpose of your business intelligence implementation. And best of all, you've made good progress toward BI success without spending a dime on software licenses or consultants' time (yet).

What can go wrong

If you move ahead with a BI *solution* but fail to properly or completely identify the problem you want it to solve, you don't get much benefit from BI. In fact, a BI implementation can be a disruptive force to your organization in many ways. Consider the following areas of impact.

Cost

If you had an unlimited budget you could try everything and keep only what works. But BI can be an expensive proposition — and it doesn't stop with new software licenses or consultant bills. There's always a need for extra hardware and infrastructure. Then you have to factor in maintenance costs, training costs, and all sorts of hidden expenses (such as a temporary decline in worker productivity as they adapt to a new paradigm, training classes for users and project team members, opportunity costs, and so on).

BI is not for the faint of heart, nor is it for the faint of wallet.

Time

Sure time is money, but sometimes time is just . . . well . . . time. Working through a fruitless BI implementation means you aren't doing something else that could be useful to the company. Waiting on a BI implementation to bake can cause delays in tackling strategic problems. The resources dedicated to the task could be repurposed to other tasks with immediate payoffs like getting a product ready for market or improving your internal processes.

Credibility

Not all high-level executives are convinced that BI is more than just an empty buzzword. If one of the doubters sees your project fail, you'll just confirm their pre-conceived notions. Worst of all, it makes it that much harder to gain support the next time around. And it's not just about the corner-office folks; a good BI implementation depends on people at *all* levels making a commitment to the process. Skepticism is a self-fulfilling prophesy, so you should take steps to ensure you get it right the first time.

Bad advice

The worst consequence of all is that you may think you're getting what you need from your BI solution, only to find out the analysis has produced recommendations that lead in the direction precisely opposite to success.

Most BI wounds are self-inflicted. When BI projects go wrong, it's not because software breaks or consultant teams lie. It's because companies either don't do adequate preparation or don't think through their goals and capabilities well enough (or both). And with this kind of self-inflicted wound, you don't get out of combat. You're back in your office on Monday morning with a bandage on your toe and an ice pack on your forehead trying to salvage what you can of your disastrous implementation.

The BI Spectrum — Where Do You Want It?

If you consider the *Big Four* characteristics of business insights produced by BI projects (*timely, accurate, high-value,* and *actionable*) you'll note that they are all abstract notions. Notice that nowhere in there does the definition include insights that *save you money,* or *help long-range planning.* The four characteristics of BI insights are intentionally left a safe distance from your company's particular success criteria.

That's because BI projects come in all shapes and sizes. The CFO might be directing a massive BI project to look at the global finance functions and how they affect the entire enterprise. Or a regional sales manager could be the "customer" of your company's business intelligence system, and have a much narrower outlook. That person is not interested in enterprise-level financial insights — and isn't particularly concerned with building knowledge about the entire company. For the regional sales chief, a successful BI implementation offers insights on the sales process alone. Any insights beyond that aren't actionable at the regional-sales level.

What makes BI insights good is not the breadth of their application in a company, it's whether they're answering the questions they were designed to answer — and producing information that is timely, accurate, high-value, and actionable.

Good BI insights can look different depending on the shape and scope of your implementation. It's for you to decide what scope makes sense. Companies are different, as are their internal processes and organizational structures. Part of the challenge of implementing a sensible business intelligence solution is managing the scope so it applies exactly where it's needed. Sometimes that means finding the place where BI insights can have the biggest impact; sometimes it's about delivering a usable solution on time.

Whatever it is, determining your project's *scope* — how far the implementation will reach, what areas it will touch — is paramount to its success. In the next sections, we talk about some of the dimensions you should consider when you're specifying the scope for your BI project.

Enterprise versus departmental BI

For most companies, the scale of the BI implementation is predetermined by the team that originated the idea, the size of the project's budget, and the level of buy-in from the company's leadership:

- ✔ For smaller implementations, the focus rests on a single department.
- ✔ Larger projects are an entire enterprise solution that affects the entire company.

As a best practice, your company's *first* BI implementation should be at the departmental level. Keeping it narrowly focused affords you the chance to learn and make mistakes, to see what does and doesn't work. Then, when you're ready for the big time, you can widen the scope for the second generation of the BI project. If you must implement an enterprise-wide BI project, at least make sure you keep the scope focused on a single function or geographic region. Trying to do it all right off the bat (multifunctional, enterprise-scale) is a challenge that has stymied even the best BI gurus.

Characteristics of enterprise BI

Enterprise BI projects are, naturally, broad in scope. They affect multiple functional areas of a business; typically they involve taking a unified view of the entire company (or of an entire self-contained business unit). Often heavy on analytics and forecasting, these projects produce insights that affect long-term decisions.

Enterprise-wide business intelligence is operated and sponsored by "C-level" people whose titles start with *Chief* — primarily CEOs and CFOs. That makes sense because they're the only ones who have the juice to force all business units to cooperate. Why *wouldn't* they cooperate? Read on.

Some CEOs run Darwinian businesses where their departments or business units compete against each other for survival. In this environment, bonuses and stock options are doled out only to the most successful pieces of the business. That's a problem because BI requires cooperation. BI projects involve — first and foremost — sharing potentially sensitive data between teams. It also requires buy-in of technology and business resources from all sides. While the surface may appear calm before work begins, internecine conflicts tend to bubble to the surface during a BI implementation. In big projects — say, installing enterprise-level BI systems — sooner or later everyone has to put their cards on the table. At that point, usually you find that someone is bluffing.

Characteristics of departmental BI

Unlike enterprise-level business intelligence projects, departmental BI exists at the *operational* level; where the rubber meets the road in an organization. Projects at this level are built to produce insights that fine-tune daily processes and improve short-term decisions. With this type of project, you're looking for insights in one narrowly defined piece of your business, such as marketing, sales, or finance.

Departmental itself is an abstract term that in essence means "anything that's not enterprise-wide." There are all levels of departmental BI, from single-team to multi-department. The word *department* itself could describe a traditional business team, or business functions that share a common geographic region or mission. There is no universally accepted definition, so when you discuss implementing a "departmental" BI solution with others, make sure you all agree on what the term means.

Enterprise versus departmental: Choose wisely

Often a BI initiative starts off with an enterprise scope in mind, along with grand dreams for producing business insights that will affect the strategic direction of the whole company. But over time, as the challenges of the project are faced and dealt with, it often becomes clear that the initial scope was far too ambitious and the BI toolset — along with the lofty expectations — has to be scaled down.

Adjusting the scope of a project downward is a natural step to take when you realize you've bitten off more than you can chew. But beware! A BI tool for a single division or functional unit can still provide excellent value to the company, as long as the solution itself hasn't been denuded to the point where the insights themselves no longer live up to BI standards. (Perish the thought!) Remember, if they don't match the Big Four characteristics, they aren't BI.

Managing expectations is absolutely essential in any discussion concerning scope. It's far easier, cheaper, and faster to do departmental BI, but you get what you pay for and nothing more. If your audience was expecting a company-wide solution, they'll be disappointed when the curtain goes up.

Smart organizations build a *scalable* solution — a departmental application that can be expanded and linked in with other data sources in the event success is encountered and the bigwigs deem it necessary to expand the company's BI out to the enterprise.

Mind the (operational) gap

Departmental and enterprise BI solutions can be a challenge mainly because traditionally there's been no smooth continuum of solutions that can handle the whole range — small-scale departmental BI, medium-sized business unit BI, and the largest enterprise-wide BI. Vendors normally produced software that covered only one specific level of an organization — perhaps even a single specialty, such as accounting, travel services, human resources, or e-commerce.

This operational gap — which separates BI into different scales of activity in one company — is one of the main challenges the industry faces today. How do you build a bridge between BI user groups at different levels of the company? The essence of the problem is that when strategic insights occur at the top of the company, there's not always an easy method of translating those changes into the company's day-to-day operations.

That task is so important, it's earned its own buzzword: *operationalizing* business intelligence. Enterprise BI tools may produce valuable strategic insights or reveal a long-term destination for the company. But that doesn't mean the way forward is always clear for individual workers or departments. To *operationalize* BI is to create an action plan of achievable day-to-day improvements that moves the company toward its strategic goals.

If your aim is to change the way workers do specific departmental tasks, but the scope of your BI is enterprise-wide, you may be asking for trouble. You have to find a way to translate those strategic insights into a tactical format. A good BI solution will account for this operational gap and take steps to accommodate the inevitable "translation" problems between BI insights and their target audience.

Strategic versus tactical business intelligence

In addition to the operational scale of BI that differentiates between departmental and enterprise-wide solutions, there's also a range of differences in the scope of the decisions that BI insights indicate. *Strategic* BI deals with the big picture and the long view; *tactical* BI handles today's immediate decision-making process and other details of getting the job done, day in and day out.

Strategic decisions

This kind of BI involves gaining business insights for long-term corporate decisions, whose arc covers the broad direction of the company or business unit as a whole. Imagine a question such as, "What is the optimal product mix for the New England sales region in Q1 2009?" The insights that can be gained from questions like that may not affect the day-to-day operation of the company: the receptionist will still answer the phone, the sales team will continue to make calls on customers, the factory will continue to run the same way. At some point, however, such questions may prompt a strategic shift that leads to a long-term change in how the company operates.

Tactical and operational decisions

These decisions guide how a company operates on a day-to-day basis; they're usually peculiar to a given department or business sub-unit — for example, a decision on the size of the discount that certain customer affinities might receive, or setting the price a business pays for a certain commodity. These are choices that affect day-to-day operations, and as such may *change* from day to day. It's difficult to fully automate these decisions; reporting and other computational tools can play a support role, but at some point in the chain, carbon-based neurons have to wrestle with them.

If transactions are like traffic, then operational decisions are like high-volume stoplights at your company. They're the yes/no gates that might approve or decline credit to a customer, kick off a coupon-awarding routine (or fraud alert), or perhaps initiate a late charge in a billing system.

The BI processes that touch these decisions — tactical BI — involve insights that might affect a business on a day-to-day or week-to-week basis. The insights might lead to immediate changes or adjustments to previous decisions. Imagine a BI application that could give you the answer to a specific question such as, "Who are the bottom three sales representatives in the Pacific sales region, year-to-date?" The answer to that might prompt an adjustment in pricing, product mix, or approach to the sales process. The decisions taken from tactical BI usually don't involve the entire business unit; they just touch a department or single functional area.

There are two scales to think about: Enterprise versus Departmental BI, and Strategic versus Tactical BI. While they often go together, there is no automatic correlation between enterprise/strategic and departmental/tactical. So be careful that the solution you design answers the most important questions for your organization.

Power versus usability in BI tools

This is really a question of your users. Are you likely to have a large population of limited-ability users? Or is your BI implementation going to be operated exclusively by a small group of experts?

BI used to be the exclusive domain of highly experienced users — IT experts, sent to expensive training classes, would then operate on behalf of the business community to draw information from the BI application. This was the model that BI vendors counted upon, and they focused all their attention on making more powerful analytic and forecasting tools.

But as BI has spread throughout the organization, non-expert business users — such as CEOs — need to be able to harness the power of the applications so they can tap into the insights. As a result, more vendors are at least paying lip service to usability, creating self-service applications, and allowing the non-experts a degree of independence from the über-nerds.

Nevertheless there is a tension between tools that focus on ease of use and those with greater power, complexity, and flexibility. Suppose you anticipate your users to ask questions like, "What are the profit margins in the first quarter of this year for the 10 least profitable products of the last five years?" Fair enough — a good SQL query writer could build that query to work against a standard database, but not all BI tools can handle a question of that complexity.

A good way to gauge your needs along the two primary BI continuums (enterprise/strategic and operational/tactical) is to anticipate what kinds of questions your users will want to ask — and then compare the complexity of those questions with the likely ability of those same users to operate the BI tools.

Even the easiest BI applications are complex. Sure, the vendors have made it easy to drag and drop dimensions and metrics into tables, but many users will be stumped by such a simple move. Some folks are going to be so set in their ways; they won't be willing to run even the most basic of reports. Better to sniff out that problem ahead of time rather than after you're deep into your implementation. If your BI system is unusable to the people you're designing it for, it puts the entire project in jeopardy.

Reporting versus predictive analytics

BI gives companies the ability to peer into the past, slicing and dicing historical data in revealing ways. But applications are available that dig through yesterday's information to form predictions about what the future will be like.

Coupled with data warehouses, BI tools give users access to snapshots of information from the organization's operational and transaction-based systems. The capability to do complex drill-downs into this historical record is where the system provides its unique value for reporting purposes.

On the other hand, some BI vendors focus on predictive-analysis tools. This software uses advanced statistical techniques to create tomorrow's forecasts based on yesterday's data. Not a crystal ball, but the next best thing.

BI that's juuuuust right

Installing a business intelligence solution requires some "TBA," or *Three Bears Analysis,* by the planners. The solution has to be relevant to the business audience you're trying to reach; if that's the executive management, then you need to measure the performance of entire business units. If, on the other hand, your users do their work at lower levels in the company, the tool will have to involve departmental metrics and operational data. In addition, the project team must gauge the kinds of insights needed; the level of sophistication required; whether the BI will do predictive analysis; and whether it looks backward, forward, or both.

None of these are simple Yes/No, Either/Or answers. They occupy a wide range of possible answers that require the BI project sponsors, project managers and business analysts to toss aside any porridge that's too cold or too hot, and to only wield a spoon when the temperature is judged to be *just right.*

First Glance at Best (and Worst) Practices

In case you're feeling a little lost, you can take heart in knowing that the path before you is well traveled. BI is an evolving field that often features cutting-edge technology, but that doesn't mean you can't learn from the successes and failures of those who came before you. In this section, you'll find a quick look at some common insiders' advice.

Why BI is as much an art as a science

Fortunately, if you're on the Goldilocks mission to attain the just-right BI, it's not like you're completely on your own. The technology is mature enough that best practices are available — and (as we mentioned) BI architecture and software are only moderately complicated. So why do so many implementations fail?

The answer is that there is an art form to juggling all the competing priorities and coming up with the right temperature for the porridge. Beyond finding the right place on the continuum, there are political considerations, budget considerations, and a host of other concerns. There are process questions that must be answered that nobody ever thinks about: How do you deal with historical data? How do you handle different levels of user expertise? How do you validate requirements? How do you prioritize them? When you're about to miss a deadline, how can you tide over the key players who were promised a solution? How do you ensure that something else doesn't go wrong because of your BI project?

It would be nice to have a salty BI project manager always handy — someone who knows (a) the answers to these questions, (b) when to draw the line in the sand, (c) when to avoid eye contact with the rabid CFO, and (d) when to back away from the keyboard and hide under a pile of old coats in the closet. But they aren't always available, and there's no chapter in this book on intuition. Hopefully by the time you finish you'll be staked with enough knowledge and understanding of the process that your gut instinct will be adequate.

Avoiding all-too-common BI traps

Statistics support that notion that more BI implementations fail than succeed. That's not meant to scare you off; it's a reality check. In some cases it just wasn't meant to be. But more often than not it was one of the well-known quicksand traps below that brought the expedition to an untimely end.

Thinking technology alone can cover it

Sheer wishful thinking. Even if you're prepared to spend millions on software licenses, it's impossible to do a plug-and-play BI implementation without getting buy-in from the data consumers — and, to some extent, the data producers.

They may be silent and invisible, but you can't spell *Business Intelligence* without the letters *T-E-A-M*. Even modest BI rollouts require collaboration among many disciplines. "If you build it, they will come," is not a valid mantra for anything other than a cornfield in Iowa.

Thinking people alone can handle it

Not to impugn the talent on your company's IT team, but there is no reason *not* to buy some components off the shelf (so to speak) instead of taking the total do-it-yourself route. The vendors may be full of themselves, but there is a kernel of truth in their hype. Business intelligence solutions aren't vastly more complicated than other software rollouts — but they are complex *enough* that building the entire package from scratch usually isn't worth your while.

Loving your data just the way it is

Data is hard to love if it's useless. One common BI failure is not paying enough attention to the quality of the data that's feeding the system. Bringing the data under one roof in the data warehouse is not (by itself) enough to ensure success. It has to be examined for a host of common problems — from format incompatibility to missing data — and then processed and integrated to make it useful.

Remember that data warehouses are typically one-way streets. Transforming the data once it gets to the warehouse doesn't put your original data at risk. You shouldn't be afraid to twist, tweak, edit, or delete the information that's flowing into the data warehouse.

Confusing causality and coincidence

Although it's true that analyses and reports are only as good as the data in the data warehouse, it's also true that the untrained shouldn't draw conclusions. It's easy to misread reports, and see things that aren't actually there. As Mark Twain famously said, "there are lies, damn lies, and statistics." What he meant was that statistics and metrics can be made to tell a story that's more fiction than non-fiction. And Huck Finn has no place in a finance department.

One more continuum: hope versus hype

That BI vendors often oversell their products shouldn't come as a surprise to you; in fact, it makes BI just like every other technology. What's a little different about business intelligence is the way it's changed monikers over the years. The different acronyms make it difficult to keep track of what's what in the industry — and that, combined with other factors, means the vendors may try to talk you in circles.

No matter which part of their pitch you listen to, there's an awful lot of noise. And to add more confusion to the mix, the industry can change month by month as companies acquire each other and go out of business. Just keep that in mind at your next product evaluation. Many of the *total* BI packages are really just hodgepodge collections of products built by different companies and acquired one-at-a-time over the years by the company that's pitching its wares to you right now. That doesn't mean the packages won't work — but as always, *caveat emptor.*

Remember, BI vendors are there to wow you, to make you think your business will transform itself overnight if *only* you would buy their products. Just remember that for every survivor in the BI marketplace, there is a company that fell by the wayside — and they said exactly the same thing to their clients right up until the paychecks started bouncing.

In fact, it's almost guaranteed the vendor you're talking to right this moment will claim to have a perfect solution for you, no matter where you are in the BI life cycle. (Isn't that easy?) If you're in the midst of a failed implementation, they'll tell you their product is the missing piece of the puzzle that will stabilize the system and make it start spitting out amazing organizational insights. If you know very little about BI and are just starting down that road, the vendor will take the role of the wise doctor — and the prescription they give you will just happen to include a healthy dose of their products and services.

As with medical doctors, when in doubt, get a second opinion, and a third, and a fourth.

Part II

Business Intelligence User Models

The 5th Wave — By Rich Tennant

"Trying to forecast with 'mind power' again?"

In this part . . .

Okay, now you know the basics. You've seen that business intelligence solutions can harness all that data you've kept over the years on your lemonade stand, bring it together, and turn them into something useful. But how?

The answer is you'll have to make those BI tools work for you. And in order to do that, you'd better understand what they are, and what they can and can't do.

First is the obvious stuff: reports. Pulling interesting data out and re-assembling it in ways you hadn't thought of. Like working out how the profit margin per cup of lemonade sold varies with the high temperature. Then you'll learn about other tools that help you get the most out of that data, like dashboards and scorecards that let you know how your stand is doing at a glance, calculating reams of data behind the scenes to give you a simple thumbs-up or thumbs-down.

Chapter 4

Basic Reporting and Querying

. . . .

In This Chapter

▶ Fitting querying and reporting in with the rest of the BI stack

▶ Getting to know the query and reports user

▶ Understanding how query tools work

▶ Seeing how managed reporting affects business

. . . .

*U*p to now we've talked about business intelligence as an abstract notion; it's the tools, technologies, and practices that produce critical business insights. But how exactly does a BI system accomplish such an ambitious mission?

Where does the *intelligence* come from? How does it happen?

You might have visions of a bunch of IT geeks huddled around a humming supercomputer, waiting for it to spit out the answer to all of life's great questions that they can then rush straight to the CEO. Or perhaps you're picturing a golden dot-matrix printer sitting on a raised dais in the boardroom that occasionally belches out pronouncements like "Betamax will beat out VHS" to the wonderment of the leadership council.

If only it were that simple.

In this chapter we talk about querying and reporting, where the rubber really hits the road on the sports car called business intelligence. Querying and reporting represents the face of a BI implementation, where all the work that goes into the back end — from the gathering and transformation of company-wide data, to its creation and storage inside a data warehouse — emerges as critical knowledge, ready to be acted upon by the team.

Power to the People!

Data warehousing and its connected functions are the exclusive domain of the pocket protector set, but querying and reporting represent pure IT democracy-in-action. These are the tools that allow individual contributors and knowledge workers to access the aggregated information inside a data warehouse, ask questions, poke and prod the answers, and finally mold them into timely, accurate, important, and actionable insights.

Querying and reporting tools aren't locked away in the server room, nor do they rest on a shiny dais in the boardroom. They are designed to go on departmental PCs and laptops. They're meant to be accessed by individuals in the middle tiers of management and lower throughout the company. Vendors design them with ease of use and flexibility in mind so they can be utilized by virtually any department — so they can handle data tasks of any stripe, from accounting and finance to sales and marketing, and everything in between.

The traditional way to look at querying and reporting applications was always to draw a solid line between the two. Querying applications were focused on enabling users to take point-in-time snapshots of a particular set of data. Reporting was always focused on the output — the presentation of the data. Today, software vendors have virtually merged the two functions. The broken record plays on, stuck on the notion that querying is forever divided from reporting; don't get caught up in semantics.

Querying and reporting in context

What you need to understand about querying and reporting tools is that they provide users with the main pathways to the data itself. To do that, they have to be designed to work closely with the data warehouse or other data sources through common communication protocols, and then interpret and display their results. And they have to do it all fast.

A *query* is nothing more than an electronic request for specific information from a database. Queries hold an important place in the world of database technology, data warehousing, and (therefore) business intelligence, because they are the most basic link between a user and the insights contained in the database. The great dramatist Eugene Ionesco wrote, "It is not the answer that enlightens, it is the question." He could have been a BI consultant; creating the correct query to get the information you're after is half the battle.

Tools

Although they're usually wrapped up in one package, here's a brief description of the important aspects of querying and reporting applications.

Querying tools

Because a query itself is a request for information from a database, querying tools are designed to help a user create that request. Common querying tools provide a graphical interface to make it easy to see what data fields are available and to give the user an insight into the *metadata* — how the fields are related, table structure, and so forth. The latest-generation tools also offer easy-to-use drag-and-drop capabilities that allow users to adjust their queries on the fly as they drill down into the results that are returned. (That's an advanced data-manipulation technique; more about those later, particularly when we get to online analytical processing in Chapter 6.)

Reporting tools

Retrieving the right information from the database is one thing; presenting it in a meaningful, understandable way is quite another. That's where dedicated reporting applications come in. They're usually either bundled with, or one in the same as the query tools. Like the query tools, modern reporting tools offer an intuitive, graphical interface that allows the user to perform calculations on the data retrieved through a query, such as averages and sums. Beyond simple presentation, reporting software helps organize and distribute query results in the form of reports.

Querying and reporting in the BI architecture

It might be helpful to take a snapshot from 20,000-feet of the entire BI architecture so you can see how querying and reporting applications fit with the rest of the components of a BI solution.

Starting at the bottom, you see the disparate data sources that may be spread throughout the company — across departments and ranging across geographical and functional divisions. The data sources are operational databases, in use by each department to record regular transactions and store data that is frequently accessed and changed.

The data sources connect into the data warehouse through a set of processes commonly referred to as *ETL, or Extract, Transform, and Load.* These processes do exactly what they say; first they grab relevant data from the operational databases, then they change it into a single, unified format so all data is apples-to-apples. After the data is *clean,* it's loaded into the data warehouse.

Querying and reporting tools sit astride the data warehouse. They act as the abstraction layer between the user and the *really* confusing, complex code that pulls just the right data from the database and puts it on somebody's desktop in a readable format.

Figure 4-1 shows how the users of the query and reporting tools — like the original data itself — can come from different departments representing diverse business functions. They can use the same query and reporting engine because that software is built to accommodate virtually any type of data, and can present it as a report that suits the needs of whichever users happen to be viewing the information.

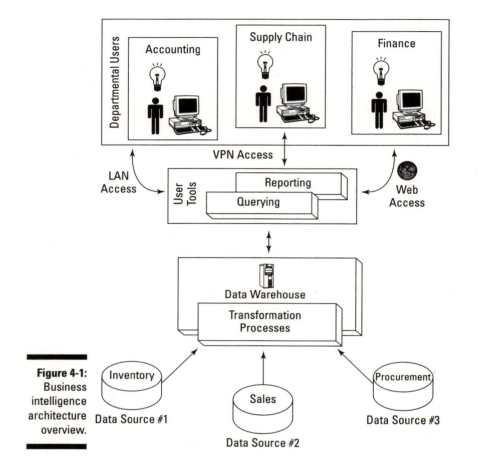

Figure 4-1:
Business
intelligence
architecture
overview.

Reporting and querying puts BI over the hump

In the old days, creating attractive and usable reports was a ridiculously time-consuming and expensive process that often required the services of a developer. That meant the process of requesting reports had to be tightly controlled by a company, lest the reporting budget get out of hand.

This bottled-up information circulated only among the upper levels of management. For the average knowledge worker, there was no choice but to utilize standard reports, make futile requests for additional information, or perhaps to try to see the same information in a different way and hope for the best.

Even as corporate computing moved away from the mainframe and toward client/server, reporting was still a challenge. What few reporting tools existed required a high level of expertise to use. Anything beyond the standard functions meant calling in a developer — just like before — except perhaps the underlying language was improved, making the reporting cycle a little shorter.

BI's rise to prominence in business can largely be traced to the advent of interactive query- and report-design tools. This allowed the information to flow outward to all levels of an enterprise, to workers without one iota of programming experience. Trendsetting tools like Cognos Impromptu and Crystal Reports allowed non-programmers to get a one-way (read-only!) look at the data in a database or data warehouse — and share the insights they gained with others — all with minimal training.

It's easy to lose sight of the value of BI querying and reporting tools because in the abstract, they look similar to any other GUI-based application sitting on a database. So what makes BI different from a plain old Access database with some slick controls and pre-designed reports? The *power* and *flexibility* of BI solutions. Business intelligence combines several key technologies in a way that can't be mimicked by a one-off application or simple database. For one thing, it provides a unified look at potentially very different data residing on multiple databases. The data warehouse is a snapshot of operational and transactional data that users can slice and dice in ways that aren't possible with traditional systems. And finally, all that's made possible by the advanced querying and reporting tools described in this chapter.

Reporting and querying toolkit characteristics

Here's a look at the latest generation of querying and reporting tools, evaluated on several key features that (naturally) vary from vendor to vendor.

Easy to use

The democratization of BI starts with making the tools user-friendly. Because these applications are no longer the exclusive domain of IT experts or programmers, they need to be usable by the masses. That means

- Making help available in the software
- Providing an intuitive and logical interface
- Making some common decisions on behalf of the user

The trade-off you make to get ease of use is a reduction in the overall capabilities of the product.

Web-based

Newer querying and reporting tools offer a Web interface that allows users to access the tool *as a service* through a common Web browser. While this arrangement places some natural limits on the capabilities of the software — and raises availability and security concerns — often the overall benefits outweigh the costs:

- ✔ Workers don't have to fuss with bulky client software, or deal with the usual headaches of software upgrades.
- ✔ It makes support a breeze for the IT organization.

Speedy

One of the biggest challenges in any data-heavy application is providing enough horsepower to manipulate millions of rows of data at a time, or to run complex queries without crashing the system. While much of the speed is dictated by the data-warehouse implementation itself, the querying-and-reporting application can drastically affect the responsiveness of the system. As the old IT-support saying goes, "Fast, cheap, reliable: You may pick any two."

Interoperable

Not only is it important for querying and reporting tools to be able to interpret data from multiple data stores, but it's also important that the output of the system can be used across different platforms like Excel.

Drill down capability

What makes a BI system so powerful is that users can dig through the data quickly — peeling layers off, rearranging the information in different formats, pivoting it to look at the data by one dimension instead of another, and focusing on the returned information with ever-increasing precision.

Versatile in communications

Sharing data between users, across departments, and up and down the levels of a company is a key factor for BI practitioners. Querying and reporting tools can facilitate that process by providing standardized and scheduled reports, as well as custom alerts that kick off predetermined querying and reporting processes when specified conditions are met.

So who's using this stuff?

Three main classes of BI users work with querying and reporting tools. Each has different needs and skills, and they're probably consuming different types of data. There are two competing goals for classifying users:

✔ Considering the users as one homogenous group creates a lowest-common-denominator effect for the BI implementation. That's a good baseline for your design but might limit your thinking.

✔ Recognizing where users differ provides an indicator for where the application(s) need to provide specialty services and interfaces.

Information consumers

Pure *information consumers* view preexisting standard reports (or perhaps receive them by way of a distribution tool), and then use the data to perform some task.

These folks aren't creating their own queries or reports, although they may use the basic functions of the reporting tools to access the standard reports.

The BI middle class

These *basic users* can create their own queries and reports using the graphical interface, but they don't know any code, and couldn't fix a SQL string in the event their queries needed tweaking.

Basic users rely on the GUI-based applications, the pre-set reports, and the simplest functions available in the tools.

Power users

Power users include developers and administrators. These folks make decisions about what information other knowledge workers need to see; they create reports and set access and distribution rights. Power users can be developers or simply experts at the particular querying and reporting tool in use by the enterprise.

Level of authority within a company plays absolutely no role in determining who's who in the user food chain. A CEO is just as likely to be a simple consumer of data as a lower-level worker is to be a power user.

Most BI users are mid-level managers and below. They're individual knowledge workers who contribute across a wide array of departments. More than ever BI is an essential tool up and down the corporate hierarchy.

One of the enabling factors of the power of data-driven solutions like BI is that SQL as a computer language has proven remarkably stable; the version in use today is much like the original. Vendors produce their own flavors that fit with the precise features of their applications, but the core of SQL is the same across all platforms. SQL is not without its disadvantages and detractors, but the language has become so ubiquitous that it has become an open standard set by the American National Standards Institute (ANSI) as well as the International Standards Organization (ISO).

Basic BI: Self-Service Reporting and Querying

Because writing queries and accessing the database used to be such a heavily restricted process, the average knowledge worker had to make requests of the IT department, await approval, and then have the results sent to them. Today the concept of self-service is ubiquitous. Knowledge workers utilizing a BI tool will interface with the data by creating their own queries, using an application that sits on the desktop or Web browser. The results of the query are returned immediately to the user, who is then free to format those results in an endless variety of report styles.

From beginning to end, the IT team never has to be involved beyond setting up the system. The power and usability of the tools themselves ensure that programmers never have to touch the reports. This naturally results in efficiency gains for the workers, as well as cost savings for the IT team.

Databases and SQL

With any application that touches a database, there's inevitable use of the term SQL (pronounced as the letters *S-Q-L* or like the word *sequel.*) SQL stands for Structured Query Language — and is exactly that: It provides a standardized methodology for asking questions of databases.

SQL grew in importance in the 1970s as the *relational database* model became the standard. With *flat-file* databases, queries could be nothing more than simple filters on the data fields. But relational systems are more complex and require a semantic model to match in order to access the advanced table structures.

The most basis of SQL queries are SELECT statements, like this one:

```
SELECT * FROM tblSTUDENTS
WHERE
tblSTUDENTS.BIRTHDATE >=
    "01/01/1980"
```

The star (*) in this query represents the word *everything*, so this query asks the database to return all the information stored in the table called tblSTUDENTS. So if that table contained the student's first name, last name, middle initial, and birthdate, the results would include all four fields. If we were only interested in the student's name, we could replace that star with specific field names.

The WHERE statement indicates that we only want certain students returned. In this case, a student's information is included in the results only if his or her year of birth is 1980 or later. The phrase tblSTUDENTS.BIRTHDATE means the BIRTHDATE is the name of the field in the table called tblSTUDENTS that contains each student's birthday.

SQL is a remarkably flexible language that allows users to perform a variety of database functions beyond just creating queries. In fact you can create, load, and maintain a database using only SQL commands.

Building and using ad-hoc queries

For BI users, it's not merely about being able to create queries and reports on your own; the second half of the equation is having access to the data in real time. In other words, workers can interact with the database as they need it, without delaying. This is the ad-hoc nature of BI; like many self-service capabilities, it provides extraordinary value for the company that enables its teams in this way.

The people in the organization who create ad-hoc queries, then, are specialists in other areas who use data from the BI system in their everyday jobs. These folks may be accountants or HR specialists or business analysts.

BI tools meet the companies' needs because these knowledge workers can easily design and deploy queries and reports using existing tools. They can do it with minimal knowledge of SQL (or other programming languages), in the same way most employees in a business can operate an Excel spreadsheet. Creating ad-hoc queries and reports is simply another arrow in their quiver that they use to get their jobs done.

Common application features

Workers will use tools to different degrees of confidence and effectiveness. The most common features called for in modern querying and reporting tools are

- SQL-free query building
- Drag-and-drop creation of queries and reports
- Basic data-analysis features (such as creating a calculation on a report)
- Graphical features that allow users to easily build charts and graphs
- Easy publication of information — e-mail, Internet, intranet, wherever colleagues might need to see it
- Export features
- Calendar and scheduler to help organize reporting functions
- Security that protects sensitive data

Building simple on-demand self-service reports

The roots of business intelligence lie in reporting. The original impetus for creating the entire system came from the need to take a closer look at transactional data to draw conclusions about the business. As the appetite for better and more powerful reports grew, so did the demand for more capable systems.

The long history of BI and its precursors means reporting tools are now well-baked inside BI packages. The best practices were devised long ago; the most popular and usable feature sets are already built into reporting environments. The next subsection provides a fast overview of these features in action.

Concealing your sources

Good reporting packages allow users to build their reports regardless of where the underlying data comes from. That means the data source may be a relational database, a dedicated analytical processing database, a data warehouse or data mart, or even another report or query.

Building your query

The front-end tool will help you build your query by sorting through the data sources you've selected — revealing usable data fields. Query tools often have wizards available to guide you through a commonly used process. After the users select the data fields that correspond to the subject they're trying to gather information on, it's time to set conditions to filter the results.

For example, you might want to see a list of history teachers at your school, along with their office hours. You'd need to access the tables that contain the teachers' names, subjects, office hours, and probably office locations too. For the fields corresponding to the teaching subjects, you'd want to set a condition so the teacher's record is returned only if it's equal to `history`. After all, the whole purpose of the query is to get exactly the information you need, and none of the information you don't.

Normally querying tools put a layer of abstraction between the user and the complex mechanics that happen behind the scenes to get your data to you. But sometimes an advanced user (or a user who *thinks* he's advanced) likes to open up the hood and access the SQL that drives the query process. It's similar to a Web-authoring tool that gives the user access to the underlying HTML that gets created from the graphical interface. Most querying and reporting tools offer a way to let users get their hands dirty if they so choose.

Perfecting the report

Once the query is run, the user should then be able to adjust the arrangement of the data, for example, looking at the revenue figures by quarter rather than by region. The software should allow the user to do this with a few simple clicks, dragging and dropping data fields. Every change the user makes will result in cosmetic changes only; it's a different perspective on the same underlying information.

One common feature of reporting tools is called *adaptive authoring* whereby the software is designed to make certain aesthetic choices on behalf of the user, for example, resizing fonts and shapes to optimal levels depending on how it fits in with the rest of the report.

Publishing the data

Because sensitive data exists throughout the enterprise, it may be necessary to set viewing privileges to ensure that only the appropriate pairs of eyes see the data contained in the report. A report's author should be able to rely on the administrative features in the reporting tool to limit distribution of the report to only those users authorized to view the data.

Most halfway-decent report distribution applications can publish that information in whatever form is appropriate — such as HTML, Excel spreadsheets, CSV files, PDF or Word documents, and even XML output.

If it's not presented in the right way, key insights can remain hidden inside reports. Sometimes the most effective way to present information is not simply as a collection of numbers, or with rows of raw data. A picture can be worth a thousand words. That's why most reporting packages have advanced graphical capabilities that allow non-expert users to create stunning graphical displays to drive their point home.

At this point, most good BI software will also allow the report to remain up to date, long after the original creator has moved on to other projects. The output of the report can be tied to another program, or perhaps a pivot table in an Excel spreadsheet. Every time a consumer of that report goes to look at it, the data will be refreshed with the most up-to-date revenue, shipping, accounting, or other information.

Web reporting

One of the latest innovations in reporting is publishing live reports to the Web for better access and ensured compatibility. Users simply call up the report using a common Web browser — perhaps entering a password along the way (as set and distributed by the original creator of the report).

The state of the art in reporting tools is to allow basic users to push complex information to the Internet without knowing a word of the underlying ASP, HTML, or other Web-enabled languages. As Web protocols grow more secure, more and more companies are becoming comfortable using this paradigm.

Adding capabilities through managed querying/reporting

For users unable (or unwilling) to operate the querying and reporting software — or for businesses that are unwilling to give their workers full access to the data sources — there is *managed reporting*. Managed reporting takes the Wild West of a completely self-service-oriented data environment, and adds a sheriff to the town.

Many BI consumers have no need to create complex reports, or to write Byzantine database queries to get what they need. They have little need to use the advanced features of the report-writing software. They just need the relevant data handed to them in a timely fashion so they can do their jobs.

Managed reporting is a bridge between simple consumption of reports and self-service report creation, where employees are responsible for getting their own information from the database. In this situation, the users are given standard reports authored by others, and are given some freedom to explore, sort, filter, graph, and drill down into the detailed data — under the watchful eye of a team of data managers who control permissions, restrict when queries can be run, specify what data is available, and so forth, all from a centralized organization.

The data managers are also there to prevent problems that can arise from a completely open environment, and make sure that help is available when needed. (Chapter 13 details how environments like this are governed.)

Accessing and using standard reports

The hallmark of managed reporting environments is a library of standard reports created by a centralized IT team. These are the most common reports used by the various functions accessing the BI solution. A user would simply go to a shared location on the company intranet to access the report, or would perhaps look at the report through the Web.

Standard reports certainly make life easier for many data consumers and BI users. There's no thought involved in creating the query or building the presentation of data; the user simply points and clicks and the report appears. The hard part's all done by someone much more interested in it than (say) Marge in accounting, who just needs to see that her numbers match with those on the monthly revenue report.

But just because your environment provides standard reports doesn't mean your company's users don't need at least some knowledge and training on the software. The snazziest reports in the world are worthless if your team doesn't know how to access them, read them, or interpret them.

Interactive reporting is a key feature of business intelligence software. When you think of normal reports, you ask the database a question by sending along a query. The database software then finds data that matches your query and returns a report, organized and presented in a predetermined way, sometimes showing every row of returned data, sometimes showing summary information.

With interactive reporting, it's possible to manipulate the results of your database query until you get just the data you need. The first time you run a query, you may not find what you're looking for. But the answer to that initial

---

Keeping control

As BI gets closer to the strategic core of many businesses, it becomes more important that it be kept up-and-running and in good health. The pieces of a business intelligence system are extraordinarily powerful, but they have an Achilles heel in that they are built on databases, which can be brought down by careless users. So with the increased role of BI, and with the increasing pressure to push more data access to end-users, vendors have developed more complex administration tools and *query governors*.

If you're thinking a query governor sounds like some kind of a statehouse scandal, you'll be pleased to know that it's nothing more than an application feature designed to protect the data systems from harmful requests. Database processing power is a finite resource — and a query governor acts to prevent poorly-written queries from executing, or from running past certain time limits. That helps keep system performance from degrading or crashing altogether. Administrators can tune their governors to balance the user community's needs and the system's resources.

---

question — the data contained in the report — may provide you with a clue of where to look next, or how to structure your next query. Interactive reporting makes it easy to zero in on the data you were looking for in the first place. If all goes well, after refining your query several times, your insight appears.

We get more into drilling down (as well as up and across) — in particular, with OLAP tools — in Chapter 5. These are analytical tools that are closely related to reports, and in fact share many common features with the front-end tools common to most BI platforms. But in the BI world, there is a clear dividing line between common querying and reporting tools and OLAP tools; we'll save that discussion for the next chapter.

Data Access — BI's Push-Pull Tug-of-War

A natural tension exists between two basic philosophies of data access, and if you've read this chapter carefully (and why wouldn't you have?), then you've picked up on it. The common challenge is connecting the right people with the right data. In some cases, businesses rely on their employees to go out and seek the data they need; in others, IT managers have determined it's best to take that potential variable out of the equation, and push the data straight to the appropriate users.

Classical BI: pull-oriented information access

In its traditional role, BI relied on a *pull* environment. In this situation, it's up to the users to go out and create queries, build reports, or view the standard reports created by someone else. Users need data to do their jobs, and it's up to them to navigate through the query and reporting systems to get what they need. It's not all that different from getting up from your desk and "pulling" a file from the cabinet. Wouldn't it be nice if somebody — perhaps a helpful robot that makes coffee, too — went to the filing cabinet for you?

One of the key tenets of BI is that the data-fueled insights must be timely. You need critical insights — that the market is going to turn, or that inventories have reached a critical level — in plenty of time to act. But in a classic pull environment, you run the risk that your workers may not gather the needed data in time. And without timely data, you don't have business intelligence, you have stale bread.

Emerging BI: pushing critical insights to users

The latest generation of business intelligence tools is moving more decisively to a *push* environment. With push technology, a power user assembles data on behalf of the user community and delivers it at critical moments. The underlying data is the same as in a pull environment, but the data "pusher" decides what data is important, the people it's important to, how it should be presented, and when that information should flow into the hands of the enterprise's critical teams.

Push environments also rely on some kind of directory service to contain all the important information about the data and user environment. It tracks who has permission to see what, keeps tabs on which reports they're receiving and when, and provides a mechanism for making changes in how the data is pushed to users as needed.

Don't underestimate how complex reporting environments can be. Two people with the same job title may be able to see the exact same standard report, but because they roll up to different business units, the users' information permissions are different. Or perhaps two people have access to the same data, but one person is not allowed to publish it while the other can distribute at will.

Red alert, red alert: different models of alerts

Alert services represent a relatively new advance in BI front-end tools that allow users more organization in a self-service environment. Users or managers can set their systems to warn them when new data is available, or simply to let them know that it's time to update their standard stable of reports. With communication options so dispersed, a good alert system can send you messages on your phone, through your e-mail, or as a message on an intranet or portal. Users can set their preferences to receive a note about the report, or get the entire report itself.

Add to that the sheer variety of ways to push information to users, and setting up a good reporting system becomes a potentially mind-blowing challenge. Too many companies fail to account for the importance (and the level) of the expertise required to manage a push reporting environment.

Chapter 5

OLAP: Online Analytical Processing

*I*f you ever watched *Star Trek,* you're probably familiar with the way the characters would interact with the Starship *Enterprise* computer when they had a problem. Mr. Scott, the ship's chief engineer would say, "Computer, please isolate why the propulsion system is only operating at 40 percent." The computer would respond (in a mellifluous, calming voice), "Fuel leak detected." After several rounds of back-and-forth, the computer might give a full diagnosis: "Broken Fetzer valve in compartment 28b causing dilithium plasma buildup. Calculations indicate a 30% chance of detonation in the next hour unless the valve is repaired, and an 84.3% likelihood that the cause of the broken valve is Klingon sabotage."

You see? The twenty-third century's not so different from today after all! Mr. Scott had what was essentially a business problem: performance in his area of responsibility was lagging and he needed answers. And since starships are ridiculously complex machines, he did what anyone would do in his position: He used computing power to examine operational metrics, find anomalous trends, and identify a solution. Presto!

The great thing about those starship computers and HAL 9000 (from *2001: A Space Odyssey*) is their *real-time interactive capability*. Querying and reporting are clearly powerful tools; they provide priceless services to organizations of all kinds. But what's missing from that process is a true on-the-fly back-and-forth, where an operator can massage the query and the data itself to get precisely the result that's required.

That's what OLAP can provide, and it's why OLAP is business intelligence's killer app.

OLAP in Context

Up until now, our focus has been on the technology foundations of a BI solution. First, you identify the important data in your company; that is, the transactional information that resides on ERP, CRM and other operational systems. Next you gather the data together into a single place, and in a single format; that's the job of the ETL processes, the data warehouse and related components. Finally, you provide access to that mountain of data in the form of querying and reporting tools.

We could stop here and the solution described would be valuable to any organization. Producing unified reports against companywide operational data is likely to increase the managers' visibility into how all the pieces interact, and make it more likely that valuable insights might come to light.

But years ago some clever programmers and database engineers realized that they could get more from company transactional data by conceptualizing it differently than was traditionally called for. The concept was multi dimensional data rather than relational data — manifested as online analytical processing, or OLAP (pronounced "OH-lap").

Instead of just aggregating and summarizing your data, OLAP tools give BI systems the ability to look at it in a truly new way. Add the increased computing horsepower and innovative software tools available at the time, and a whole new paradigm was born.

OLAP Application Functionality

An OLAP application is software designed to allow users to navigate, retrieve, and present business data. Rather than taking data from a relational system, writing complex queries to retrieve it, then manually inserting it into a report to analyze, OLAP tools cut out the middle steps by actually storing the data in a *report-ready* format.

Traditional data processing was like plumbing: Your query would get flushed down into the system. You'd wait a while, and hope that what came out of the pipes on the other end was what you wanted.

That's not the case with OLAP. While it's true you have to make choices about the kind of data you want to get a look at initially, it's possible to twist and cut the results immediately. There's no need to work through confusing query logic or write long SQL strings. With a little drag-and-drop action, you're looking at the data in a whole new way.

How to get "online" without the Internet

Both OLAP and *OLTP* (*online transaction processing*) use *online,* yet both were invented well before the Internet came into widespread use. As a point of reference, *online* used to mean something completely different.

In the early days of computing, the systems were used strictly to store data and to run specific programs thought out and coded well ahead of time. Programmers and engineers would feed code into the system, wait for it to execute, and see what the results were on the other side (as the vacuum tubes and transistors cooled in preparation for another round of processing).

OLTP and OLAP include the term *online* to indicate a revolutionary shift in the actual process of working with computers. Instead of working with reports and figures offline, and then feeding the results into the computer for processing, users could now work directly with the stored data.

For OLTP systems, that meant a user in the accounting department could change an invoice status from *unpaid* to *paid* by sitting at a terminal, accessing the invoice's data record, and changing the record in real time. We take such an action for granted today, but it

wasn't always like that. Accounting clerks used to have to aggregate transactions, and then have them fed into the computer in batches by programmers.

OLAP changed things on the other side of the data path. Knowledge workers would request grouped data in the form of reports that would then be processed at sparse intervals. If a user looked through the paper printout and discovered a need to see things in a different way — say, sorting the data by date rather than by amount — the programmers would have to build a brand new report. Moving these processes online meant the report's consumers could see the data on a computer or terminal first, make changes to the report as needed, and *then* print the report.

OLAP actually takes that process a step farther than merely playing with reports online. It allows the users to get their hands directly on the data — changing queries on the fly, altering perspectives, adjusting the scope of the data. Before OLAP, analysis was something that happened away from the computer. Taking all those intermediate steps out of the process saved time and money, and (best of all) people thought it was really cool.

If you're thinking this is just a snazzy way to create the same old weekly TPS reports for your boss, you're missing the point. The *O* and the *A* in *Online Analytical Processing* aren't just there for looks: the *online* and *analytical* aspects of OLAP add up to a key difference. Consider: Rather than a set-in-concrete report, OLAP allows for fully interactive sessions between users and software. If it used to take you a week to build the report of your dreams to hand in to your boss, you're in luck: OLAP can take you through the process in a matter or minutes and leave enough time to do the analysis yourself.

Okay, the *P* isn't all that important in OLAP; it's no surprise that *Processing* is going on here. But a nice consonant makes an otherwise-forgettable acronym sound more like a real word.

Multidimensional Analysis

An OLAP data-and-reporting environment is different from a traditional database environment — mainly because of the way data is conceptualized and stored. And we aren't talking about putting it on magnetic tapes instead of floppy disks (how twentieth-century). In an OLAP system, users work with data in dimensional form rather than relational form. OLAP's bread and butter is multidimensional data.

Don't worry about geometry right now (or how you would fit such data into a table). Some people freak out at the word *dimension* because they think it means they have to understand Einstein's Theory of Special Relativity and the space-time continuum. For now, just remember that a dimension is nothing more than a way to categorize data.

The *A* in OLAP is not just any old kind of analysis — it's specifically *quantitative* — based on good old number crunching — rather than qualitative. OLAP software is designed to work with numeric data. That's why most of the examples you'll see are accounting, finance, or some other calculation-heavy subject.

Lonely numbers

At their core, financial records and sales data are really just numbers — prices, costs, margins, quantities ordered, and time periods. A list of numbers means nothing unless you know something about what those numbers represent. What makes numbers meaningful (and available for analysis) is the details: their *descriptions* and *qualifiers*.

If you see a number in a vast table, it will mean little to you without the context provided by the *title* of the table (or chart or graph) and the names and elements of the axes.

One-dimensional data

Consider a table whose title is "Sales Data" with the vertical axis labeled "Region" — and you can begin to draw some business conclusions right away, as in the Table 5-1.

Table 5-1	A One-dimensional Table
Annual Sales Data	
Region	*Amount*
Northeast	$45,091
Southeast	$73,792
Central	$88,122
West	$63,054
TOTAL:	$270,059

Although the data is (of course) displayed in two dimensions (horizontal and vertical), in OLAP terms this is considered one dimensional data. In other words, we're looking at sales data from one particular perspective (or dimension): in this case, by region.

Since companies usually record lots of information about each individual sales transaction, you could probably look at the same batch of transactions in a different way. Table 5-2 shows the same underlying sales data in a different dimension: by product type. The total sales amount is identical with the total in the sales table by region because the exact same transactions are used to calculate both. We're just looking at it broken out by product types rather than by regions.

Table 5-2	The Same Data from a Slightly Different Direction
Annual Sales Data	
Product	*Amount*
Gizmo	$88,697
Widget	$181,362
TOTAL:	$270,059

Another important factor in OLAP analysis is time, so let's take a look at what the sales figures look like through the time dimension. Table 5-3 shows the same underlying transactions broken out by calendar quarters:

Table 5-3	Yet Another View of the Sales Data
Annual Sales Data	
Quarter	**Amount**
Q1	$55,887
Q2	$87,659
Q3	$23,598
Q4	$102,915
TOTAL:	$270,059

Setting the table

By running reports that show a breakdown of annual sales figures by region, product, and quarter, we know what the total sales figure is — and we can recognize which of those dimensions shows sales strength and weakness. But where we go from there is a different story.

One option is to combine two of the dimensions into a table like Table 5-4.

Table 5-4	Two Dimensions of Data Combined		
Annual Sales Data			
Product			**Totals**
Quarter	**Gizmo**	**Widget**	
Q1	$23,199	$32,688	$55,887
Q2	$24,798	$62,861	$87,659
Q3	$14,555	$9,043	$23,598
Q4	$26,145	$76,770	$102,915
TOTALS	$88,697	$181,362	$270,059

With two-dimensional data, you can begin to think of dimensions as a kind of *coordinate system*. With quarters listed down the vertical axis and product type listed across the horizontal axis, each unique pair of values of these two dimensions corresponds to a single point of data. For example, we know that Quarter 2's Widget sales were $24,798.

Okay, let's not dislocate our shoulders patting ourselves on the back for this "breakthrough" — tables date back to the Stone Age as a way to store two-dimensional data. Any spreadsheet application can handle table data with ease.

But remember: We also have regional data as well, so how can we incorporate that information here? One way would be to create a series of two-dimensional tables. We could map regional sales figures by quarter, and we could map regional sales figures by product type.

But that doesn't necessarily get us where we ultimately want to go.

Seeing in 3-D

An analyst or a manager would find it especially helpful to be able to see all the dimensions — regional, quarterly, and by product type — on the same table at the same time.

But since spreadsheets and tables render all information in two spatial dimensions, we have to rig our table to handle the extra complexity. In Table 5-5, we've drilled deeper into the sales data. The individual data points from our original three one-dimensional tables are now the subtotals on the edges of this lone three-dimensional table.

Table 5-5	All Three Dimensions in One Table				
Annual Sales Data					
Region					
	Northeast	*Southeast*	*Central*	*West*	*Total*
GIZMOS					
Q1	$1,543	$14,098	$1,991	$5,567	$23,199
Q2	$6,811	$2,822	$13,300	$1,865	$24,798
Q3	$5,190	$5,050	$2,106	$2,209	$14,555
Q4	$2,347	$8,005	$5,900	$9,893	$26,145
WIDGETS					
Q1	$3,555	$5,520	$6,828	$16,785	$32,688
Q2	$9,158	$15,999	$18,096	$19,608	$62,861
Q3	$2,486	$1,297	$4,247	$1,013	$9,043

(continued)

Table 5-5 *(continued)*				
Annual Sales Data				
Region				
	Northeast	**Southeast**	**Central**	**West**	**Total**
Q4	$14,001	$21,001	$35,654	$6,114	$76,770
TOTALS	$45,091	$73,792	$88,122	$63,054	$270,059

With this table, you begin to see the value of multidimensional analysis. The totals and subtotals are the same, but with all three dimensions represented together, you begin to see how these factors interact with each other in an operational sense.

As an example of some analysis you might do, notice how the Northeast and Central regional sales figures are disproportionately lower in the first quarter for Gizmos, relative to those of the other regions and the other products.

Taking note of that anomaly might spur a call to the regional managers, who would then explain to you that Gizmos don't work well in the snow, making them hard to sell in Q1 because it's wintertime.

Beyond the third dimension

There's (theoretically) no limit to the number of dimensions you can use to describe your data. It all depends on what information your operational and transactional systems capture — and how finely detailed you want the picture to be. For example, your company's CRM system might also have data on specific sales reps. The accounting system could probably break down the time dimension further into months, weeks, and days.

There are practical limits on the software you use. Storing and manipulating multidimensional data is resource-intensive; it takes a lot of number crunching. So you should make sure the OLAP application you work with matches with your data model.

Even though *multi* means more than one, *multidimensional* in the OLAP world typically refers to data that can be described in three or more dimensions (as in our earlier example where you have sales data by time, by product, and by region). OLAP applications can certainly handle two-dimensional data, but one of the main reasons you'd use it is to handle information you can't easily generate with a table.

The output or results of an interactive session with OLAP data is often just a one- or two-dimensional data view. OLAP gives the analyst the freedom to

Data hierarchy

OLAP data is viewed in terms of dimensions, but some dimensions are related to others in the form of hierarchies. When you look at annual figures for how many products were shipped, it's the same as taking the quarterly figures and adding them together; the annual figures just occupy a "higher" level in the hierarchy of abstraction — they provide more of a bird's-eye view. Both quarterly and yearly data represent the time dimension of the shipping data — they just do so at different levels of *granularity* (a common term in OLAP circles meaning *detail*).

Multidimensional data almost always has a logical hierarchy with multiple levels. Successful analysis can only occur if the OLAP user is viewing the data at the hierarchical level that's appropriate for the job in hand.

For example, if a team of analysts wanted to look for fluctuations in store sales based on the weather outside, they'd need to see information at a certain level of granularity or the analysis would be impossible. If they had sales figures by year, for example, they'd be out of luck; if they had daily sales figures and were looking only at national sales numbers, they couldn't do much analysis either (since, presumably, the weather is different across the country). But if they had per-sales-rep sales figures by the hour, the data would be *too* granular; it would be difficult to spot the larger trends they were looking for.

Data hierarchies spawn several other important concepts. If your company has two different systems to track Web sales and in-store sales, those two figures in the OLAP system would represent *child* dimensions of overall sales, the *parent* dimension. Good OLAP tools let you move easily up and down the hierarchies of dimensions to the level that suits the scope of the analysis you're doing.

view information from different vantage points and in different ways. After cleaving and rearranging the multidimensional data, the analyst will find or calculate the essential data and put it into tabular form.

OLAP Architecture

OLAP systems are fundamentally different from other forms of data conceptualizations because it handles data in the same way people do when they're creating reports.

These systems are designed to work in concert with the other tools in the business intelligence architecture. The OLAP system typically comprises two distinct categories of software:

- ✔ The *OLAP cube* houses the multidimensional data (Figure 5-1 shows how it relates to the rest of your BI implementation).
- ✔ The *access tools* allow users to build and massage information into forms appropriate for analysis.

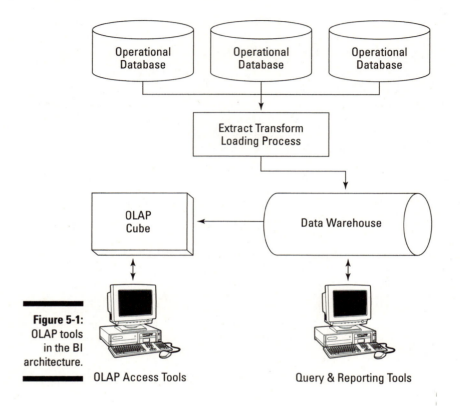

Figure 5-1:
OLAP tools
in the BI
architecture.

Figure 5-1 shows a traditional view of OLAP architecture. The operational applications store their data in disparate database systems strewn around the company. That information is brought together into the common data warehouse environment. The OLAP system extracts information from the data warehouse and stores it in an easily changeable, multidimensional, hierarchical database called a *cube*. The OLAP access tools then link users to the data in the OLAP cube to help them produce multidimensional reports and analyses.

The OLAP Cube

The table is the most common representation of numeric data because it's a highly useful and easily recognizable structure. It also lends itself to the two-dimensional world of paper and computer screens. But tables are, well, flat.

Company data is intricate and multifaceted, which makes tables of limited value in storing and representing information. We know that the table's natural state is to show data in one or two dimensions — as either a one-column tabular list or a row-and-column matrix that uses the vertical and horizontal to represent the key characteristics. So when it comes time to add more complexity — in the form of extra data dimensions — tables quickly lose their utility.

It's a data structure

To store multidimensional data, we conceptualize it as a *cube*, where each of the three axes represents a different dimension of the same information. A cube version of the previous example would look like Figure 5-2.

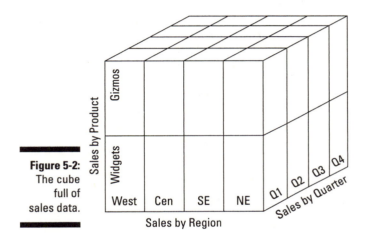

Figure 5-2: The cube full of sales data.

The cube has 32 cells of data, just like the three-dimensional table we drew. Another way to think about it is that we're taking two 2D reports and stacking them on top of each other — in this case Gizmo sales by region and by quarter, atop Widget sales by region and quarter.

That's the concept of a cube — but how does it work in real life?

In an OLAP environment, a cube is a specialized data store designed specifically to handle multidimensional summary data. But rather than being held in relational tables (which are built to process transactions rapidly), cube data is stored in cells; its structure is like a 3D spreadsheet.

You say "dimension," I say . . .

In OLAP-speak, a *dimension* refers only to a characteristic of the data, not a direction in space. So when you hear talk about a cube with 25 dimensions, don't give yourself a headache trying to picture the thing. In reality, it's just a list of sales figures that can be jockeyed in many different ways. Likewise, *cube* is a convenient proxy term for *any* multidimensional data structure. After all, if you add a dimension to a flat two-dimensional table, you've made a cube. And since we don't have words for any shape beyond three-dimensions, *cube* is the closest we can get.

Some vendors use the term *cube* as a general term to describe all multidimensional data in an OLAP environment; others say their software employs many cubes at once, one for each general data subject. For example, one vendor may describe an OLAP system where the tools access several different sales cubes, inventory cubes, and so forth. But another vendor may simply say that all tools access *the* cube. There's no difference beyond semantics.

OLAP access tools

The OLAP access tools are the client environments that allow users to twist and turn the cube's data and ultimately produce meaningful business intelligence.

The goal of the OLAP access tool is to present large quantities of information to the user in a way that lets them produce business insights without losing sight of the larger context of what they're doing. That means the tools need to have the following characteristics:

- **Easy:** The coin of the realm with OLAP end-user software is its ease of use. That means not only its ability to quickly and intuitively navigate what can be extremely complicated data arrangements, but also drag-and-drop controls, and simple administration of the data views and files.

- **Beautiful:** Spotting anomalies can be a matter of turning a river of numbers into just the right kind of visualization. The best tools will also have lots of charting, graphing, and reporting options.

- **Smart:** Users need to be able to tune the OLAP access tool to the right kinds of tasks. That means intelligent searching functions and robust analysis capabilities to help the user identify trends or create forecasts.

In the early days of OLAP, vendors packaged their cubes and access tools into a single pseudo-client-server package; there were two distinct applications that had to be deployed together. That approach is still common today, but plenty of companies specialize in one application or the other, building their software to work with that of other companies.

What OLAP Can Really Do

Ask someone what you can do with an OLAP cube and they'll likely immediately revert to the tired old slice-and-dice cliché; they might even throw the Veg-o-Matic joke at you if they're past a certain age (and remember those old television commercials from long ago). Okay, cheap jokes aside, you can take specific actions with data in an OLAP system that you can't do in other environments:

✔ **Consolidation:** This is another word for rolling up data into the next higher level of abstraction. For example, sales offices can be rolled up into districts, and districts rolled up into regions or complex expressions that connect interrelated data.

✔ **Drilling into the data:** With OLAP applications, you aren't just looking at a static report. Nor are you forced to thumb through 1000 different reports covering different areas of the business. OLAP lets you work through the data in a natural, intuitive way. See a data point on which you need more information? Click it — the software will re-orient the view around that piece of information. Consider our three-dimensional sales report showing subtotals by quarter, product type, and region. Clicking on one of the sales figures might take you to a view of the individual transactions. Clicking on a product category might open up detailed sales information on that category. OLAP drilling lets you go straight to the information you need.

✔ **Computation:** The formal word for number crunching. Because OLAP's focus is typically vast amounts of numeric data, the applications have built-in mathematical functions to help users turn more raw data into *less* raw data. For example, if your data warehouse contains sales and production-cost numbers, you can include the derived data in your final report that shows profit margins.

✔ **Pivoting**: If you've worked with a pivot table in Excel, you know the value of being able to view your data or report from different perspectives. If you aren't familiar with pivot tables, read on.

Members only

OLAP has its own peculiar lexicon that you need to become familiar with if you do any work with multidimensional analysis and reporting. Different vendors or consultants complicate matters by using their own proprietary glossaries that may not correspond to everyone else's. Nevertheless, here are some common terms for the OLAP concepts you'll encounter most frequently:

✔ **Attribute:** A descriptive detail, or a way to subdivide or categorize dimensions. In a way, attributes are members of dimensions. For example, if you are storing sales in a multidimensional environment, your dimensions might be time, product, and location. Each of the three dimensions has attributes that describe it; product's attributes might be "product name", "product type", "product family" and "product ID#". Attributes often have meaningful hierarchies too; you could create your multidimensional table so that certain product families combine to make a single product type. The time dimension is made up of "month", "quarter", and "year" which are all related to one another in ways familiar to everyone.

A word about pivot tables

The example in the previous section shows that it's fairly easy to represent three dimensions on a table — but then, that *was* a relatively simple example. Imagine if there were 18 regions instead of 4, or if you wanted to look at sales in each day of the year rather than by the four quarters.

And for every new dimension you add to the table, you must add as many new embedded cells in the table as there are elements in that dimension. For example, suppose you wanted to explore the dimension of sales channels — and divide the regional, product, and quarterly sales data according to whether the product sales go through corporate-owned stores or franchise stores. You'd need to add *two* cells for every one that exists in the table right now — one for corporate stores and one for franchises.

Microsoft Excel offers a good analysis tool for doing fairly routine multidimensional analysis in

the form of pivot tables. Pivot tables are built from raw dimensional data (as opposed to relational data); users can design and alter their tables by dragging and dropping particular dimensions onto the two axes of the tables.

Suppose, in our previous example, that you thought it made more sense to place the time dimension across the horizontal axis instead of on the vertical axis. You would simply click a design screen that allowed you to drag a representation of the time dimension to the horizontal axis. Excel would then recalculate all the fields to fit the new perspective of the data.

Users often find pivot tables handy for working with OLAP data. That's because a pivot table is a consistent way to picture the overall multidimensional nature of OLAP, and the two play well together, even if a pivot table is not the same thing as an OLAP cube.

 ✔ **Cell:** A single data point — like $5439 — identifiable by a coordinate system. A table is made up of axes and a lot of cells.

 ✔ **Measure**: Think of the title of your report as the long version of your measure — the general description of what's going on in the table. The measure usually corresponds to a description of what is represented by the cells (data points). In our example, the data points were dollar figures representing daily sales by store; the measure would be simply "sales."

 You sometimes see the word "measure" used to mean much the same as "fact." Technically there are some subtle distinctions between a measure and a fact, but to get a handle on the basics of OLAP, it's usually okay to consider the two terms synonymous.

 ✔ **Member:** One discrete element within a dimension. In the preceding example, we listed out stores by number along the horizontal axis of the table; any individual store (like Store #49) as a member of the "location" dimension.

Remember the Big Four BI criteria

Think for a moment about the essential characteristics of business intelligence. Regardless of how you get them, what applications are used, and what acronyms are involved, you need insights that are timely, accurate, high-value, and actionable. Here's how those criteria look from an OLAP perspective:

- ✔ **Timely:** Manipulating data in a modern OLAP system is a much faster way of producing relevant business data and presenting it in an intuitive, intelligent way than querying and assembling data from a relational database.

- ✔ **Accurate:** Multidimensional data doesn't just provide mere accuracy; you can trace it. You can dig into any cell instantly and find out what its constituent data elements are. In an OLAP report that shows quarterly sales data (for example), you can drill down and see monthly, weekly and daily information as needed to make your point.

- ✔ **High-value:** Even though an OLAP system deals in multidimensional data, it's still the same information that's housed in the transactional systems. Using OLAP, you can perform advanced data manipulation and analysis on just about any data stored in your enterprise. That means you can move quickly through data that doesn't matter to get to the data that does matter. And when high-value data is easier to get, good valuable insights are likely to appear.

- ✔ **Actionable:** This is where your OLAP system really earns its keep. Your OLAP system is especially good at aiding in analysis, allowing precise trends to be plotted and activities to be monitored. That means analysts can recommend immediate action to take advantage of a situation — or prevent a problem from growing worse.

Drill team: Working with Multidimensional Data

Users get more utility from reporting-and-analysis applications when they can explore the data on the fly. A typical *dumb* report is just a list of numbers, a table, or a series of tables. OLAP links all the data together at various levels in the system, then gives users access to it.

If all you're after is to taste the soup, you can stop there. But OLAP allows you to see the recipe and taste each ingredient. Going the other metaphorical direction, if you *like* the soup and want to see it in the context of the full meal, OLAP will set the table and serve you salad and a nice steak.

Because OLAP data dimensions are usually arranged in terms of hierarchies, it's important that the users be allowed to navigate up or down the different levels as their jobs require. That lets 'em get granular and settle on the right level of detail for performing a mandated analysis.

OLAP terms this maneuverability *drill capabilities*. Viewing a data point's constituent parts is called *drilling down*. This allows you to see business insights in greater detail. If you're examining how a data point aggregates into broader figures and calculations, you're *drilling up*. And viewing related data is called *drilling through* — a metaphor of moving sideways instead of vertically.

Gaining insight through drill-down analysis

Most users start their analysis with figures that are broad in scope, and from there they move into finer levels of detail as they see anomalous data or interesting trends. This is the *drill-down* process, an essential tool in the OLAP user environment.

Specifically, drilling down is the action of moving through the data hierarchy to the next (more specific) level of detail. As an example, a user might take an initial look at the OLAP cube and see quarterly production data, as shown in Table 5-6.

Table 5-6	A Drill-Down Example			
2007 Production Data				
Quarter ⇨	**Q1**	**Q2**	**Q3**	**Q4**
Factory A	577	529	499	442
Factory B	301	306	299	280
Factory C	753	731	819	648

The user might notice that each of the three factories were down in the fourth quarter of production — and double click the Q4 cell to open a new table that looks like Table 5-7.

Table 5-7	The Drill-Down Destination		
	2007 Production Data		
Month	**Oct**	**Nov**	**Dec**
Factory A	122	116	104
Factory B	93	107	80
Factory C	220	227	201

Okay, here's the user's action translated into OLAP-speak: Looking at the "2007 Production Data", the user double-clicked one of the dimension members (Q4) and drilled down by one level, opening a new table that displays the next level "down" in the hierarchy. This table shows more granularity — finer details of the fourth quarter. The user is still looking at factory production data — but can now look at each factory's production for the three specific months that make up the fourth quarter.

Okay, this is a simplistic example, but it gives you an idea of how useful an OLAP access tool can be. Instead of having to rewrite a report, the user can simply drill into the data to reach the desired level of detail.

Going in the other direction: drill-up analysis

As with drill-down analysis, the user can also take advantage of multidimensional data's hierarchical nature by looking at larger groupings of data — also with a single click. This is called *drilling up* in a report. Drilling up effectively telescopes the more detailed levels of the data hierarchy into the next level up, and consolidates (*rolls up*) their data totals.

If the user in the previous example wanted more of a bird's-eye view of the data, he or she could *drill up* from the quarterly table and view (say) the *annual* production total (that is, the quarterly totals combined). The table would provide a context across other years of output numbers, as in Table 5-8.

Table 5-8	A Drill-Up Example			
Production Data				
Year ⇨	**2007**	**2008**	**2009**	**2010**
Factory A	2047	1998	2166	2141
Factory B	1186	1094	1101	1136
Factory C	2951	2795	2788	2993

Again, the rest of the table remains the same, as it was in the drill-down analysis. We're still looking at production data over time, but now we're seeing yearly data with less granularity (detail). You'll be comforted to know the totals for 2007 by each factory are the same as before — and why not? It's exactly the same underlying production data.

Getting to the source: drill-through

Lying behind any item of multidimensional data are the many — sometimes millions — of rows of source information. The OLAP cube aggregates this data and transforms it into the multidimensional form you see in your OLAP front-end tools. But what if you need to go back and look at the original source data? If you've ever daydreamed about being able to walk through walls, here's your chance: *drill-through* capabilities.

Drill-through allows analysts to move between the OLAP table view and the source data. For example, suppose an auto dealership has an OLAP cube in place to provide instant analysis and reporting — but in the process of producing the annual sales report to the ownership group, the lot manager notices that the margins on a certain car model are far lower than they are for other models.

In this case, drilling down into more granular levels of the data hierarchy won't help. The information that's really needed is the individual transactions themselves — and that data is stored on the relational databases of the operational systems. OLAP access tools that can drill through to those databases (on the same level of detail) give the user quick and seamless access to the source transactions that make up the aggregations shown in the OLAP cube.

So why not just keep all your multidimensional data in a relational database? Well, there are some really good reasons not to — and they have to do with the difference between OLAP and OLTP, detailed in the next section.

OLAP versus OLTP

The reason behind building an OLAP database is because it excels where regular relational databases don't do such a good job. It might be useful to remember what's involved in an OLTP system.

For day-to-day operations such as running the accounting department or call center, almost every company relies on transactional databases. Transactional systems are built to perform data actions in a few fundamental ways:

- **Rapidly:** Transactional systems must allow their users to read, write, and delete data quickly. For example, picture a point-of-sale (POS) system of a large retailer where the back-end database must allow rapid, simultaneous processing of cash-register-like transactions. Every time a customer buys a stick of gum, the cashier scans the gum's bar code, accesses the database, and retrieves the price and product information. Then the system adds a record of the final purchase — all fast enough to get the customer out the door with minimum wait time.

- **In vast numbers:** In addition to working rapidly, transactional systems must be able to address billions of rows of data. Imagine an inventory system for a multinational enterprise with hundreds of warehouses all over the planet. Every addition, deletion, and change to a warehouse's contents must be recorded in a database.

- **In real time:** Transactional systems operate on a more or less continuous basis, reacting to user actions immediately and processing transactions on demand.

Transactional systems that support a company's basic operations are called *Online Transaction Processing* systems or *OLTP*. Even though ERP software provides some unity in the back-office applications and data, most big companies must run a variety of OLTP systems to support day-to-day operations.

Looking at Different OLAP Styles and Architecture

A multidimensional approach to data can be useful in different kinds of architectures. Unfortunately it involves another helping of alphabet soup (as if you aren't full enough already).

MOLAP: multidimensional OLAP

MOLAP — *Multidimensional Online Analytical Processing* — is the architecture based on cubes. It's a version of OLAP that's built for speed: MOLAP stores data in logical structures uniquely constructed to accelerate retrieval; these are separate from the relational database system (RDBMS).

In spite of its unappealing acronym, this is the traditional cube architecture described so far. The M for *multidimensional* simply indicates that in a MOLAP environment, a cube structure sits as a layer between the OLAP access tools and the relational database.

Old days of MOLAP

OLAP can trace its origins to the 1970s, when the relational database model was starting to gain a foothold in the programming community. An IBM engineer named Ken Tomlinson developed a high-level language called APL (you might expect it to stand for something technical and important, but APL was really just A Programming Language.) APL was radical because it included built-in functions to handle multidimensional data.

APL was as much mathematics as computer science. The old saying "It's Greek to me" applied (literally and figuratively) to APL; many of its programmatic operators were letters from the Greek alphabet, making it difficult to code on a standard keyboard and ASCII-based system.

APL did, however, spark some interest in the multidimensional approach. Although relational databases became far more prevalent, the ancestor of OLAP continued to evolve in the shadows through products such as TM1, an early spreadsheet application. There were also analysis and reporting companies such as Comshare and Information Resources (IRI) that produced databases with many multidimensional characteristics.

MOLAP in modern times

MOLAP-based systems began to hit the mainstream in 1992 with the release of the Arbor Software (later Hyperion) product Essbase, which IBM later integrated with its DB/2 relational-database product. Then Oracle (the 800-pound gorilla of the database world) bought IRI's product with the intention of turning it into a packaged layer of their traditional relational product. About that time, the term OLAP came into being, often attributed to Dr. E.F. Codd, best known as the father of the *relational* database.

Other OLAP products came on the market in the 1990s — Cognos Powerplay, SAP BW, and early versions of Microsoft Analysis Services — each of which still holds an important position in the market today.

If there is a downside to a MOLAP environment (versus other analysis-and-reporting architectures), it is that MOLAP necessarily involves an extra layer — the cube — and the architecture is already complex. It requires specific expertise beyond what the average database administrator can offer.

ROLAP: relational OLAP through "normal" databases

RDBMSs didn't get along well with OLAP at first; they were designed for transaction processing and efficient storage of data, not for analysis and reporting.

Nevertheless (to the shock and consternation of many OLAP traditionalists), a breed of OLAP that goes completely cubeless — ROLAP (Relational OLAP) — emerged, and is still alive and well.

Instead of proprietary multidimensional databases, ROLAP *emulates* a cube layer, inserting a semantic layer between the database and the end-user tool that mimics the data cube's actions. The OLAP access tools access the semantic layer as if they were speaking to OLAP cube.

The downside here, of course, is that relational databases weren't traditionally structured to deal with data in a dimensional format. When the information takes on more dimensions and increased hierarchical complexity, performance lags. A decade ago, there simply was not enough computing horsepower to handle such a load — but today's relational databases are more capable.

On the other hand, using ROLAP allows companies to use the relational database they've already installed (say, Oracle or DB2). What's more, they don't have to hire experts in building and maintaining multidimensional cubes and integrating all that stuff with the relational system.

HOLAP: Can't we all get along?

There are strong arguments on both sides of the ROLAP-versus-MOLAP debate. And the acronym-slinging doesn't end there. HOLAP (Hybrid OLAP) is an attempt to combine the best of both worlds.

In the early 1990s, it was necessary to make a firm commitment to one technology or the other, but these days vendors have taken serious steps to integrate the most useful functions of both worlds. Products like Microsoft SQL Server, with its integrated Analysis Services package, mean that organizations don't have to choose either ROLAP or MOLAP.

It's a lot like the hybrid automobiles on the market today. After all the questions about whether to buy an electric car, the manufacturers ended the debate by building a hybrid. When the driver needs power, the good old gas-guzzling, exhaust-spitting, V-8 internal combustion engine roars to life and boosts the car onto the freeway. But when the car is cruising, the gasoline-powered motor shuts off and gives way to the more efficient electric motor.

HOLAP systems perform the same kind of behind-the-curtains tricks as hybrid automobiles, switching modalities back and forth outside the view of the user. The cube structure is in place to handle large numbers of dimensions spanning many levels of hierarchy. They offer rapid performance and fast refresh times for workers performing analysis and creating complex reports.

Meanwhile, the hybrid systems can rely upon the space-saving ROLAP architecture to store larger volumes of raw data, funneling only the necessary summary information to the cube. And when the user needs drill-through capabilities to dig into the source transactions, the OLAP access tools can work directly with the relational system without a hitch.

And they do all that without contributing to global warming.

Chapter 6

Dashboards and Briefing Books

. . . .

. . . .

Some executives like to describe businesses in nautical terms. Start-ups are like speedboats they say, able to change direction on a dime as called for by market conditions. The huge multinational conglomerates on the other hand, are the supertankers, lumbering and powerful hulks, which take lots of planning and foresight before they make the slightest move.

Well, consider the supertanker *Knock Nevis,* the world's largest ship. It tips the scales at nearly 600,000 tons (eight times the weight of the biggest battleship ever constructed), and is about 1500 feet long. In spite of this enormous and complex mass, the many systems of the *Nevis* can be controlled from a small room in the superstructure by just a handful of sailors.

Every business, like every ship, has to have someone at the helm, reading conditions, navigating a course, and making the big decisions. But executives don't have the benefit of a ship's bridge, a single place where every operation can be monitored and controlled at the flip of a switch.

The closest a CEO can come to that kind of command are IT tools powered by business intelligence systems. For example, business dashboards provide what is essentially a control panel for monitoring the vital functions of the business. They supply immediate information and indicate when and where performance is lagging. With the help of the dashboard, its user might be able to keep the ship afloat.

Dashboards' Origins

In the 1980s, as virtually every company was adding to its technology infrastructure, managers and executives began to demand — and get — some benefit for all that computing power. Blossoming technologies were making life easier for everyone else in the company; whether you were a secretary, an accountant, or a salesman, computers and networks were encroaching on your day-to-day job functions, allowing for more informed decisions, and making you more productive. But it took a new class of software — even a whole new technology paradigm — for the suits upstairs to begin to reap the rewards of all that silicon muscle.

EIS: information gold for the top brass

The normal decision process for company leaders involved analyzing reams of data and combining that with subordinates' interpretation of that data. *Executive Information Systems* (EISs) changed all that. In the early 1980s companies began working with their IT departments to funnel key company information into the corner offices and boardrooms. These programs — typically built internally — harvested operational data from around the company mainframe and minicomputer systems. They brought all that data together, combined it, manipulated it, and presented it in easy-to-read summaries. Instead of raw numbers, executives now had some context, analysis, and intelligence to go with it. They got more than just *data*, they were now being fed *information*.

The foundation for the EIS concept was the *Decision Support System* (DSS) — early software that quantified how business decisions were made, and used computing power to support that process. For companies that had dabbled in DSSs throughout the 1970s, the EIS was the logical next step. It applied decision calculus to a wider array of business problems — and it got the attention of senior executives.

In the beginning, DSS and EIS software packages were mostly built in-house by corporate technology teams. In the mid-1980s, vendors started getting into the act. Pilot Executive Software started installing its Command Center application in 1984 and was quickly followed by others like Comshare, Metapraxis, and Execucom. Most packages cost in the neighborhood of a quarter of a million dollars; by the early 1990s, EIS was a $100 million business.

Most old-style EIS software was built with a fourth-generation (4GL) programming language, using pre-written queries and predefined parameters to summon the needed data from operational or transactional systems.

EIS versus classic reporting

The value of having an EIS package installed was that it allowed decision makers to avoid the difficult and time-consuming process of sifting through reams of reports for key information, and they short-circuited the upward-cascading feedback loop in which field personnel reported results to their managers — who in turn summarized local results for *their* managers, and so on until the information finally found its way back to the company leaders.

The user interface of an EIS program could be set up to show the most important information, metrics, and trends. The programmer or administrator could set ranges and parameters that defined when items needed attention and triggered visual alert messages. That way bigwigs with limited time to spare could quickly flip through the pertinent information, only pausing to dig into the nuts and bolts when they saw the flashing red light.

From the executive's point of view, it was perfect: No Byzantine queries to be written, no mountain of data to be scaled. The software took advantage of emerging database standards and could be hooked into any of the leading database and mainframe systems of the day. The information could be controlled and given out on a need-to-know basis only. The screens were all menu-driven; the graphics were beautiful.

EIS: Everybody's Information System

Although EIS was originally designed to supply only the top levels of the company with operational data, the rest of the organization quickly became interested in the same capabilities. After all, EIS software's job was to grab data from relevant data stores, summarize it, and present it to the user. Why couldn't it help mid-level managers make decisions about their particular domain, just as it did for executives making decisions about the entire enterprise?

The only difference between executive-level EIS and mid-level EIS is the scope of data that feeds the system. A COO might view sales metrics from all 250 stores around the country — checking status, looking for trends in product category sales and inventory cycles, perhaps comparing the figures with previous quarters and years. The regional manager would be interested in the same kinds of information — if only for that particular region's 32 locations. If the boss cares about it, the lower levels should care about it too.

EIS and dashboards can also have a unifying effect on a business that wasn't part of their original mandate. When the vendor or IT team is customizing the system to suit the company during the installation, the executives have to define their criteria for success and failure. Formulas based on those criteria must be attached to the key metrics that get scrutinized. Knowing how the boss judges the company's performance can help focus the efforts of the sub-ordinates on hitting those target metrics. That gets the entire team pointed in the same direction, working to meet that unified goal.

EIS gets left behind

As revolutionary as the Executive Information Systems were, there were certain limitations that pushed the approach out of style by the mid-1990s. EIS began to be associated with a primitive, static display of data — if you wanted to customize the data or change the questions that the system asked, a programmer still had to adjust the code.

But several key concepts came to light during the EIS era; they evolved and were woven into the business intelligence systems that companies use today:

✔ **The dashboard:** Presenting a user with an interactive GUI (graphical user interface) as a way to summarize information was a notion that stuck. In an airplane cockpit or on the dashboard of a car you find gauges and indicators for the most important elements of the system — but not all the information that exists. A 777 cockpit (for example) doesn't need a display showing whether the passenger in seat 17F had the chicken or the fish for dinner; it's not important to the pilot's job (except in the movie *Airplane*). The captain and first officer see things that matter to flying the plane — such as altitude, attitude, and heading. The key to a dashboard's utility is the presentation and position of the gauges: All the necessary information should be conveyed with a glance. Depending on the metric, that might mean using a graphic such as a red light/green light indicator, a chart, a graph, or a table. That technique — boiling down and expressing information in its essential form — has become an important business intelligence tool.

✔ **Interactive controls:** Most EIS software that flourished in the late 1980s and early 1990s was good at following a prearranged process with a dataset laid out well in advance. But it was not so good at tackling unforeseen problems, looking at data outside the expected domain of the EIS, or creating advanced projections, calculations, and what-if analyses. As the systems evolved in the 1990s, it became clear that the products would need some new features:

  • A customizable interface to match the level and function of the user

  • Adaptability to work with any data source in the network

  • The capability to present the data in a variety of ways

This increased level of flexibility and on-the-fly interactivity was part of the foundation for today's BI.

The Metric System

What exactly are users looking at when they turn on their dashboards? Businesses are complex animals, and they can be measured in a thousand different ways. But every enterprise has just a handful of metrics that reveal the essence of how the business is performing — its *Key Performance Indicators* (KPIs for short). It's one of the most important concepts in the realm of business intelligence.

Defining KPIs

KPIs go beyond simple financial measures and get at the heart of a company's operations. But KPIs have to be carefully selected, regardless of whether they appear in a dashboard application, a standard report, or some other tool. They must measure what's important to a company's success — and do so in a way that summarizes other, more granular measurements to provide a larger, more general measurement. A KPI occupies a middle ground between specific and general:

- ✔ Specific enough to indicate where to find the source of a problem if one exists

- ✔ General enough to keep the reader or user from getting lost in the minutiae and complexities of a large organization

A good analog to KPIs is a grammar school report card. For starters, even though a kid could be measured against many different criteria, report cards showed only items of importance. For instance, your report cards didn't include a grade for your posture or how well you tied your shoelaces. They were restricted to subject areas the school board deemed academically important (such as math, English, and social studies).

But there was no specific indication on the report card for how well you could diagram a sentence or do long division, even though those skills were critical to academic success. That's because report cards show *composite* metrics — they blend all of your test and homework scores in certain related areas under more general headings. Your math grade, for example, is a broad measurement that reflects your ability to do long division, convert fractions into decimals, complete word problems (ugh), and so on.

Why not list every single test and homework score on a report card? Because it's much easier to gauge a student's overall academic performance by showing a few *general* marks, rather than by displaying every single grade received during a semester. So, in effect, your grades were your childhood KPIs.

Business KPIs

Companies are complex beasts. The marketplaces in which they operate have a vast array of moving parts. How can you tell whether a complex organism like a corporation is moving in the right direction? There are the obvious measures — for example, those that deal with sales and profitability — but are they telling the whole story?

Financial metrics may indicate the overall health of the business, but they can do no more than hint at what's happening behind the curtain. It's like measuring the health of your car by the speed it's traveling down the road. You may be going 65 mph, but that doesn't help the fact that you're leaking oil and that there's a mailbox tangled up in your front bumper.

To get a better look at what's really happening inside their organizations, business chiefs turn to KPIs. Business KPIs help measure success — not of the company as a whole, but of individual processes. They are the benchmarks that encompass nearly every operational aspect of the business, and they allow companies to manage their overall success.

BI grows in popularity every day because it puts better KPIs in the hands of managers — developed through business intelligence processes, designed from the get-go to be accurate, meaningful, and timelier. On top of that, the KPIs themselves are precise enough to point at the actions required to make them better.

Consider the following example KPIs:

- ✔ Average waiting time in a customer call center queue
- ✔ Number of times inventory turns over in a year
- ✔ Percentage of defective units manufactured
- ✔ Average sales-cycle time
- ✔ Sales per square foot of retail floor space

There are endless permutations of key performance indicators; this list is only the lightest smattering. They cover a wide variety of operational disciplines, from customer service to sales to manufacturing.

While the success of any business always boils down to money, notice that that the preceding measurements don't *necessarily* include a direct dollar measurement. Through business intelligence processes, operational data is collected and evaluated that shows (for example) that call center wait time rises and falls at specific times of the day. With this information, a call center manager can then act to change staffing levels. A few weeks later, the BI system presents the manager with a follow-up report that demonstrates the results of the staffing changes.

It goes without saying (but we're going to say it anyway) that every organization is a little bit different. Even companies selling the exact same products or peddling identical services have their own peculiar strengths and weaknesses. Each company's position in the marketplace is unique; each one has a certain admixture of talent and skill that no other organization has. And most of all, corporate philosophies vary throughout a market. As a result, KPIs vary from company to company.

Looking at BI Dashboards

Today's dashboards are direct descendants of the old EIS and DSS systems — with greatly improved functionality and appearance. That's because they're linked to today's powerful data systems (the backbone of modern business intelligence solutions) and utilize tightly focused KPIs.

Mission control to the desktop

As with the BI query-and-reporting tools or OLAP drill-down reports, the latest generation of dashboards can be made widely available to people throughout the company — at all levels and in nearly all job types. The shipping department might have a system that keys into the production, inventory, and logistics databases, in addition to hooks that lead into the road and rail companies' systems. Their dashboard might show the status of shipments, collated daily and weekly delivery statistics, damage and late arrival rates, and other metrics understandable and relevant only to shipping department personnel.

The fact is, 80 to 90 percent of individual contributors perform analysis of some kind. Not all those workers have the skill or training to write complex queries or direct an intricate application to produce the desired results. A well-designed dashboard can make a marked difference in workers' productivity because it allows them to make immediate decisions based on real-time information.

Dashboards are flexible tools that can be bent into as many different shapes as the users call for. They can be customized for all levels of an organization and can be set up to be backward-looking or focused on the present situation, depending on the users' needs. Administrators may populate a dashboard with historical data to show a general strategic situation or they can feed low-latency (that is, almost real-time) data to act as an up-to-the-minute status report on current operations.

Each screen and control on a single dashboard should represent information that's relevant to the user's office domain. A call center rep's dashboard (for example) might display a running graphic of call volume, average hold times and call times, calls handled per employee, and other metrics peculiar to that environment. The accounts-receivable clerk might have other metrics such as late payers, weekly and daily revenue received trends, and outstanding collection notices.

Dashboards might show high-level abstract data about the company (say, aggregate financial measurements), but they are equally effective — if not more effective — if they show real live operational information that relates directly to tasks that teams and individuals perform every day.

Dozens of dashboard vendors exist in the marketplace. Some offer general packages to sit atop a BI solution; others provide specialized controls that focus on certain areas of the business. But most dashboards share a set of common features:

- ✔ **Navigable layout:** Computer screens are only so big, so dashboards allow for multiple, easily accessible screens. Whether it's tabs, bread-crumb trails, or some kind of menu-based system, most dashboards have a global navigation feature that allows for more information to be displayed than a single screen can handle. That means there's a lot of information at the users' fingertips.

- ✔ **Appealing and differing graphics:** Conveying information on complex subjects is not always easy or intuitive. A good dashboard allows for the presentation of metrics in a variety of ways, such as charts, graphs, tables, and speedometers.

- ✔ **Interactivity:** When a user sees an important measure that needs attention, the dashboard presents a pathway to deeper layers of information. For example, if the speedometer control dips from the green into the red section, a user might want to see the component measurements that make up the larger measure in an effort to get to the source of the problem. Clicking a dashboard control might do something simple (say, sort or expand a list or pivot a table around a more relevant dimension), or it might lead to another application, or even automatically produce an OLAP report that can then be drilled into and analyzed.

- ✔ **Customizable interface:** Users should be able not only to navigate to different subject areas, but also to set up their dashboards in a way that gives them the ideal mix of information relevant to their jobs. Except for specialty packages, dashboards offer customization and personalization.

- ✔ **Embedded content:** This feature allows administrators and users to mix in external content with the application-fed indicators and graphics. It might be appropriate for a financial analyst to have a dashboard window that had a stock ticker crawl. Or the accounting team might need to have an interactive calendar available.

- ✔ **Browser-based capabilities:** Dashboards can be standalone applications, or they can be made available over standard browser software. This makes distribution and control of the information easier.

Dashboard best practices

The old cliché about a picture being worth a thousand words rings true when it comes to dashboards. Rather than working through a mass of reports and hours of meetings and briefings, knowledge workers can take a quick glance at their dashboards and understand in an instant whether or not their team, department, or division is performing up to snuff.

Picking the right kind of dashboard

We've talked about the different business areas that can be modeled with a dashboard approach, from accounting to shipping to human resources. But the other dimension is just as important: What level of the company *needs* the dashboard? It's worth asking; the approach to installing dashboards is actually quite different depending on the view required.

In *Performance Dashboards: Measuring, Monitoring, and Managing Your Business* (Wiley Publishing, Inc., 2005), dashboard expert Wayne W. Eckerson defines three main breeds of dashboards: *tactical, operational,* and *strategic.* Here's how those differ:

- **Tactical dashboards** measure short-term productivity and effectiveness; their output is often used by an individual contributor. As an example, a network engineer might have a tactical dashboard that actively monitors real-time IT infrastructure statistics and trends — say, a Web site's hits and dropped packets. Such metrics would give the engineer an immediate tip-off when something is wrong — and a pretty good notion of whether it's with the servers, the software, or the connectivity.

- **Operational dashboards** quantify the short- and medium-term effectiveness of a specific business function (or family of business functions) at the team or business-unit level. This level of dashboard could potentially be deployed for an individual knowledge worker or a local team manager. The trends and metrics displayed will have an impact on short-term decisions. Call center managers might watch customer-satisfaction metrics on their operational dashboards, looking out for negative trends that would spur them to take immediate action and make changes to the way the reps handle certain kinds of complaints.

- **Strategic dashboards** are built for the policy-setting levels of the organization (such as the chief-level executives or business-unit directors). These dashboards display metrics that represent corporate strategy and direction. They correspond to large-scale business activities, and usually have designated teams responsible for monitoring them, interpreting them, assessing their status, and making recommendations for the indicated course corrections (if necessary).

Building the best dashboard for you

As useful as dashboards can be, there are still ways to mess it up. Dashboards are designed to offer a first indicator when something is amiss, but they aren't meant to completely replace all other decision processes. Fortunately more than two decades of best practices are available to offer aid and comfort to the project manager facing the dashboard wilderness.

- **It all starts with two simple questions.** What is the scope of what you're measuring? What kind of data will you be displaying? Answer those, and you can move on to even more "best practices."

- **Select your KPIs wisely.** Start with your business objectives, then look at the available operational data to find appropriate metrics — not the other way around. Some companies have a tendency to let the tail wag the dog and slap any old measurement on the dashboard. If your goal is to monitor manufacturing performance, the factory manager's dashboard doesn't need to display the company stock price.

- **Don't succumb to dashboard overload.** It's possible to cram so much data — so many gauges and widgets — into a dashboard that the clutter nullifies the advantages of having at-a-glance summary information. Remember: Dashboards should show essential information only.

- **Watch the dashboard, but check the oil occasionally, too.** Dashboards can be incredibly useful on their own, but they're at their best when used in concert with other BI components, such as OLAP-driven querying and reporting.

- **Take dashboard design seriously.** That means considering the placement and type of gauges, simple user interface best practices, and careful management of the depth to which users can dive into the data so they don't get tangled in the weeds of too much detail. A dashboard, like any other application, is only as good as it is usable. If the user community has trouble navigating or interpreting the data, then your dashboard won't offer much of an advantage over standard representations of information.

Briefing Books and Other Gadgetry

Dashboards are excellent at delivering real-time information, but they're only a part of the overall business intelligence equation. What if, as a knowledge worker, you need regular access to reports and other application output beyond your customized dashboard screens? Or what if you want to share specific BI insights with others in your company? To collaborate on dashboard metrics or other complex reporting, many BI application suites offer a briefing-book tool. A *briefing book* gives the user the capability to save and collect dashboard screens, scorecards, and reports to create a *book* of related information. But briefing books aren't just screen shots or Power Point slides.

Scorecards

In discussions of BI end-user tools, *scorecards* are usually lumped in with dashboards — but they have different functions: Scorecards are designed to measure progress toward meeting strategic business goals; dashboards are only designed for ongoing monitoring of specific activities. Dashboards are not meant to convey information about how close operations match the intent of the business and associated targets.

A scorecard usually appears as a graphical list of specific, attainable strategic milestones, combined with metrics that serve as benchmarks. Measurements of how well the company actually executes specified activities are linked to the scorecard; the resulting display is the status of each goal, often with some kind of graphic indicator.

For example, a scorecard might display green when a given profit margin is meeting or exceeding company expectations. But once the bloom is off the rose and profits sag, the scorecard fill color turns to red — indicating that attention is needed to shore up the business. Like a dashboard, the scorecard gives a consolidated at-a-glance view of key information.

Scorecards are designed to help managers and executives quickly identify company initiatives that need extra attention. They're also an excellent way to distribute accountability to mid-level managers — if you have to explain to the boss why the goal associated with your name is blinking bright red, it's a motivator!

This figure is an example of one of Hyperion's BI strategic scorecard screens. The strategic objectives have status lights that indicate whether the company is on target. Another important aspect of this product is that the objectives are linked directly to subordinate objectives — and (later) to specific activities that must be accomplished to meet the objectives. In this example, the objective "Profitable Growth" links to sub-objectives "Increase Revenues" and "Reduce Costs" — which are in turn connected to specific actions that the company must undertake successfully to hit those component objectives. The overall effect is a traceable story arc about the current business situation that a manager could quickly transform into actions to correct any strategic shortcomings.

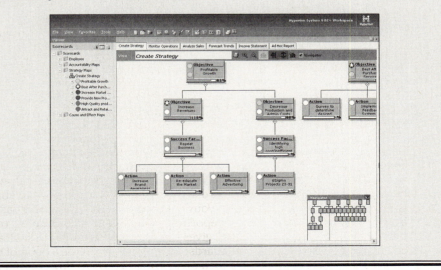

Users can actually create and organize a dynamic, interactive collection of data from a number of sources — and tightly control its presentation. For example, in your briefing book you might assign a certain dashboard control to the first page, but have it appear only if it falls into a certain range of values. If you have a project scorecard, for example, you might set your briefing book to display only those phases and steps that are overdue and appear as flashing red lights on your dashboard.

Other tools exist to help users manage the volume of information available to them. Tickers can be set to crawl across the users' desktops, constantly updating the metrics of their choice. BI vendors are also increasing their capacity to display KPIs as interrelated measurements through cause-effect diagrams and process maps. In essence, though, all these tools are attempting to accomplish the same basic task: inform the user with timely, accurate, important, and actionable insights.

Chapter 7

Advanced / Emerging BI Technologies

In This Chapter
- ▶ Making choices with guided analysis
- ▶ Shafting the competition with data mining
- ▶ Seeing visualization clearly

*F*rom its humble beginnings, business intelligence continues to evolve today as vendors offer more powerful and innovative solutions. With all those changes, the purpose of BI systems remains the same — timely, accurate, high-value, and actionable insights. The new capabilities all serve those simple goals in one way or another.

Some of the advances happening today are taking current capabilities and making them better, such as more powerful graphic representations of data. But BI innovation goes beyond simply adding bells and whistles to existing applications. The evolution of BI is happening along a broad front with the technology growing more powerful, more meaningful, and capable of putting business insights into the hands of more people.

Transforming data from raw facts into meaningful observations and rules about business operations is not so different from scientific research; every year sees incremental advances, not just in the conclusions reached, but in the research methodologies, tools, and technologies that the researchers rely on. The pace of change in BI is steady; occasional minor breakthroughs in how environments are built and used become next year's best practices and top-selling tools.

Of course, in a BI environment, *innovative*, *imaginative*, and *powerful* are all relative terms. Vendors are always rolling out new tools, but there's no guarantee that the newest thing can help you with your business problems; that's for you to evaluate, and for your team to make a reality.

Some of the areas where research is expanding rapidly include the following general categories:

- ✔ **Visualization:** using advanced graphics to make critical business insights clearer and more meaningful

- ✔ **Guided analysis:** interactive, goal-oriented BI that answers a specific set of questions in a structured way, prescribing certain actions based on the user's input and analysis

- ✔ **Data mining:** finding *the* needle you really need . . . in a huge stack of needles

- ✔ **Unstructured data tools:** turning irregular data into business insights with search and indexing capabilities for hard-to-quantify information formats

Does that mean you can install these things today? In some form or another, the answer is usually yes. Implementations tend to lag BI innovations. That's a nice way of saying that companies rarely want to be the first on their block to try an untested technology. A new tool that blows away the current paradigm will take time to find its way into immediate widespread use — and it takes even longer to make everyone's "best practices" list.

Of course, a tool or feature that is so common in today's BI environments started as little more than a gleam in the collective eye of a team of software engineers in the design shop of a particularly innovative vendor. When it gained popularity in the marketplace other vendors would have copied that success by building their own version of that feature. Before long, it would become a must-have for any BI system. That process is still going on today as vendors continually seek to gain market share by building a better mouse trap; it's a continuing cycle of development in the BI world.

Catching a Glimpse of Visualization

The mission of any business intelligence program is to get information to people when and where they need it. But as a secondary task, a BI system also has to make that information usable once it reaches its destination. One of the ways BI software can make information more usable is through visualization techniques.

 Visualization means presenting numbers, statistics, metrics, and other facts in a graphical format that makes them easier to understand and interpret. Representing poll results as a pie chart is a simple example of visualization. As the old saying goes, "what the eye sees, the mind knows."

Basic visualization

As data-warehousing and querying software grew more powerful and widespread, so did the need for ever-more-complex ways to present the output data. The result was stand-alone reporting software — either separate from or packaged with basic query tools — that could help the user arrange, transform, and present data to audiences in a variety of formats. Reporting software made the information as easy to understand as possible.

As BI was applied throughout the organization, the insights it provided grew in strategic value. Presenting data in a compelling format was no longer a luxury; in fact it became a top priority. Companies turned to tools that could transform their numbers into charts, graphs, and other accessible and understandable representations. The lesson was clear: as important as standard row-and-column reporting is, presenting data graphically can make the communication of complex data more efficient and more powerful.

Worth a thousand words

Data has to be understood as having an impact on business. And representing data with charts, graphs, and other images is a powerful way to communicate insights to team members, managers, partners and customers. A concept or trend that may not be dramatic, or even clear, in tabular form, often comes alive in the right graphical format.

But this bit of everyday magic is easy to dismiss as insignificant. By creating a bar graph, all we've done is represent numbers from the table as proportionally sized bars on a graph. But that simple change is powerful: Instead of seeing numerals sitting in a table or on a page — thinking to ourselves, "Self, that number sure is bigger than that other number," and then analyzing the results of our assigning relative sizes to each data point — we can actually *see* those relationships. The bar graph allows us to skip a cognitive obstacle between us and the *meaning* of the numbers.

It's true that in such a simple example, you might well have spotted the sales pattern just by focusing on the 12 numbers in the table. But imagine a table with a *thousand* points of data, or a million. In those cases visualization isn't just a bonus or a shortcut; it's a necessary step to performing meaningful analysis and obtaining business insights.

Just as Excel grew beyond mere grid-style representation to include its well-known charts and graphs toolset, BI reporting tools have grown to include basic visualization techniques, similar to those you find in spreadsheets.

Off the charts

The charting tool is the core of a visualization tool set. At the most basic level, that means static representations of data points like pie charts where the size of a given "slice" of a disc shows its relative share of the total amount.

BI reporting tools available today include visualization packages — but most of those are still fairly simple. Analysts who need to translate their visually barren reports into compelling stories do have some special tools available that can help them with that job. Just as reporting tools ride atop the rest of the BI stack, visualization tools plug into reporting engines — and can translate data into cool pictures that convey the message about the data much more immediately than the data itself can.

Turning large complex data sets into meaningful images is the domain of advanced visualization tools. Instead of simple charts and graphs, graphics packages allow users to render data into complicated geometric shapes and vector graphics, all in vibrant colors. The goal is to make that information easy to interpret; instead of poring over tables to find profitability hot spots in a company's product line, a visualization tool can create an image that will bring the full profitability picture to life, and put it into context with other business factors.

Visualizing tomorrow

Vendors have to grapple with an unavoidable challenge inherent in visualization techniques: A graphical representation of data must be compelling enough to look at, informative and truthful in its portrayal of the data — without giving the user a severe case of visual overload.

This balancing act is no mean task. As visualization software expands to include charts with multiple layers, drill-through capabilities, and navigation links, they risk becoming just as challenging to comprehend as the report they're attempting to simplify! BI administrators and visualization tool users must be vigilant that users and information consumers aren't getting buried in too much detail.

Nevertheless, graphical representation has given BI a jolt of life by making business insights compelling and convincing. In addition, users in many different jobs are used to graphics-based interfaces — and high-end visualization is the next logical step. Dashboards have become permanent tools for BI family; vendors such as Microstrategy are taking advantage of dashboard space as a place to represent data with visualization.

The newest visualization tools offer some fairly jazzy features, especially when you think of BI and processing truckloads of numerical data:

- ✔ **Aesthetic appeal:** Vendors have realized that rendering data in a visual format is only useful if the audience is willing to read, view, and digest the information — and to do that, they have to *look* at it first. Making a control on a dashboard beautiful, rather than just giving it bare-bones functionality, helps attract the user's attention in the same way a memo or position paper can do if it's engaging, reader-friendly, and suited to its audience.

  Most knowledge workers with dashboards on their desktops aren't pilots, engineers, or mathematicians; accuracy by itself isn't enough to make a graphical representation of data useful.

- ✔ **Interactivity:** The original dashboard model relied on graphical controls to be read just like any other static report; the data was translated into a chart or graph that could then be interpreted by the reader. The next generation, however, takes advantage of greater computing power and speedier data transformation — and turns a static report into more of a dialogue.

  This goes beyond simply clicking a dashboard control to see a second, deeper-level control. Imagine putting the mouse pointer over one word on the report and having all the other graphical controls transform or pivot in reaction — can do. The newest controls also allow for rapid toggling and tabbing.

- ✔ **Customizable tools:** Vendors can't anticipate everything, so they build programmatic hooks into their tools to allow developers on your team to dip into the toolbox and make the dashboards and controls just right to fit with your system. This approach also allows developers to import and use a wide range of third-party tools.

Really cool, next-generation visualization

Quality visualization goes beyond just more slippery sliders and tastier-looking pie charts. BI vendors are trying to incorporate enough visual tools to allow design professionals to turn data into meaningful presentation material. We're not quite to the point where you can surround yourself with a hologram of your BI data (as in the movie *Minority Report*), but anything that helps audiences understand data better is fair game.

These days most tools present complex, three-dimensional geometric renderings of data, overlaid with traditional visualizations such as bar graphs or pie charts. For example, a tool might render the data points of a simple two-dimensional table into elevation points on a smooth 3-D terrain; on top the terrain would be a bar that corresponded to each elevation point and could show another dimension of the data.

Advanced visualization tools are only worthwhile when there is an expert there to create the graphics. That means a BI manager needs analysts who can not only build queries and reports, but also pilot the tools that create the advanced representations. Vendors make every attempt to make the tools easy to use, but to take full advantage of the latest tools that create scientific-grade charts, advanced geometric representations, and other next-generation visualizations, you'd better have somebody on the team who can both

- ✔ Understand what's going on with the underlying BI process.
- ✔ Use the visualization tools that present the information most effectively to a specific audience.

On top of that, visualization requires good data-management practices. Companies typically need visualization tools when they're dealing with massive data sets that resist interpretation by other methods. If you've reached a point where visualization tools make sense, then your BI environment as a whole must be able to move and manipulate gargantuan volumes of information. If it can't do that, it won't be able to support the kind of visualization tools you need.

Spatial visualization

One of the hottest trends (and latest buzzwords) in business intelligence is presenting data by way of *spatial visualization*. This approach takes advantage of today's mapping technologies to weave business information into maps and other geospatial representations. What you get is an immediate impression of (say) where business processes are taking place and how they compare with each other, as in Figure 7-1. Of course, using space as a data dimension is nothing new. (After all, where else *do* you visualize something but in space?) But its burgeoning integration with business intelligence is a symbiosis that allows companies to represent information about customers, vendors, shipping points, or any other entities that reside in the real world, and whose locations are an important business consideration.

These tools have grown with the advent of ever-more-accurate GPS technology that can create data with a coordinate system in much the same way that transactional data might be stamped with date, marking its "location" in the time dimension.

Steering the Way with Guided Analysis

Part of the challenge of business intelligence is that powerful tools create so many possibilities. It can all be overwhelming to an analyst. Capabilities keep proliferating — usually way too many for the limited range of problems that need to be solved immediately. Wouldn't it be nice if someone could just show you what to *do* with all these buttons and options and toolbars?

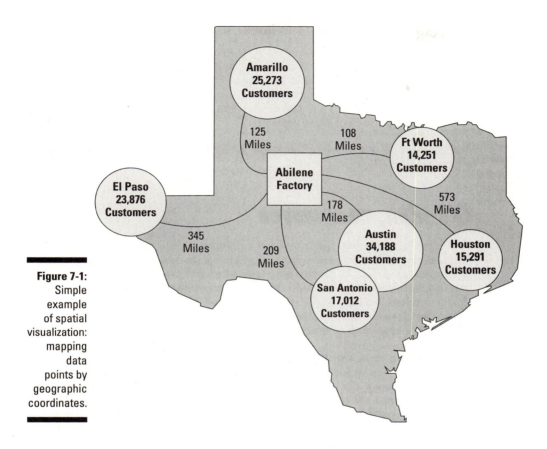

Figure 7-1:
Simple
example
of spatial
visualization:
mapping
data
points by
geographic
coordinates.

That's where *guided analysis* can help. It's an application that sits atop other BI tools and literally directs the user to take certain follow-on steps that depend on initial results. It's like having a BI tutor sitting next to you saying, "Okay, now you'll want to rerun that same query, except expand it to include the Northwest region."

Having trouble visualizing what guided analysis is like? Think of a piece of well-designed tax software. The goal is to complete an overall tax return, but the software helps break up the task into manageable chunks. The application guides the user through a series of steps that build to an ultimate solution.

Dancing the BI two-step

The typical BI process is still very much a two-step sequence:

1. The user poses a query of some kind to the system, or perhaps signs up to receive a certain array of information on a regular basis. Then, when

the system delivers that information to the user, the second step begins: analysis.

2. The user takes the information set and performs whatever manipulations and data gymnastics might be needed to draw a useful conclusion. For many complex business tasks, this involves performing a series of queries, followed by intermediate steps of data manipulation, and finally producing the necessary answer.

Guided analysis is a process that helps users get from point A to point B more efficiently and effectively.

Old idea, new moves

The more BI spreads to the masses of a company, the more important it is that the end users have some form of guidance as they manipulate data to make decisions. This is particularly true when a department or team makes regular decisions where the variables are well understood, even if those decision processes are long and complicated. Guided analysis is an element of BI where developers configure decision-support tools to offer users direct help during their regular processes.

For example, a bank employee processing a mortgage application might have to enter hundreds of pieces of information about the customer and the loan. That process likely has dozens of branches that are taken depending on what data gets entered. On top of that, the employee might need to access BI systems to view market reports, credit profiles, and other information on the fly. Guided analysis wraps this complex process into a single "skin", prompting the user from one screen to the next, delivering contextual information as needed.

The basic idea of guided analysis is nothing new; software vendors have always sought to combine computing tasks into sequences to create applications with broader reach. And since BI systems are built to support the decision-making process, you'd think guided-analysis techniques would be a natural fit with BI-driven tasks. But because BI tools were built to be strictly functional, users were expected to design their own workflow to solve their specific problems. Designers rarely considered wrapping tools into a consistent package that could link insight-gathering processes together for users.

With so much data being stored and analyzed in so many different corners of the today's business world, it only makes sense that vendors embrace the guided analysis paradigm. Users in any discipline can combine transactional tasks with analysis tasks — two actions that were traditionally separate. Teams can build playbooks and end-to-end processes around BI tools, making an already-strategic function that much more powerful.

Guiding lights

Guided-analysis systems do more than simply add a few help icons to a reporting tool. BI tools with guided-analysis features might have (for example) process wizards that walk users from step to step, or set up event alerts that monitor the system — or the user's activity — and only offer help when it's needed.

When certain trigger conditions are met, the user is alerted and the guided-analysis tools step in to direct the user on how to proceed. The trigger may cause any of the following to happen:

- ✔ The user is alerted to a problem and given advice on how to resolve it.

- ✔ The system automatically runs processes or queries that the user might need to perform the task that's been identified.

- ✔ The system leads the user down a known best-practices path, presenting screens and tasks that have been pre-scripted.

Using complex, multistep processes, the guided-analysis engine serves several functions:

- ✔ Helps keep users on track and ensures that they've supplied complete information

- ✔ Keeps track of the progress of branch tasks that might need to be revisited later

- ✔ Gives contextual help about progress made toward the solution

Result: users don't just work in a vacuum of numbers and spreadsheets; they work in the context of broader business goals. Tight process management combined with established best practices to help with users' workflow and collaboration make guided analysis a useful manifestation of business intelligence capabilities.

Data Mining: Hype or Reality?

The amount of information maintained by companies has reached levels that are truly astonishing. Most of the corporate packrat habit can be traced to the rapid advances in storage technologies. Data that used to require an entire storage room full of documents can now be digitally rendered and put on a few square millimeters of magnetic tape or a hard drive platter. There's also a just-in-case attitude that many corporations take: Hang on to your data because in a more litigious society, you never know when you'll need it.

But it's probable that *hope* drives some of the trend in data storage. There are people who dedicate their lives to finding hidden trends in stock prices and economic indicators in the hope that they can transform that information into profit. Top-level executives take the same attitude: All that company data must be harboring secrets and trends that, if harnessed, could help make the business more successful than ever before.

That's what data mining is all about — examining oceans of past business data to find useful insights about the past that can act as a guide to the future. The twin trends of increased information storage and the steady advance of processing power means that dream may not be out of reach.

Digging through data mining's past

The concept of data mining has been around since the 1950s when the first computers were moving out of entire floors of buildings and into single rooms. As scientists' eyes were being opened to the possibilities of machines that could resolve math problems, they also dreamt about far more complex problems, and even of machines that could find their own problems to solve.

The term *artificial intelligence* was coined in 1956 at Dartmouth. But what they had in mind wasn't the brand of AI that involves a robot mowing your lawn while deftly avoiding your begonias. Computer scientists originally saw AI as a way to tackle evolving problems by including feedback loops in code. The idea is simple: When an AI application attempts to solve a problem, it "learns" from its incorrect guesses by noting what variables change — and is programmed to look for why they change.

AI gave birth to so-called *expert systems* (a trend that peaked in the late 1980s) — computer programs that accept inputs and apply to them a set of *heuristics* (a fancy term that computer scientists use to refer to formulas and rules) to produce a result. Programmers typically fed the system a vast amount of past data and worked in a randomness that the system would use as a model for its predictions of future results.

In theory, you turn the power of the computer loose on the data and wait for a solution to emerge. In practice though, it was hard to implement. If they weren't set up correctly, or if they weren't fed the correct data, expert systems turned out to be not so smart.

But the idea was sound, and as other information technologies around them improved, the expert systems of the 1980s evolved into ever-more powerful pattern-matching software of the 1990's and the twenty-first century. Data mining came into its own.

Digging for data gold

Like "business intelligence," *data mining* is a catchall phrase; it refers to any computational technique that attempts to transform reams of raw data into meaningful business insights. Data mining software often includes advanced pattern-matching algorithms and high-end statistical analyses — anything to help the user draw useful links between the past and the future.

No matter what it's called, these are the questions that get answered:

- ✔ **What *really* happened in the past?** This is where the mountain of data points comes in. We're not just talking about showing you reports of yesterday's sales. Data mining tools use advanced mathematical models to find patterns and themes in historical data that wouldn't otherwise be evident.

- ✔ **Why did it happen?** Knowing *what* happened is valuable — but it's even better if you know what the root causes were. Data mining compares many different variables and looks for subtle correlations over long periods of time.

- ✔ **What is likely to happen in the future?** If you can apply the patterns of the past to the current conditions of the company, it might be possible to predict the outcome of certain business activities.

Those three questions lie at the heart of all doctrine, whether it's business, medicine, warfare, or any other discipline. If you can recognize that you're currently following a specific chain of events that has happened before and led to a certain outcome, it gives you the opportunity to act to improve that outcome this time around.

It's worth saying again in the context of data mining: Don't confuse causality with coincidence. Just because two things happen at roughly the same time doesn't mean that one event caused the other.

Data mining today

Data mining has been successfully applied to business problems, especially over the last decade. Some industries (for example, banking and insurance) use it to attach likely outcomes to certain behavioral patterns — which helps determine major business variables such as financial risk.

As data mining techniques have become more refined, it's become a mainstream tool for non-financial businesses as well. More software vendors now view data mining as an essential BI component, and are starting to include it in their core DBMS (database management system) products. For example,

Microsoft installed data mining tools in the latest version of SQL Server 2005, allowing you to work all kinds of cool statistical wizardry upon your data. If you know how to take advantage of things like multiple regression and non-parametric analysis, data mining is for you.

If you're using data mining, make sure you don't become the sorcerer's apprentice and unleash magic you can't control. Advanced data-mining and statistical tools are like weapons: Only those well trained in their use and application should be allowed near them. The problem is simple: It's both hard to create meaningful results and (unfortunately) easy to turn perfectly good data into total highfalutin garbage through the miracle of statistics.

In spite of the challenges, data mining should be on every BI project manager's roadmap as a critical part of the overall toolkit. Used wisely, it can add tremendous value to the business.

BI 2.0 and the world of tomorrow

Technology buyers are enamored with version numbers, and no number is more significant in terms of hype than *2.0*. You see it associated any so-called "next generation" technology. (Of course, when that generation actually arrives, they'll probably just think of a new buzzword for it, and then they'll apply "2.0" to the follow-on generation. And so it goes.)

As BI has matured in the marketplace and become widely accepted, executives far and wide are authorizing BI installations in their companies. But the fact is, BI is already a little long in the tooth; the term has been around since the first George Bush was president. So it's only natural that vendors are competing to claim more mental real estate as *the* provider of next-generation BI. No wonder *BI 2.0* has entered the lexicon as a common buzzword for "emerging business intelligence tools."

Of course, BI 2.0 means different things to different vendors and experts:

✔ For some vendors and experts, 2.0 involves specific capabilities we've listed in this chapter, such as advanced visualization techniques.

✔ For others, it's about architecture — such as the very stylish service-oriented architecture (essentially building business intelligence tools without a data warehouse, and using other methods of collecting and aggregating data before funneling it to the BI tools).

From a more general perspective, BI 2.0 encompasses broad improvements in existing BI trends — a shorter time from analysis to action, a wider user base as BI spreads throughout the organization, and potent encounters with other IT products and processes such as ERP (enterprise resource planning).

Okay, nobody has the one true definition of BI 2.0. But rest assured that you'll continue to see the term pop up in articles and in the literature of vendors. For now, you won't go wrong if you think of it as a general acceleration of existing BI trends.

Other Trends in BI

The business intelligence universe is in constant flux. Read an article in one of the many magazines or Web sites covering the field, and you'll likely learn about another hot topic on the minds of BI professionals. Whether it's how to organize a team, the latest in applications and architectures, or manage ongoing BI processes, keeping up with trends can be a full-time job. Below are a few examples of other broad directions in business intelligence.

BI for one and all

The consistent trend in business intelligence is to offer the ability to retrieve and identify useful insights "down" the corporate food chain from the great white sharks to plankton. Whether it's high-level executives, senior managers, mid-level managers, or individual contributors, if an employee makes better decisions, it's a good thing for the organization.

Unstructured data

Oceans of corporate data reside in non-standard formats. Imagine the wealth of information stored in documents, Web pages, or even video. And up until now, that information has been untamed — difficult (if not impossible) to search, sort, and report on.

That's why there's a veritable gold rush to develop tools that reach into a business's nooks and crannies to ferret out hard-to-reach information. This growing element of the BI space is centered on new search technologies that allow a user to find — and make use of — information that doesn't fit into a known pattern.

The problem with unstructured data that exists in documents — or other formats — is that there's no context to explain how that data is arranged and what it means. As a result, the tools have to be extremely complex to be able to interpret what they're looking at.

For example, Business Objects has a technology called *Data Feed as a Universe* that accepts information from just about anywhere — including Excel files, Web-service feeds, RSS feeds, and any other source for external data. The idea is that users can combine information from varied sources with data warehouse data to create a richer environment for analysis and presentation.

Part III
The BI Lifecycle

The 5th Wave By Rich Tennant

"I started running 'what if' scenarios like, 'What if I were sick of this dirtwad job and funneled some of the company's money into an off-shore account?'"

In this part . . .

So you've figured out the concepts of BI, and you understand how users work with the tools to obtain business insights. Now you're ready to make that lemonade stand hum.

In this part, you'll learn about how BI solutions are assembled. Where do you start? What goals are you working toward? How does the structure of your company play into these tasks? What factors are important to your lemonade stand that may not be important to your competitors?

Before you know it, you'll be hammering out a BI strategy for yourself.

Chapter 8

The BI Big Picture

*I*f you're waiting for that chapter where we talk about the one-and-only BI methodology that will bring about world peace in addition to guaranteeing your project's success, you're in for a disappointment: Such a thing does not exist.

As anxious as you may be to get started, making careful first steps is one of the best things you can do for your project. You're faced with a thousand decisions early on — including selecting a scope for your initial implementation, which vendor(s) to choose, and how to staff your team.

But the consequences of rushing headlong into the project are too far-reaching and expensive to do anything but the best planning beforehand. In this chapter, we talk about just what kind of mousetrap you want to build, some of the key choices you have in front of you, and some tips on making good decisions in the early stages.

So Many Methodologies, So Little Time

There is no shortage of pathways to the end of your BI project, but there may be only a few that will truly lead you to BI nirvana. Because while they may look nice on paper, it's likely that only a few of these "secret recipes" will actually fit your project's particular needs.

So open up a magazine, crack a book, or fire up a Web page, and you'll likely come face to face with yet another methodology for installing a business-intelligence solution.

When you take on the challenge of selecting a BI methodology, you're evaluating not only what you can afford to do with the technology budget; you're also thinking about what your company can actually do within the allotted timeframe, and why you're doing BI in the first place.

Starting at the beginning

What's your BI implementation going to accomplish? Have you settled on a precise scope and timeline for the project yet? If you haven't, then you should consider doing so before looking any farther down the road.

Once the strategy for the project's been laid down, consider some roadmapping exercises where you match the project goals with some concrete steps on how to achieve them. A roadmap is like a Gantt chart on a project plan; the results and ending of one phase become the inputs and starting whistle for the next phase. Working through the critical stages of the project gives you early perspective on the challenges of timing and coordinating activities, availability of interconnected resources, and the kinds of decisions that have to be made — now and in the future.

Every methodology you see will probably look easy on paper. And not just easy to do, but easy on the eyes as well, what with all the richly colored diagrams of technology stacks and process flows where circles and boxes get magically connected by big, thick arrows that virtually scream "progress!"

If only it were that easy.

It's unlikely that a single, out-of-the box methodology pitched by one vendor or consultant will suit all your needs. There will inevitably be unexpected twists and turns in the implementation, and your organization will have nooks and crannies that won't be covered by a canned solution.

That's actually okay. It's to be expected that no one methodology will be exactly what you need. In the end, the best BI implementations are hodgepodges of ideas, best practices, and even vendors. In the end, your technology solution will likely be a collage of software and processes that attach perfectly to each piece of your problem.

The exception to the rule: Micro-BI

It's possible to get away with a single-vendor, single-methodology BI solution if the scope of your project is narrow enough, and the needs are perfectly defined. A good example is when your BI problem concerns a single area of the business, like Shipping or Human Resources. Single-facet BI challenges

Wait, what's a "methodology" again?

The word *methodology* is one of those overused buzzwords that makes an appearance in just about every high-tech arena. In the context of BI, the methodology refers, in broad terms, to how you are going to build and deliver your business intelligence solution.

Different experts or vendors may have different definitions of what exactly a BI methodology covers, depending on their perspective (and on what they're selling!) One dimension to consider is how you're going to import the expertise to install the BI software solution; valid answers might be a vendor-driven, consultant-driven, or internal-focused methodology. In other cases, the methodology refers to how you divide up the many tasks at hand — for example, splitting up strategy tasks from development and support, or splitting individual tasks into phases similar to those in standard project-management steps.

So don't fear the word. BI methodology just means what *strategy* or *approach* you're taking to meeting your goals. If you want to include what kind of beer to serve at the launch party as part of your own . . . er . . . *proprietary* BI methodology, hey, nobody's stopping you.

can often be met with an off-the-shelf solution from an established vendor. In the case of HR, you'll find capable tools like the one from Knowledge Workers Inc. that can be installed and used right out of the box. Knowledge Workers is a specialty vendor that's been around for a long time providing a tightly-defined solution with a well-established methodology to match. Companies shouldn't feel obligated to make their solution any more complicated than it needs to be.

For situations like this, where you are using a single vendor to solve a problem of limited scope, it's advisable to *not* seek out ways to custom fit the methodology to your company's contours. In fact, in these situations your best bet is to follow the vendor's step-by-step instructions as closely as possible.

If your BI installation involves creating a solution for a single department and a minimal collection of data, it's possible to follow the recipe exactly. But sometimes things get more complicated than you originally planned — and you have to consider customizing or expanding your BI solution. Here are a few telltale signs that an off-the-shelf solution won't cut it:

- ✔ It goes beyond the one department you had in mind.
- ✔ It requires anything beyond static reports or light OLAP.
- ✔ It uses resources shared by other systems.

At this point, it's good to know when to throw the single methodology out the window and light out on your own path.

How does the old saying go? "A project plan does not a methodology make," or something like that. There is a difference between a BI methodology and a canned project plan. There's a temptation to confuse the two, but they encompass divergent ideas. A project plan only discusses steps and resources, while a methodology encompasses motives, vendors, and a strategic outlook. You might be able to get by with just a project plan on a small-scale project. But for true BI solutions, you have to consider full methodologies if you want the job done right.

Customizing BI for Your Needs

No two BI implementations are the same, but how your company's system differs from the one at the company down the street is a mystery that you need to unravel one step at a time. As Glinda the Good Witch told Dorothy: "It's always best to start at the beginning." So you should begin by taking a look at what you're company's doing already to develop business insights. Then you can move on to more formal reviews of existing resources, software and hardware components, and needs. And if you do a good job, you might just find yourself on the yellow brick road.

Your not-so-clean slate

The ideal situation for any BI project team would be to build a solution from the ground up. The landscape would consist only of operational data sources, with no tradition of information aggregation, few established reporting standards, and no analytics to speak of. With no preexisting conditions to distort your design, each system component and process could be built to meet the business needs to a tee.

In the real world, there's no such thing as a clean slate. Every company has developed some form of decision-support apparatus, whether it's a Ouija board in the snack room or a full-fledged technology-based system. And like it or not, you'll have to consider what's there today before you can think about tomorrow.

Even if the words *business intelligence* have never crossed the minds of any of the managers or executives, it's a sure bet that reports get created and routed to an established schedule and with agreed-upon standards. There are processes for applying lessons learned and operational information to decision-making. Whatever it may be, someone at every company is attempting to find, use, and distribute business insights, and you must account for it in your process.

✔ **What is it?** Make an inventory of existing methods being used to deliver business insights — whether it's spreadsheets on desktops, old mainframe applications, or departmental data marts.

✔ **How does it overlap with your planned BI scope?** Concern yourself with how your planned system will either use or replace existing resources, but don't stop there. Think ahead, too — about what might happen when you make future upgrades to your BI implementation.

✔ **How effective is it?** This is the most challenging part: assessing whether anything in your current process is really worth keeping.

Some elements of the existing system probably *are* worth keeping. Just because a technology is old doesn't automatically mean it's bad. Your job is to search for kernels of good, reusable business intelligence, if they exist. There may be reports or processes that are perfectly fine the way they exist today. If that's the case, be careful before you mess with them. Taking a step backward won't win you many friends in the user community, and it will take up precious time.

Initial activities

The early phases of the BI project consist of a set of evaluations on the organization's needs and an assessment of the company's current BI readiness, both in terms of technology and culture. With this information in hand, you're ready to start developing more concrete plans that will drive your project through to its conclusion.

Assessing your current BI state

Does your company have a good solution in place that supports decision-making? If so, what's it made of and how effective is it? You'll find parts of it (or maybe the whole thing) to be good, bad, or just plain ugly.

If you understand the general information needs that are driving the BI solution, then assessing the current systems' effectiveness is really just a process of comparing what's supposed to be delivered with what actually is being delivered. In most cases, the company's information needs are not being met. (Otherwise, why would you be installing a BI system in the first place, right?) To mitigate the problems, you need to understand their sources.

We get into evaluation of asset capabilities in Chapter 10, but for now it's best to start at the natural flow of data and work your way toward the user.

After you identify the operational data sources, you need to evaluate their readiness to be integrated in a BI solution. Is the data entered accurately to begin with? Is it structured in such a way that makes it accessible down the line?

If your organization is merging data in a central repository, you need to assess how well that process is working. Does the quality of the end data meet the standards you need for your reporting and analysis systems? You should judge whether the current data-warehousing environment — if it exists — can handle the tasks you have in store for it.

Finally, there's the reporting environment. It's safe to say that just about every company has an existing reporting environment. During the assessment phase, you need to evaluate whether that system can create the kinds of reports that will be commonplace in the BI solution — and whether the system can distribute the information in a way that meets the new standards.

Developing a sound BI strategy

It's best to develop your BI strategy in parallel with — or directly after — your assessment of the current BI state. Once you've figured out what your company can do now, it's time to really begin locking in the specific reports and functions that you expect the BI solution to handle.

This is the time to begin talking about who will be using the reports and other applications — why they'll be using them, and what they hope to get from them. You also have to make judgments about who will be setting the rules, where the administrative responsibilities fall, and how you expect to keep the data secure.

There's a tendency to go straight from the assessment of current BI capabilities into evaluating software vendors, specific technology approaches, and products. But be cautious. Selecting a vendor inevitably narrows your solution options. One common pitfall in BI projects is a tendency to lock the project *mindset* in to one solution or another too early in the overall process. It's tempting to do because it gives the team a tangible starting point and some specific direction, but it also invests you in certain applications and protocols that may not (in the final analysis) be best for your organization.

Developing your BI architecture

At this point, you've got an idea of your ultimate destination, you've got a map to tell you where to go, and now it's time to plan the vehicle that will get you there. How well you assemble this plan will have a grave effect on the success or failure of the project.

Piecing together the components of the solution is where you begin to see your BI vision start to take on a real form. When you're confident that you understand who needs what information and in what form, you can begin thinking about the kinds of systems that will meet those requirements.

The end result of this stage is a document (or set of documents) spelling out the specific requirements of the project — from an overall business perspective and in terms of a project-specific technology. Whether you label that document "Architecture" or "Systems Requirements" doesn't really matter. The point is what's in it:

✔ An itemized list of the components and major sub-components of your system

✔ Detailed functional requirements for system components

✔ Information about the data that flows through the system

A good architecture document usually includes information on the following areas:

✔ **Source data:** You should inventory the general domains of information that will be handled by the BI system, such as finance, human resources, or sales data. There's also the matter of assessing the current state of that information, as well as the databases and storage systems that house it.

✔ **Extraction, Transformation, and Loading (ETL):** With the sources of data identified, a huge part of the architecture document will be devoted to how that data is moved to the central repository and made available for queries and reports. The architecture document will also cover data cleansing, and lay out thresholds for minimum data quality.

✔ **Data warehouse:** The architecture document will include decisions about the final makeup of the dimensions and metrics tables, the metadata, the normalization mix in each table, and the business rules.

✔ **User tools:** This will be a description of the functions available to the end users and administrators in the form of queries, reports, and analysis tools. Include descriptions of how precisely users will be able to manipulate the information they find, whether it's (say) drill-through capabilities or more advanced analysis.

Other sections of the architecture document will cover logistical concerns such as governance, administration, security. It's imperative to know where and how decisions get made during the ongoing use of the BI tool.

Architecture documents are typically long on narrative and short on convoluted diagrams. But there should be some basic boxes-and-arrows artwork included to help readers picture the end results.

In the end, the architecture documentation is not just about the components and logistics of the system, but it will tell you how everything actually fits together. In complex systems such as business intelligence application suites, the individual pieces are also complicated; how those pieces should interconnect and interact isn't always intuitive.

Could-be versus should-be alternatives

Like any complex system, a business intelligence implementation boils down to making some key choices (read: "a whole lot of" key choices). Your team will have to make calls on some tough decisions throughout the design phase; your best bet is to look at more than just the first alternative that surfaces. These multiple choices are the *could-be* alternatives.

What makes it harder is the fact that no single prescription can meet all of your enterprise's BI needs.

But the good news is that there's almost *always* more than one way to get to Poughkeepsie. So don't feel as though you must find the single perfect path; in most cases it doesn't exist. There certainly may be a solution that's preferable to the others, but as long as you have examined several *could-be* choices, you can just make your best call and move forward.

A perfect example of many *could-be* solutions is in selecting your overarching BI business and technical architecture. If you want to do an enterprise-scale implementation, you have at least two ways to go about it:

- ✔ You could make your system highly centralized around a hub data warehouse.
- ✔ You could create a more distributed architecture, setting up departmental data marts.

Either alternative is a viable choice, but one or the other will make more sense for your company — depending on your available resources, the company culture, and how the business is organized. But it's up to you to weigh those factors and make the best possible call.

 Seek outside expertise when you're confronted with a tough call that you worry might come back to haunt you down the road. Even better, you don't have to call a consultant or a vendor to get in touch with somebody who's been there before: There are multiple user communities open to BI professionals (and dabblers); there you can get in touch with people who might have just the right piece of advice.

Selecting BI products and technologies

With the strategy in place and the architecture plotted, it's finally time to begin speaking to vendors. Because you're fully prepared — with your assessments, documentation, and general knowledge about how you expect to integrate the BI application into the company — you're in great shape to evaluate alternatives among applications.

Picking the right vendor

One approach to selecting the right product for your system is to focus first on finding a vendor the matches what you need, and then digging into their offerings to decide which pieces you need. If you want to evaluate vendors, you'd first assemble a list of companies that offer everything your BI project needs in general — and then narrow the list by examining criteria such as the following:

✔ Approach to license pricing: *site* (where use is limited to locations or servers) versus *seat* (where use is restricted to a certain number of people), and *concurrent* versus *individual* users (which concerns whether licenses are interchangeable between people).

✔ Availability of technical support and willingness to answer questions before you've issued a purchase order for a million bucks worth of licenses.

✔ Vendor stability and longevity.

✔ Product maturity and reputation in the marketplace.

Picking the right product

If you're simply going to go product by product and make evaluations, the questions get more granular, and focus on the specific capabilities of the tools each vendor offers:

✔ Suitable cost of ownership, including initial license costs as well as fees for ongoing support, training, and upgrades

✔ Compatibility with existing systems

✔ Response time and processing speeds

✔ Usability and ease of use that matches the profile of the user community in your organization

✔ Data-handling capabilities that fit with your variety of source-data platforms

✔ Customization capabilities so your BI developers can create tailor-made applications and reporting

Implementing BI: Get 'er Done

We've taken a high-level look at all of the preparatory steps necessary in any business intelligence project. Your team has done assessments, made a detailed plan, and selected vendors and software platforms. Now it's time to put your money where your mouth is and start installing the system.

For the professional who's comfortable with managing standard software-implementation projects, the analysis phases are complete at this point — now you're ready for the detailed design of the main components that will make up the system:

- the database design of the software infrastructure that will power the data warehouse
- the metadata repository
- the ETL process design that will wrangle the herds of data from the pastures and drive 'em home to the corral

When you get to this point, the theorizing is over. Now it's time to turn the general principles into specifics and start powering up pieces of the system one at a time until the BI solution is up and running. (Translation: It's time for this choo-choo train to hit the rails and start getting somewhere.)

Zeroing in on a technical design

The assessments and high-level strategy and architecture documents will point the way to the technical design itself. This is the heart of the system, where there are no more abstractions, no more generalities. The technical design includes precise data definitions and user-interface designs.

The central decisions surrounding the design of the data warehouse and data marts include the level of data granularity, working out how the fact tables and metrics will be constructed, the level of summarization of the data, which tables get normalized (and to what degree), and so forth.

This same technical design process continues for all pieces of the BI solution. That includes the user facing-tools — in most cases the querying and reporting applications plus any analytics software. Standard UI design processes apply here, just as they would with any application.

User interface design is a key factor in whether a BI solution is a success or not. That means it's a good idea to use tried and true methods for assessing usability — these, for example:

- Mock-ups and wireframes to ensure basic form-by-form or screen-by-screen usability
- Cases and other UML tools to ensure that the system's navigation and activity flow makes sense in the context of the system's business purposes

UML is a great overall modeling tool for any kind of software system. If it's a standard your team plans on using, check out *UML 2 For Dummies* by Michael Jesse Chonoles and James A. Schardt (Wiley Publishing, Inc.).

For companies that buy packaged solutions, much of this work is already done; standard forms can be customized to suit specific needs. For companies building their own front-end applications, this is the moment when it's time to work out how information is presented to the user and which controls are in place.

In other words, the BI implementation team already knew *what* needed to be done; now it's actually working through the process of *how* to accomplish these tasks.

This stage in the implementation will be dominated by the developers, data architects, database administrators, and other techies. But make sure the team isn't stuck on a virtual technology island, with no connection to the business "mainland". It's always important to maintain buy-in from every business organization affected by the technical design. This is where it becomes important to identify power users in the key business functions who can help the tech team stay grounded in the business strategy as they make technology side decisions.

Putting together the BI project plan

The *project plan* ties the many tasks of the technical design together, accounting for resources and dependencies. The project plan is at once the schedule for the BI implementation as well as a detailed inventory of the remaining steps, and a running assessment of the resources that are available to the BI team.

Standard tools are fine

There's nothing special about a BI project plan relative to other technology implementation project plans. Any software that offers the standard project planning, reporting, and display tools for tasks and resources will usually be fine. Microsoft Project is the most commonly used application for building and maintaining project plans, but there are certainly other capable offerings on the market.

To learn about the capabilities of Project, check out Nancy C. Muir's *Microsoft Office Project 2007 For Dummies* (Wiley Publishing, Inc.).

Policing the process

As with any large-scale implementation, you need to maintain an adequate level of control over the quality of the technical development. It's best to build in such features as inspections, walk-through sequences, and a thorough quality-assurance and testing program to ferret out any bugs and defects.

Finishing the job

At the end of the line, when all the plans have been made and adhered to, when the development is complete, and the processes have all passed a white-glove inspection (and survived every QA scenario you could possibly dream up), the project is finally done. Or is it?

There's more to it than just building the solution and flipping the switch. Once the BI system is working the company has to be ready to actually *use* it — and benefit from the results.

As you get closer to the end of a long implementation, it's not uncommon for the troops to start grumbling. With the light at the end of the tunnel growing brighter, it's tempting to speed up, take shortcuts, or deviate from the plan. Without warning quality drops on the final phases of development. And even if you keep your team motivated and on target, sometimes the late-game pressure comes from the outside. Prospective users, managers, and others begin agitating to see the fruits of your labor. They'll grow more and more anxious to finally light the fuse and start taking advantage of the system before it's completely ready. They figure, *just because the dashboard application hasn't gotten out of the quality-assurance testing phase doesn't mean we can't start querying the data warehouse, right?* Wrong. There's nothing wrong with planning a phased rollout, but once the plan is set, stick to it. Hold the line at all costs. If you roll out the BI soufflé half baked, you risk it falling flat before anyone's been able to enjoy it.

Part of the project plan should include time for training classes for the user community. The training strategy deserves just as much attention as other parts of the high-level plan, because it is one more area that can make or break the BI project. Here's a sample of the issues you have to wrestle to the ground:

- ✔ Will you have technical people train the user groups? Or will you hold *train-the-trainer* sessions and trust that the first round of learners can pass on the right information to their teams?

- ✔ How much material will you provide for the training? Will it be different for different user groups of varying skill levels?

- ✔ Will there be ongoing education as the system evolves?

These are not trivial questions. And they'll crop up again from time to time.

Do yourself a favor and have a ribbon-cutting ceremony — and associated party! — once the implementation is complete. Invite as many people in the organization as you can. There are several purposes to this pleasant ritual (beyond getting the company to pay for the beer):

- ✔ It rewards the BI team for a job well done and marks a milestone on the project plan — a phase shift from *building* the tool to *supporting* the tool (which will be a challenge in its own right).

- ✔ The ribbon cutting is an opportunity to show off the full capabilities of the new system — and to build support and goodwill in the early going. (If something goes wrong, you may need it.)

Chapter 9

Human Factors in BI Implementations

*E*very successful business intelligence implementation, no matter the size and scope, must address how the project is affected by human factors. You can assemble the best possible plans and purchase high-grade software and infrastructure components, but when it comes down to it, you'd better have the right people in place, or the whole thing could come crashing down around you.

You can't just have brainiacs and geeks in your team. You need some *people skills*. That means you need internal salesmen, facilitators, negotiators, and diplomats. And in some cases, you need many of those skills packaged in one single person.

Companies are microcosmic societies, where egos, rivalries, and prejudgments are in constant motion — usually in the form of individuals and groups united for one cause or another. The business intelligence system will be a two-way street. It will have to draw on the resources of the community of experts, users, allies, and champions, and it will need to provide benefits, direct and indirect, to those same groups.

This chapter dives into the people elements of your project. They are easily as important as the technology factors, so take heed.

Star Techie: Skills Profile of a Core BI Team

Business intelligence projects are bridge-building exercises like no other. To guarantee success, the implementation team must develop linkages between the business goals and operations of the company and the elements of the IT infrastructure.

Key performers

Some members of the team will work on the BI project full time, while others will be *on loan* from other teams, or will supply expertise on an as-needed basis when the implementation touches their particular area.

- **Project manager (PM):** This person will be the linchpin role for the entire implementation. The PM is tasked with oversight of the project, meaning they will establish the initial plan of attack, coordinate the necessary resources, and do whatever it takes to adhere to the schedule.

  A BI project manager should have the requisite skills inherent in good PMs; they should have a good grasp of both the business and technology side of things. They must understand how the BI project dovetails with the company's business objectives. The PM must be able to exercise all the key "soft" skills such as negotiation, mediation, and mentoring.

  It's often said that a good business intelligence PM has a sixth sense: able to *see* project dead-ends and pitfalls in time to avoid them, and able to *feel* when it's time to deviate from the plan to keep the project moving.

- **Business Analyst (BA):** The BI business analyst shares the same basic qualities as counterparts working in other technology fields, with a few notable exceptions. All BAs are (in effect) translators who move between the technical staff and the business teams, enabling communication in both directions.

  Because they must create a common platform for communication, BAs, like PMs, must have a good understanding of the underlying BI technology as well as a solid grasp of the business goals. BAs operating in a BI environment must have a particular handle on how data moves — not only within a company's operational systems but between those same systems — to succeed. Armed with that knowledge, their main objective is to help the user community get the reports and application functionality they need. For later phases of the project, they must also be able to grasp the complexity of analytical tools, especially when the requirements aren't as cut-and-dried as those that apply to simple transactions and reporting.

BI BA, Private Eye

Documenting a BI implementation is an incredibly important task. . The business-analyst role sits closest to the users, whose participation will ultimately determine the success or failure of the project. That makes the role of business analyst (BA) as important as any other role on the team.

Documenting business requirements has a cascading effect on a project because it drives so many other branches of the process — testing, support, and troubleshooting, for openers. Creating that initial set of requirements usually requires investigative skills much like those of a reporter or a detective. The BA must be able to interview business users and any area's subject-matter experts to find out where the BI capabilities are needed the most, and how the tools are going to be used in the final solution. It's then necessary to filter those business requirements through the projected capabilities of the project and distill them down into a core

business requirements document (BRD) that spawns further documentation of the functional specifications — which the development team will use to actually build the solution.

A talented team of BAs can make the difference in a difficult implementation. Like project managers, business analysts have to have a sixth sense — to be able to elicit definitive information from people who may not know or understand what's on the line, or from people who have trouble articulating what they need. The BA must be able to weigh requirements that are at cross purposes, and make supportable decisions that settle whose #1 priority is #1a and whose is #1b. And finally, the BA must be a talented writer who can create crisp, well-organized documents. In the end, a solid requirements-gathering and documentation process helps a good technology solution graduate become a good all-around business solution.

✔ **Data architects and designers (DAs):** These folks work at the lowest levels of the data itself — designing data models, database structure, and information flows through the various elements of a BI solution. They also make decisions about which methods to use for key processes. For instance, ETL (extract, transform, load — the essential processes of data warehousing that are responsible for moving data from source databases into the warehouse) can be performed in multiple combinations of pre-built tools and home-grown code; the DAs must recommend a combination that works best for the project. They must also work with the rest of the team on how and when to make new data available in the data warehouse. The developers may have designed the front-end tool based on (say) 30-minute data-refresh intervals, but the architect may determine that such a requirement is impossible to meet.

This is one position where the BI version of the role is quite different from the *normal* version. Unlike a *transactional* data architect, the *BI* data architect must understand dimensional modeling (which you'll recall from Chapter 5 on OLAP), and be able to design a platform for multidimensional analysis.

The data architect must be prepared to work closely with the business analysts to keep the data model in synch with the business model. As with many positions in the BI world, the DAs have to know just when to break certain rules, deviate from best practices, and mix in their own brands of solutions as they design the data model.

- ✔ **Data-quality analyst (DQA):** When a system relies on a data warehouse, a data-quality analyst in the project is a must. The DQA is there to assess the fitness of the data that courses through the operational and transactional systems for use in the data warehouse. The DQA has a strong hand in the ETL process, making the call on which cleansing routines must be used on data from each source before it's transferred into the warehouse.

The rules about how and when to implement the multidimensional data model (as opposed to a relational data model) are no longer as hard and fast as they used to be. Some experts will carry a copy of their favorite database-design textbook around and refer to it reverently as if it contains those missing Five Commandments (the ones Moses dropped in Mel Brooks's *History of the World Part II*). Most database designs follow one of two traditional directions:

- ✔ Relational databases are built for storing and accessing information.
- ✔ Multidimensional models are tailor-made for analysis.

But the lines are blurring; more systems aspire to do both these days.

Your other techies

The following folks don't have lead roles, but their support is important to the project nonetheless.

Front-line IT folks

This is the crew that actually wrestles the machines, programs, and data into submission:

- ✔ **BI infrastructure architect:** The person in this role oversees the technical foundation of the project, ensures that all the software parts work together, and ensures that the hardware is in place to handle the load.

- ✔ **Application lead developer:** This is a programmer who is responsible for assembling the front end tools. They are likely tasked with cobbling together the various querying, reporting, and analytics environments into a smooth, usable application.

- **Database administrator (DBA):** The database administrator's job is to take the logical model handed down by the data architect and turn it into an efficient physical model — selecting database hardware and software, and assembling the foundations of the data-handling software that will be accessed by other areas of the application.

- **Quality-assurance analyst:** In any technology environment, the testing phase is the first of many moments of truth. In a BI implementation, you're looking not just for classic script-testers and bug-finders, but also (in fact, especially) for people who will work to actively challenge the environment you've created. Once it's gone through the paces set by an experienced BI testing team, you can be confident that the system is rugged enough to handle any level of user and abuser.

Getting help from the IT-free

People in the organization who aren't necessarily technology professionals still have an important role to play in your BI implementation:

- **Users:** Yes, these people are effectively part of your team (even if they don't always want to be!). You need to identify and classify them in order to build the application to suit their needs. Remember how very different users can be across different business units and functions — and yet, if you can find the common aspects of what they need from the BI tool, your job is that much easier.

- **Subject-matter experts (SMEs):** It's important not just to get information and opinion from the end-users, but also to identify experts in the fields you're touching directly. For example, say you're building a BI tool that will serve the supply-chain team. Just because you speak with a few individual users doesn't necessarily mean you're getting the big picture. In fact, you can be led astray if you don't identify SMEs who can show you the 30,000-foot view of the company's supply-chain operations, the data that gets exchanged with the manufacturers and suppliers, what metrics are used to judge success inside the organization, and so on.

Your team will inevitably develop a small army of SMEs to rely on again and again to resolve development dilemmas such as selecting from two competing business priorities. An SME can be anyone with full knowledge of that specific business function and how it fits into the overall business model.

Ideally your SMEs will be people of considerable experience, but you don't necessarily want to aim for the most senior people; they're prone to mix opinion in with fact. Instead of a snapshot of reality from 30,000 feet, you could easily get an oil-on-canvas picture of how your SME would like it to be.

Overruling Objections from the Court of User Opinion

Who knew that a company is filled with tollbooths and drawbridges? You don't see them, of course, but they're out there — in human form: Team leaders, mid-level managers, and people of all levels will seek to exact a toll of some kind from you in exchange for their cooperation in the BI implementation.

Okay, we're not talking direct bribes here, but you need to be prepared to bend the project plan to meet the wishes of certain key people who control resources you need to make the project work. Whether you're paying a symbolic toll or paying homage, you should be prepared to do whatever it takes to get across that bridge or through that gate.

After winning the fight to get the BI solution implemented, after duking it out over budget and resources, the final test awaits you: the user community. Even if you do a superior job in every other respect, there will always be people who touch your implementation that will express mild doubt, skepticism, or downright antagonism.

The "other" half of the people battle is winning over the user community, as well as areas of the business that you must pass through

Ch-ch-ch-ch-changes

Did we mention that the BI project management team has to be part psychologist as well? It's obvious why there are so many doubters, gainsayers, negaters, and resisters: People naturally fear change because change means . . . well . . . that things change.

For worker bees in a department that's about to get a shiny new BI application, it means learning a new skill. It opens them up to someone being "better" than they are — that is, losing their place in the pecking order. They might fall out of line for that promotion they were bucking for.

Just lay off, okay?

Worst of all, people will often fear for their jobs. So as you lead a BI implementation, you need to be able to reassure all those affected by the implementation that their jobs are absolutely, positively, *not* on the line. Except there's one little problem: Sometimes they're right. Their jobs may *be* on the line. Knowing that better decisions will result from the BI implementation is cold comfort for those who lose their jobs in the process; they won't be around to experience the fruits of those better decisions. It's an unfortunate side effect of working with *any* program that has the power to transform a company.

At the risk of sounding melodramatic, companies who don't adapt get left behind and eventually go out of business. Your company must be as efficient and smart as its competitors or *everyone* is out of a job. So (if you're looking for a little rationalization) think of BI as a way of saving jobs, not chopping them.

Cut through the buzz

Business intelligence is a powerful and far-reaching technology concept (its starry-eyed adherents call it a "paradigm") that has the power to transform organizations, both in action and in structure — in ways that can frighten the rank and file. BI solutions are often implemented right along with organizational restructuring initiatives. Frequently those involve putting processes under a microscope through programs such as *TQM, ISO 9000,* or *Six Sigma* — all of which are beyond the scope of this book but will produce millions of hits when run through your favorite search engine. Such efforts often go hand in hand with re-jiggering teams, moving employees around on the organizational chart, and (yes) downsizing.

Turn and face the strange

Being aware of the ramifications of a BI implementation is an important first step in combating the problems that can arise. Fear, uncertainty, and doubt will spawn resistance to the program through the ranks of the teams touched by the BI implementation. But there are some proven techniques and actions that can mitigate the drag-effect on your BI project:

- ✔ **Get sponsored:** Here's where top-down clout comes in handy. A BI implementation is far more likely to succeed if it carries the weight of a corner-office mandate with it. Anyone whose title starts with *Chief* and ends in *Officer* will do, because when they say something *will* happen, one of the main effects is that critics are immediately silenced.

Your company's Chief Executive Officer is a case in point; you need that person's buy-in from the beginning. So show the CXO how the BI project will have an impact on things he or she cares about. Then keep that person in the loop — invitations to the kickoff meeting, the launch party, and as many points in-between as a busy exec is willing to attend. Run big decisions by the higher-ups you get on your side — both to get the benefit their expertise *and* to reinforce buy-in as they contribute what they know. Best of all, if you can generate enough enthusiasm for your project that your exec allies chat about it in the executive washrooms, you gain momentum.

- ✔ **Employ champions:** No, don't hire Tiger Woods or Garry Kasparov to do your data cleansing. In this case, *champions* are any managers or influential users who are willing not merely to set aside their antagonism toward the project, but to sing its praises.

    Long-time employees are especially good in this role because they not only hold the respect of their coworkers, but they also operate within networks of friends and colleagues that extend far and wide throughout the company. A few well-placed champions can generate more positive buzz about your BI implementation than a full-fledged marketing campaign.

- ✔ **Convert heretics:** Is there a particular user group or team whose participation is essential to the functioning of the entire program? Then focus your best sales effort on them — especially potential doubters — and bring them into the tent. If you involve skeptics early on in the process, ask their advice, and take their suggestions whenever possible, you're more likely to tamp down their negativity.

- ✔ **Accentuate the positive:** Simple positive reinforcement goes a long way for the implementation team, the extended technology resources, and the user community as well. While you don't want to oversell BI capabilities, it's important to remind the relevant players of the end result, the magnitude of the anticipated improvement, and the level of value it will create within the company. It's what politicians sometimes refer to as *the vision thing:* where you give voice to a version of future events that people in the trenches sometimes lose sight of while dodging everyday bullets. When they're reminded of how great it's going to be (rather than being threatened or cajoled), they're more motivated to do their part to create that positive outcome for the company.

- ✔ **Do what works:** The wheel's been invented already, so there's no need to sit down at a drafting table with a picture of a manhole cover and a pencil. The biggest favor a BI project leader can do is simply to adhere to best practices. In almost every area of BI — from data management and integration to application design, training, and support — a standard has already been set. The lessons are all there: incremental rollouts, highest-value-first, and so on. Lean on that combined wisdom provided by the myriad experts who have gone before you down this path.

- ✔ **Archive knowledge:** BI implementations are not one-shot deals; they're designed to be a long-term transformative force inside companies. The systems will inevitably evolve over time as business priorities change, new technologies become available, and the people involved in the project rotate off or out of the company altogether. Preserving the lessons and institutional knowledge that accumulates over the life of a BI implementation is essential to keeping it efficient and relevant. Whether you create a competency center, invest in knowledge management software, or find some other solution, responsible stewardship over the BI archives ensures the project's survival.

Major in Competence

Just building the BI solution can often be a multimillion-dollar enterprise that takes dozens of months to accomplish. But the enormity of that challenge is nothing compared to what it takes to actually *maintain* the BI system over several years.

Setting and maintaining the ongoing business intelligence strategy is a role that often has no obvious home within an organization. And yet, it's a must for companies that want to protect their BI investment and get the most from that complicated system moving forward. A common trend in the BI world is to set up a permanent organization tasked with maintaining the company's BI effort.

Enter the BI Center of Excellence (BICOE) — or (as it's also known) the Business Intelligence Competency Center (BICC).

The two terms essentially mean the same thing. While there are no hard and fast statistics to prove it, *BICC* seems more commonly used so we use that here to talk about the organization in general — but if you have a choice, go with *BICOE* over BICC. The word *competence* has a connotation of bare-minimum proficiency, giving the feeling of being damned by faint praise. Even though a BI Competency Center will go well beyond mere proficiency, it sounds so *average*. It's like advertising your restaurant with a billboard that says "Eat at Tedd's Hamburger Joint, Where Our Food Won't Make You Sick!" But if you put *excellence* in the title, right away you have something everyone wants to identify with.

Find your center

The purpose of the BICOE/BICC — okay, the BI *center* by whichever name — is to act as a permanent body whose sole focus is to address every aspect of BI throughout the organization, from establishing standards and priorities, to driving the overall BI strategy.

BICCs don't issue orders or hand down mandates that must be followed. They make formal recommendations to the appropriate executive and management teams that actually govern the company. Even so, that advice — coming from a team of experts and representative users — typically carries a lot of weight. Their evaluation of a vendor (for example) can make or break the relationship. If the BICC center deems one project a success or failure, it can impact the future of the individuals involved. And the BICC will give a thumbs-up or thumbs-down to every major BI activity being considered — from new installations to upgrades to changes in the architecture. And it's all accomplished from one central organizational node.

If you think that a BI center might be overkill in your organization, keep in mind that part of its purpose is *coordination*. BI activities often involve so many different players and teams that it's almost impossible to make a move without a central committee that gathers everyone into one place to hash through issues. And remember: There may be more than one BI effort going on at once. A BICC ensures that the multiple data warehouses and dozens of data-mart environments all follow the same standards and protocols.

Organization-based competency centers

In this model, the BICC acts as a cross-functional committee, filled with representatives from every relevant business unit and division that has a hand in the BI process. The committee members manage tasks like managing relationships, both internal and external, such as establishing lines of communication with the legal department and bodies that govern the company as well as vendors and BI organizations. There are also sub-groups concerned with establishing common protocols and standard processes in the technology environment, as well as guiding principles for how projects are run.

Like competency, the word committee also has some negative connotations and/or bureaucratic baggage (think *Committee for Public Safety* during the French Revolution). But the BICC doesn't have to fall into the standard committee traps of doing too much or too little. As long as the mission and agenda of the BICC is clear, and all key players are required to participate, it has a good chance for success.

Competency centers — budgeting

A common sin committed by companies is to create a BI center without adjusting the mix between primary job responsibilities and committee responsibilities. If representatives from around the company are to take an active role in the BI center, it must have people who can take the time to participate without jeopardizing their jobs. But at the same time, the BICC can't become a home to full-time committee members with no other responsibilities.

In the former case — the "PTA model" — the Competency Center is made up of BI specialists who are essentially volunteers. Management doesn't officially make their work on the BICC a part of their performance plan. That leaves the BI center devoid of a steady source of energy and influence as members drift in and out of the organization.

On the other hand, creating a fully budgeted BI center — where members have no primary responsibility other than the work of the committee — creates another set of problems altogether. When members have no tasks in the day-to-day functioning of the BI system, they're likely to become divorced from the truth of what's working, what isn't, and where the company's BI initiative should go from there.

The spreadmart phenomenon

Almost every company in the world faces a problem with *spreadmarts.* Yep, another buzzword (in this case, mashing up *spreadsheet* with *data mart*) — but it describes a potential obstacle to integrating data in companies where important operational data resides on desktop spreadsheets.

Part of the problem is that spreadsheet programs are so powerful these days. Back when it was just a young pup, the spreadsheet was a true killer app, forcing the abacus, slide rule, and pocket calculator off people's desks and changing the way individual workers handled data — particularly figures — for good. Today's spreadsheet applications are so powerful that

employees can emulate fairly advanced database and analytical applications if they know the right tricks.

The problem is that spreadsheets remain mostly isolated from the central population of company data. What's more, a spreadmart environment is the Wild West when it comes to standards, security, access, and other basic governance functions.

As long as the data remains out of reach of standards committees — and as long as the individuals maintain their own micro-BI spreadsheets — there will be a roadblock to integrating all operational data, and there will be resistance to implementing a full BI solution.

A BI center that's juuuuust right

You guessed it — the Three Bears are right again: The middle ground is the safest place to be when it comes to forming a BI center, somewhere between the two extremes mentioned earlier. Membership should be mostly voluntary, but those who serve on the committee should be compensated for doing so by their originating organization. That allows the members to stay in touch with the BI strategy without becoming so far removed from their primary jobs that they lose unique professional perspective on BI's direction in the company.

It's also beneficial because there is no question of member loyalty. Everyone on the committee has a known dual allegiance: to their primary organization as well as to the company's BI strategy. This balance provides a natural and positive tension that means actions won't be rash or hasty, and BI conclusions will only be reached by active compromise where the company's needs are placed ahead of all others.

Raising standards

The simple act of setting standards in a business intelligence environment can be daunting when you consider the number of source databases that the effort may have to draw from — and the sheer volume of reports that may be created. Sure, decisions can be made in the field, but that makes coordination and integration harder. Competency centers step in and apply best practices when it's time to set standards throughout the company. Even something as mundane as column widths or report layout spacing isn't out of reach for a BI Competency Center, although such niggling attention to detail is rare. But when it comes to big-picture decisions — such as deciding on ETL timing and data-refresh rates for data warehouses throughout the company — standards are necessary to making the system run. The BI Competency Center provides a mechanism for making such decisions.

Chapter 10

Taking a Closer Look at BI Strategy

This chapter drills farther into business intelligence strategy. Before you start making specific plans for your solution, however, take a quick, hard look at certain realities that will become very important during the implementation. (This chapter helps with that step, too.)

The Big Picture

The first part of your second look at BI strategy (as shown in Figure 10-1) includes a more detailed examination of the BI capabilities you already have (versus *desired* capabilities). The goal here is to collect information about your organization's current BI capabilities, assess its current BI needs, and chart a way forward to the next step: creating a roadmap, project plan, and requirements documentation. From there, you can begin building the project.

Figure 10-1:
BI strategy:
gathering
ideas and
information
to shape
implementa-
tion
decisions.

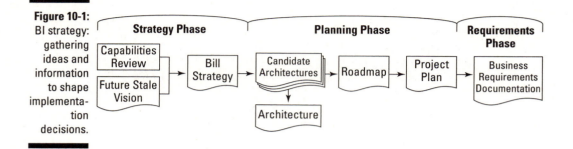

Your Current BI Capabilities (or Lack Thereof)

Traditional strategic planning begins with a (usually long) analysis-and-planning phase: Leadership assesses a company's current situation, defines the finish line far over the horizon, and then goes through the long laborious process of developing the route to get from here to there.

A BI implementation is no different: To know what's needed, you have to understand what's currently in place.

How you approach this assessment depends largely on the shape of the organization, and the scope of your planned offering:

- ✔ If the focus is going to be on a single business function (for example, customer-relationship management), you might look at how that function affects the entire organization: How does the sales department track customer data versus the service delivery group? How does the billing department use customer information, and which pieces of data do they use? You'll need to understand the ramifications of a focused BI solution everywhere it plays a role in the company.

- ✔ If your BI project is going to involve a comprehensive overhaul of a single business unit or department's processes, you'll start with that department or division, and then move outward to all the connection points throughout the organization.

Assessing your business infrastructure

Before you move into an assessment of the technology that's currently in place throughout the company that supports business intelligence capabilities, you'll want to understand the existing processes that govern the operation of your business.

You're not yet at the point of gathering data on specific requirements. This is still preliminary discovery work to give you a good view of how a BI solution *would* fit. By stepping back to look at the big picture, you can work out the right questions to ask while you're identifying requirements. For now, it's about listening to individual contributors, middle management, and executives as they tell you how they go about normal work processes — as of today. Here's an overview of what to look for:

✔ **Business functions:** These are the broad categories of an organization's operational activities. When you make a map of them, what you get is a cousin of the organizational chart, which diagrams the divisions and teams of the company in a hierarchy of activity. For example, your company might subdivide the business into divisions based on the markets they serve, or perhaps base the divisions on different product lines. Within each of those divisions there might be a sales team, a sales support staff, a marketing arm, and a shared-services entity (further subdivided into accounting, finance, human resources, and so on).

Chances are the company's functional breakdown has already been documented in some form; most people who've worked in an organization have a general understanding of how the company's large pieces fit together. For areas of the company that might be affected by the BI implementation, you'll want to create a pretty granular functional map. Don't just list (for example) "Human Resources"; you'll want to do some detective work on *how* the HR department is assembled, and then list its major parts (such as the Benefits, Recruiting, Training, and Employee Relations teams).

✔ **Operational processes:** This category describes how things actually get done within each business function listed on the map you created earlier. This is a specific, step-by-step map of the major activities performed every day by each team. For example, in the payroll team under the accounting department, you'll build a list of the basic steps, roles, and interactions for the day-to-day functions like adding and deleting an employee from payroll, or changing employee withholding information.

You're not looking to map out every single step the workers on a team take; there should be no entries in your notes that say, "Employee pulls out chair. Employee sits in chair. Employee sips coffee. Employee opens ReportWizz application by clicking the *Run ReportWizz* button. Employee waits 8 seconds." You want detail, but don't go overboard. You're trying to get down to the point where you understand at a high level only what data individuals use to perform their key everyday tasks, how those employees are using data to make their critical decisions, where they get their data from. You don't need to a play-by-play of every second of their day.

The questions you'll ask will cover the following broad areas:

✔ **What are your current pain points?** In other words, what processes or applications don't serve your function well, and seem to be without an obvious or easy fix?

> ✔ **Are there any opportunities being missed because the data, reporting, or analysis infrastructure aren't working well?** What would be needed to take full advantage of those opportunities?
>
> ✔ **What are the positive and negative aspects of the tools and processes you work with every day to perform your job?** Does everyone in the department feel this way? Can that view be backed up with specific instances or evidence?

Business intelligence has to produce insights that are *timely, accurate, high-value,* and *actionable*. Anything less than that and you're probably talking about a failed process or a tool that's not doing its job. That definition should never be far from you at any time during your evaluation process. It should inform your detective work and guide you as you gather information about quality of the business processes and their specific contributions to how the business functions. In most cases, when employees deem a process or tool to be inadequate, they can identify the *absence* of at least one of the four key characteristics of BI.

As you discover more about how your company's current processes work, you also build an understanding of general policies and business rules. You're learning what people are doing, but along the way you also build a picture of why they're doing it that way. You figure out cause-and-effect relationships between the elements of the processes, along with business rules and team policies that affect business operations.

Mid-level managers are perfectly capable of expounding on the processes within their team and how their team interrelates with other teams. You'll want to understand how things are *supposed* to work as well as how things *actually* work. But ask a fundamental question about a business issue as a whole, and the answers start to vary widely. For example, you might ask a basic question like, "How do you calculate the profitability of a particular sales account?" or "Who are our main competitors?" and two different managers might have perspectives that are completely at odds with each other.

Part of the task ahead of you, as you assess current capabilities, is to find "the truth" about how the business actually functions. That means finding agreement across divisions and teams about business rules and procedures, and sometimes even forcing agreement between opposing parties who have been doing things differently. It may actually come down to putting two managers into one room and letting them hash it out. That means you're going to interview lots of people, including representatives from the current end-user community, those performing analysis work, those making decisions based on the analysis, and just about everyone in-between. (It can be a long process. But you knew that.)

You may uncover some uncomfortable facts about business operations — say, a disagreement between managers over what constitutes the correct business process, or the correct data definition or rule. This is where your executive sponsor can go to work for you. Businesses are like families. When there's a dispute among siblings, it's up to a parent to resolve it. And when there's a dispute among managers at a company over how the business works, your task is to move up the organizational chart until you find the appropriate executive with enough power over all parties to get (read: force) an agreement.

Don't look at disputes about business rules as a bad thing necessarily; it's an opportunity for business intelligence to add value.

Now that your team has a clear picture of business policies and processes, as well as a solid understanding of how information is used within and between departments, you can move on to the technology assessment, another important step on your way to developing a sound BI strategy. During this phase, you're attaching the processes described to you earlier by the managers and individual workers, and associating them with the technology tools currently in place.

Assessing the technology stack, top to bottom

The technology assessment proceeds similar to the non-technology assessment. At first you're involved in a simple discovery process where you gather vital statistics and basic information without pausing to perform a lot of analysis. Later you'll want to align what you found out with the project goals.

Looking at the technology stack, here are the key points for each level:

- **Infrastructure:** This category starts with hardware; we're talking mostly about PCs, servers, and networking gear. But it goes beyond that and includes some low-level foundation software as well. The key variables to nail down are these:

    - What hardware platforms are currently in place in the departments in question — what is their life-cycle and are there any planned upgrades or changes to the company's approach to hardware?

    - What type of network are we using? Is the proper network in place to carry an adequate quantity of data between the appropriate business units? Are all departments connected in the way(s) they need to be?

- Is enough server horsepower available to handle the kind of reporting, analysis, visualization, or advanced statistical tools that we're looking to install?

- Are all potential end-users properly equipped to run the BI tools and applications? For example, if you're building a supply chain and inventory application — designed for your managers to access as they walk the warehouse floor — it is essential to know whether your managers carry personal mobile devices or tablet PCs that can run the application.

✔ **Security:** Because a BI initiative often involves moving large quantities of data (whether in raw form or as reports), you need to feel comfortable that the network and PCs are properly protected. That means understanding everything from data encryption on the network backbones to basic user management.

✔ **Information management:** Any software that has to do with the storage and manipulation of data is covered in this technology layer. For a BI project, this layer gets as much scrutiny during your current-state assessment as any other:

- Is the company standardized on one database-management system (DBMS) or one single vendor? If not, what's each division using?

- Are there any compatibility limitations with the DBMS used throughout the company?

- Where does the relevant operational and transactional data reside right now?

- How many different versions or views of each key data dimension are in use?

  For example, if you're planning to implement enterprise BI for the field sales team, it's important to know whether every entity in the company defines *customer data* in the same way, or whether you're dealing with islands of data, each with its own definition.

- Is there a unified data-stewardship council that maintains the enterprise data model for companywide applications?

✔ **Application and user interface layer:** *Applications* can include middleware and other software that constitutes the foundation of the business technology environment, housing business logic, security, and communication functions. The *user interface* consists of any tools that stand between knowledge workers and the company's computing environment.

- Is there an Enterprise Resource Planning system in place? For that matter, are there any other enterprise-wide tools that handle data that may be important to the BI implementation?

- What software tools does the prospective user community currently use to perform its analysis tasks? How are queries built?

- What is the current state of reporting in the organization? How are they produced and distributed, and when does that happen?

In the same way that you mapped out the business functions and operational processes, you're going to want to do an application inventory. This is essentially a list of all the major software being used by the teams that can potentially be affected by the BI implementation. A good application inventory should include

✔ a high-level view of the role each application plays in the delivery and manipulation of information

✔ an understanding of the users' subjective view of its effectiveness

✔ the relationship with the software vendor, sales and service points-of-contact, and an overview of any contractual agreement (such as the license status)

Keep the good stuff

It's always possible that you're starting from a pure-green-fields situation, where nothing in the way of business intelligence is happening in your organization yet. But that's not likely. In most situations, companies have some existing elements that should be accounted for. You'll eventually have to evaluate whether it's best to use them in the BI implementation or simply leave them alone.

You're looking at both *processes* and *software*. And it's important you keep them separate in your evaluation. Sometimes the software tool being used is not adequate and you'll want to replace it. But that doesn't automatically mean the underlying process (or set of business rules) surrounding that BI function is no good. And the opposite may be true — good tools, bad rules.

The goal is to put an effective BI solution into place, but in all likelihood you've got a limited budget and limited time. So if you have software or processes in place that cover functions you've targeted for change during your business intelligence initiative, take advantage of it.

Improvement projects

As you assess the efficacy of a specific BI element, pay attention to the conversations you've had with the managers and workers in each department. Their opinion of what's working well and what isn't is your starting point — but it shouldn't be the final word. Evaluate their opinions in light of the overall goals of the project, keeping the future state (and your BI goals) firmly in mind.

In many cases, employees are so focused on their daily tasks that they miss the forest for the trees. In the case of a BI infrastructure assessment, it means they don't recognize that their current process could either be drastically improved with a new system (likely to a degree they can't envision), or that their current process will be inadequate for the future state of the team. In these cases, the user gives the tool, report, or process a thumbs-up, but the BI project team decides it must go anyway. To make sure that team stays on board with the implementation, be prepared to make your case to the folks who really like the old tools.

Beware the sacred cow. Some applications, protocols, or processes may be inextricably ingrained into the company's operational framework, not because it's the best-in-class, but because of politics. It happens all the time. Maybe the CEO's brother works for a software vendor whose product is doing a poor job supporting the call center reps. Good luck upgrading your call center in that situation! You know that cluster of little old ladies in the accounting office who perform the audit that could be done in half the time by a simple piece of software? Forget it; they're a corporate institution. Make your recommendation, but do so knowing you may have to back down. Before you take on any sacred cow, be aware that there will be plenty of battles ahead, so pick the ones that count, and make sure the brouhaha is well worth it.

Hidden technology gems

At this stage, there's another task your team can do: Keep an eye open for functionality that already exists in the company's technology infrastructure, but which (for whatever reason) hasn't been utilized to its fullest.

This can happen in several different ways. Sometimes an application that's been rolled out across the organization has a feature set that employees haven't been trained on. Rather than buying new software and installing it, you might be able to get by with developing a training class and getting your people to take full advantage of *assets that are already in place.*

In other cases, there is an application being used by one team or department that can be extended across the company. For example, if the company is looking at rolling out an advanced dashboard tool to all mid-level managers and above, it may be possible to take advantage of the fact that the vice presidents in the Finance organization have been using a dashboard for years. If the tool has been successful in its limited role, maybe it's time to make it the star of the show. Of course, if it's no good, and the veeps are ready to pull their hair out over its limitations, then you needn't go any farther with it. But think of the advantages of expanding an existing installation:

✔ The IT guys are already familiar with supporting it.

✔ You have a history with the vendor.

✔ You have some record or the software's performance.

The anti-incumbency bias

Experts in their fields (or, for that matter, product specialists) have a certain affection for that which represents their livelihood. A worker at a Ford factory can talk for hours about why a Mustang is better than a Camaro. And the same is true of the growing ranks of BI specialists; they probably got involved in business intelligence technologies because they found the solution compelling, and would probably come down on the side of BI should a debate start with a BI skeptic.

That enthusiasm is an important trait to have on your project team. New implementations being rolled out to a cautious (or downright skeptical) user community need to be evangelized, not just explained. Just be careful that enthusiasm doesn't turn into jingoism.

Often BI professionals have to deal with BI-by-spreadsheet: A lot of folks still do data storage, manipulation, and analysis on spreadsheet tools such as Microsoft Excel. Your instincts might tell you to press to have such simple and generalized tools replaced with dedicated, specialized BI reporting-and-analytics software. But before you jerk that knee, consider: In some cases, the Excel-based solution might be better than what your project will offer. It's a question of which technology is *appropriate* to your organization, your project, your people, and your situation.

Excel has some huge inherent advantages that redound to your benefit. First and foremost, it's everywhere. And we're not just talking about the installed user base; it's pervasive *inside the minds* of your potential user base. They are already comfortable using it; many are experts at the intermediate and advanced features.

So take stock of existing BI functions being performed already. But don't just assume that all the tools being used currently must be plowed under to make way for the shiny new business intelligence software. Such a move could backfire with the user base, and cost you a very real opportunity to make the most of an existing tool.

Don't assume that an old or ugly process should be chucked out just because there's a replacement technology that's slicker and newer. Sometimes whiz-bang new technology isn't the answer to every single problem in the world. (What a concept.) In some cases, the $100,000 application simply doesn't add *enough* value to a manual process to make it worthwhile.

Throw out the bad stuff

Of course, there's plenty of technology that can't be redeemed, no matter how hard you try. Since your organization is considering a BI initiative to begin with, in all likelihood there's a good deal of it that's either ineffective or doesn't exist at all. Figure 10-2 shows a typical relationship of processes to keep, remove, and add.

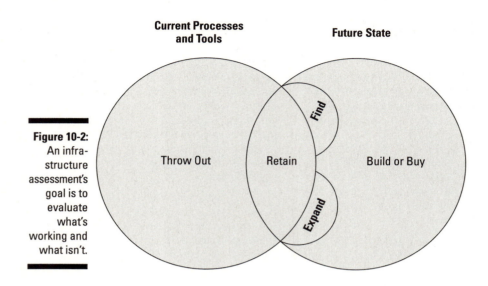

Current Processes and Tools

Future State

Throw Out

Retain

Find

Expand

Build or Buy

Figure 10-2:
An infra-
structure
assessment's
goal is to
evaluate
what's
working and
what isn't.

The process of doing an infrastructure assessment is to evaluate how much of what you currently have is getting the job done. The future state of your BI tools and processes will be a combination of elements from the old days — whether used as-is, expanded from their original limited roles, or found to be underutilized — and (of course) lots of brand new elements.

Exploring "Should-Be" BI Alternatives

Lots of folks you encounter during this process will have ideas about what it takes to fix BI-related processes. And at the same time, you'll be developing opinions of your own about where the company has gone wrong, and what tools are needed to make it right. These ideas are your *should-be* states; they're roughhewn ideas about the direction BI should follow. They may involve changing processes, changing tools, altering corporate standards or policies, adjusting the way departments interact, tweaking data definitions, and any of a hundred other ways complex processes can be taken apart and put back together.

Our goal is to find the best path between the way it is today, and the way it could be. The best path might be the shortest path, but often it isn't. Sometimes it's best to walk downstream until you find a bridge to cross; you may be tempted to wade right in, but you never know whether there are gators lurking.

Utopian BI

After the assessment process is complete, an excellent exercise is to suspend reality for a moment. Remove the Earthly time and budget constraints and build the perfect imaginary team to go along with the highly cooperative user base.

So, what's it going to look like? Think of these areas and what your dream scenario entails:

- ✔ Changes to the technology infrastructure
  - Hardware
  - Networking
  - Storage
  - Personal computing devices
- ✔ Data management
  - Transactional database systems
  - Reporting systems
  - Changes to data definition
- ✔ Changes to the business infrastructure
  - Re-arrange organizational chart
  - Adjust corporate policies
  - New business processes

This is an important exercise because it gives you a baseline of sorts. Having a far shore to aim for is a good way to instill your team — and the rest of the stakeholders in the BI project — with a sense of common purpose. Plus, it helps to start thinking about what you want and why you want it. That's the first step to doing some real quantitative analysis on what needs to be included in the BI release, and what can be left out.

Don't skim over this step. While you certainly don't want to linger in la-la land forever, there are some genuinely important lessons that come from this exercise that you can really take advantage of down the road. So don't just think about what you want in an ideal world; think about why you want it, what the direct benefits would be, and what successes would be spawned by its implementation.

Coming back to reality: examining barriers to achieving your desired future state

Okay, fun's over. You caught a glimpse of what your BI dream-state is, but now it's time to come back to Earth. Hopefully you'll descend filled with optimism and a sense of wonder at what *might* be. Truth to tell, most of us mere mortals aren't likely ever to reach that far shore. The utopian dream will never be, but, as Hemingway asked, ". . . isn't it pretty to think so?" Sometimes it's even useful.

With the utopian BI vision planted firmly in your still dream-fogged head, slowly come out of your trance and begin thinking about what stands between you and that alternate BI universe.

Set money and time aside for the moment and address other factors that play a role in technology implementations. What are the barriers that prevent you from getting to each item on the list? For starters, take a look at these thorny factors . . .

- ✔ **Human:** The company doesn't have the right people in place to make the necessary changes.

- ✔ **Methodology:** The company doesn't foster an appropriate amount of cooperation, communication, or some other quality that's necessary to make it work.

- ✔ **Process:** The company doesn't follow sound or universal processes to achieve its strategic objectives.

- ✔ **Technology:** The company's technology environment is woefully inadequate to handle the load of such a system.

- ✔ **Political:** There are too many forces resistant to changes to think that such a system would even be possible.

After utopia, of course, this exercise can get a little depressing. But what makes it useful is that you'll start to identify potential obstacles to the BI initiative. You'll want to determine what the biggest barriers are, as well as which ones can be overcome, and what effort will need to be expended to do so.

From this stage of the analysis comes the diagnosis that can get you past the barriers — a game plan for dealing with negative forces while you try to build the system.

Deciding "Could-Be" Alternatives

In case you were wondering, the "correct" solution isn't likely to jump out at you. It's rarely the case that a single, obvious path presents itself (or even exists). For now, it's your job to winnow the choices that *don't* fit for whatever reason, keeping those that *do* for later consideration.

After you've gone from Utopia down to Hades and lived to tell the tale, you should be able to step component-by-component through your strategy and for each, build a short list of combinations that would work and what wouldn't.

Judging viability

In this stage of the process, you want to ask yourself if the alternatives swirling around your mind are even possible. Focus on the current state of the company; don't factor in your pipedreams about how the business *might* evolve to become a more appropriate vessel to carry all of your BI hopes and aspirations. Here's a quick list of questions:

- ✔ Does the company have the technical capability to build, integrate, and support this approach?
- ✔ Does the user base have the appropriate skills to take full advantage of the tools that would be offered to them?
- ✔ Does sufficient budget exist to make this level of investment?
- ✔ Does this element or solution conform to existing corporate standards and policies?

If the answer to any of these questions is "no," you've identified an option that should be set aside. The hour is getting late, and this is the time to consider only those options that could actually get past all the usual hurdles and *be implemented*.

If every one of your alternatives produced a "no" answer, it's time to go back to the drawing board and create a smaller, less invasive set of BI options. Consider this to have been your feasibility study and the final verdict came down that your initial approach was infeasible.

Identifying risks . . . and also how to mitigate those risks

Slowly but surely, you're eliminating the impossible strategy elements from your list of candidates. What's left are the possible solutions (and pieces of solutions). That doesn't mean every choice remaining is *practical* or a version of the right choice, but you're getting warmer.

The next step is to identify potential risks with the remaining choices. Before you go too far down the road with one of the alternatives, it's important to understand what risk exposure — and how much — you'd be subjecting your team and the company to.

Risks to BI projects come in all shapes and sizes. Some can be identified; others are latent, and won't show themselves until they've damaged your initiative. The first step to mitigating risk is to identify as many possible (realistic) risks as you can. Start with general categories and work your way to more precision as you go:

- ✔ **Data risks:** How stable is the data? How much clean up will be required?
- ✔ **Application risks:** Are we familiar with the tools? Are they reliable and easily integrated?
- ✔ **Organizational risks:** Are the users ready to accept this initiative? Will other teams cooperate with the implementation?
- ✔ **Financial:** Is this project fully funded? What could cause it to break the budget?

It's impossible to overcome every possible risk. Shoot, a human being (even a talented one such as yourself) won't even be able to identify all of them. But by choosing one alternative over another, you might be able to reduce the likelihood that the identifiable risks will cause a problem. You might even reduce their impact if the worst does occur.

Gauging business value

Just as every strategy alternative has risks, each one also comes with rewards. The question is, how much of each? In the same way you identified the things that could go wrong, now it's time to talk about what could go right. Two principles help here:

- ✔ **Remember the Big Four.** The whole purpose of the BI initiative is to deliver a solution that provides business value in the form of insights that are *timely, accurate, high-value,* and *actionable.* But each will deliver its own unique combination of benefits and business value. As you did with risk, you have to create a matrix or list of business value attached to each potential strategy, along with some means of quantifying. And as with risk, you'll need to consider how likely the benefits are to be delivered, and how significant those benefits really are to the business.

✔ **Business value is not always tangible.** Improving a familiar metric — like wait time in a call center, or profit margins — shows compelling value. But it's not the whole story; sometimes business value is indirect, hard to measure, or both. It's hard to quantify, but make sure you're considering more than just easily-measured benefits. For example, the BI initiative includes finally doing away with that clunky old application in the shipping department. Presumably there will be some tangible value produced in the form of improved departmental efficiency, but there's also the improved morale at the loading dock and the warehouse where the team is better managed, and doesn't have to wrestle with the old software. That could have cascading benefits throughout the entire supply chain.

The balanced-scorecard approach can be very helpful at this stage, as you attempt to measure the impact of the business value of certain strategy alternatives.

Aligning your alternatives with your organizational structure and culture

This process involves more than merely identifying costs, benefits, and risks that go along with each alternative. You have to consider the political challenges you might face as well. You must consider how any potential solution might align with the corporate culture. If it doesn't, even the utopian solution is destined to fail.

Any business intelligence strategy should work in concert with the power structure of the company. A decentralized organization, for example, lends itself to more entrepreneurial strategies. That's because decisions are made in the divisions rather than in a central control unit; the target users have more control over their experience, and are relied upon more to get the most value from the business insights they develop and find.

The power structure goes beyond centralized versus decentralized, however. The planning team must consider other aspects of the culture that may view certain solutions in an unfavorable light. For example, imagine a BI strategy that involved an aggressive fraud-detection system. It might be low-risk and provide tremendous business value in the form of reducing abuse. But if the corporate culture isn't accepting of intrusive technologies, installing the application might cause more trouble than it's ultimately worth.

If one choice seems to keep popping up as the right way to go, don't settle for less. Don't short-circuit the process just because there's an easy way to skip all those planning meetings you have on your calendar. This decision is important; it takes time for all the possible ramifications to bubble to the surface. Let the process run its course so there's no doubt you've made the right choice when all is said and done.

Making Your Choice

Deciding on the BI strategy is the first step of the rest of your project. So take care in how you approach it.

Considering everything

An inevitable chicken-and-egg feel infuses this process: One decision affects another, which affects another, so it's hard to know where to start. You'll need to channel your school days — in particular, algebra class, when you had to solve simultaneous equations.

The way to solve simultaneous equations is simple: You find a way to hold one variable constant, and then adjust the other variable until it fits. In the BI world, that translates to making an assumption about what one or two important elements of your company's strategy will look like, and then seeing how that assumption affects the other pieces of the equation.

Don't just think about the technology. This process requires a holistic approach to your business intelligence strategy and thinking about every possible variable — these, for example:

- Technology versus work processes
- Operational needs versus long-term goals
- Scope versus schedule
- Budget versus time
- Governance and control versus user flexibility
- Data integration versus performance
- Needs versus wants

Imagine you've identified the ideal reporting tool that suits the needs of your target users perfectly. But if you go with that tool, you likely cost yourself a month in implementation time because it doesn't integrate well with the existing applications you have in place. Optimizing one variable will cost you somewhere else, so the trick is finding that safe place where the high-priority needs are met, but the rest of the project doesn't pay an excessive price for it.

Deciding on your strategy

You have enough evidence to make a decision now. No really, you do. So just step off that cliff any time you're ready.

What if there isn't a standout? If there's time, you can revisit the best available options, but more than likely, you need to make a choice and move on. At this point in the game, the reason you have two choices is because both are viable, so don't drive yourself bananas trying to make it perfect.

Several good techniques exist for picking two equal finalists. One way is to "game out" the next steps of the project, talking through likely scenarios that pre-suppose one of the two choices have been made. You've selected your path, so what happens next? At each fork in the hypothetical road, you'll talk through the likely impact on the core business processes, and assess the options available from that point forward. Most important as you walk through the imaginary architecture planning steps is to take note of any obvious road-blocks or problems that emerge by taking one path versus the other. It involves making a lot of assumptions, but talking through a deployment path is a window into what the future just might hold.

Another way to choose between two seemingly even paths is to select a default choice and continue the debate. Pick one single fallback position that you'll take if no clear winner emerges. Then continue the discussion with a hard-stop time limit. After time's up, if you haven't reached a different conclusion, move forward with the default selection and don't look back. If the differences between the two approaches are so minimal that you can't reach a definitive conclusion about which one's best after a full-throated debate, it's unlikely that some unrecognized disaster is lurking behind one of them. Flip a coin.

With that decision made, it's time to get approval. If you don't, the project plan you're about to write won't be worth the paper it's not yet printed on.

Getting the necessary buy-in

Just because your planning team thinks you've made the right call doesn't mean the rest of the company will. It's imperative that you get some outside perspective. A business intelligence initiative isn't just a technology installation; it precipitates real business changes in the way processes flow and decisions are made. Making such grand decisions in a vacuum is a sure path to failure.

You'll need some level of buy-in from the teams that will be affected by the new systems. That means the folks who will be supporting the technology, contributing data, reaping the insights, and dealing with those systems at every point in between. And the best way to make that happen is to get everyone in the same place, and give them a single version of how it's going to go.

Conducting the stakeholders' summit meeting

One important option in making the solution choice is holding a *stakeholders' summit*. This meeting will introduce many of the key solution concepts and present some of the outstanding choices still to be made — to the people who will have to deal with their effects.

The breadth of the company should be represented at the summit, with the attendees being as high-level as possible. But this isn't a conference for bigwigs only; invite some mid-level managers and director-level folks who can provide solid expertise in their operational areas. Invite ambassadors from the user community as well; they'll be able to comment on what's likely to happen where the BI rubber hits the road. Finally, make sure there are a few people from the technology team as well, who can speak to the constraints and impact on the rest of the IT infrastructure.

The goal of the summit is to increase the participants' understanding and sense of ownership in the initiative. You'll be getting a lot of vital input that will help you determine the strategy to use, but more important is the buy-in from critical personalities inside the company.

Don't underestimate the importance of a good facilitator at a stakeholder summit. There will be a lot of strong, loud voices in the room, each thinking what they have to say is more important than what everybody else has to say.

During the meeting (or series of meetings) you'll be presenting the main approach you're planning on taking, and how it affects each department, both good and bad. Listen to the stakeholders' concerns and do your best to address them. At the end of the stakeholders' summit, there should be a general agreement on the company's BI strategy.

Locking in your decision and moving ahead

With any luck, you'll reach a point where one strategy stands out above the rest. At that moment, it's time to lock the decision into place and move on to the next phase without looking back.

Different camps might emerge within and outside the BI planning team, and inevitably one will be miffed when their first choice isn't *your* first choice. Take it all in stride. Criticism is part of the process. Stay positive, don't reenact the same debate over and over. When the course is set, quickly move to the next phase of the project.

Knowing when to revisit your BI strategy

The Hudson Bay Company was founded as a trading firm in 1670, and survives today as one of the largest department store retailers in Canada. Zildjian Cymbals was founded in the seventeenth century as well, and still supplies instruments to the world's musicians.

While some companies are rocks of stability, most foster an environment in which change occurs rapidly. And when conditions force a company to evolve, even in a tiny way, it might indicate a second-look at the business intelligence strategy that is needed.

Certain conditions are obvious red flags: When a serious economic event rattles the market, the company may shift into survival mode, necessitating a downsizing or refocusing of BI efforts. If the company is in an acquisitive phase, or if the company is a buyout target, it may make sense to plan for rapid-fire small releases so that when a change occurs, the BI initiative will be ready to turn on a dime in concert with the company.

Even smaller events can prompt BI project managers to re-examine the direction they're going. Say one of the program's key executive sponsors leaves the company, or the company launches or re-tools one of its leading products, or enters a new market. Any of those developments can affect your BI project.

Changes aren't permanent, but change itself certainly is. A good BI organization is one that can roll with the punches. So never assume that the BI strategy you develop is a permanent fixture. It should provide a guiding light for the current project phase, as well as the next few in the planning stages. But after that, remember that anything can happen.

Chapter 11

Building a Solid BI Architecture and Roadmap

Good news! The Chief Operations Officer has accepted your BI strategy recommendations, and the Chief Financial Officer is prepared to fund the project.

Bad news: Now you actually have to figure out how you're going to make it happen.

Right up to this point, a lot of the focus has been on theoretical issues — defining tools and technologies, and assessing how one piece fits together with another piece. But now it's time to put that knowledge into action and begin to build the project roadmap.

As with any map that helps you on a journey, your BI roadmap is just a general guide to help you get from point A to point B. Defining those two points is the *whole* point of the content in the first half of this book. Now you have to find the best route between them. Plan well; the road may get rough.

Notice that we're looking for the *best* route between where you are now and where you want to be, not simply the fastest or the cheapest route. As is the case with any IT project, the "impossible triangle" (Figure 11-1) is in effect for BI implementations. The concept is simple: You may strive to create a project that's cheap, good, and fast, but you can't have them all. For example, if you want an inexpensive system that works well, you'll have to sacrifice time. On the other hand, if you're looking to install something immediately on a limited budget, it's not going to be very good.

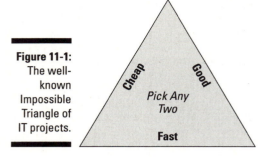

Figure 11-1:
The well-known Impossible Triangle of IT projects.

What a Roadmap Is (and Isn't)

A business intelligence roadmap is one or more documents that lays out the formal objectives, high-level requirements, and specific activities of the project. It is, in effect, a founding charter that the project team will use as a guiding North star to set schedules, allocate resources, and even to market the project internally. Your roadmap should tell you what you're trying to accomplish, what tools you're going to use to get the job done, how you plan to do it, and (to some extent) the justification for the approach you're taking. Here are some examples of sections of what to include in your roadmap:

- Statement of overall business problem(s) and the specific scope of the solution.

- Business perspective of the solution — for example, what information needs your system will meet that it wasn't meeting before.

- Initial financial analysis, including ROI projections.

- Current condition of the organization's information infrastructure — including a discussion of where all the relevant data is being housed and what condition it's in.

- High-level review of hardware requirements, emphasizing any new platforms you may need to implement.

- Discussion of existing and new software that will be utilized for the BI solution.

- General make-up of project team and division of responsibilities.

- A section on risks, constraints, and assumptions that lays out where things can go wrong, as well as the known limits of the BI implementation. (It's always good to be explicit about what the project will *not* deliver.)

What you won't see anywhere on your roadmap is a detailed work plan. A roadmap is not a comprehensive task-level project plan (though if you use Microsoft Project as one of the tools to represent your high-level sequencing of activities and milestones, you can build your project plan starting from your roadmap). It's a strategic-level document that outlines the major decisions about how the business intelligence solution is to be implemented. Unlike a project plan — which lays out every step — a set of major choices transforms the goals and requirements of the system.

Before you can finish your roadmap, you'll be forced to make some big decisions about the architecture of your BI solution. Those initial decisions will determine what kind of tools you'll need, and what kind of talent you'll need on your team to get the job done.

As President Dwight D. Eisenhower famously noted, plans are nothing; planning is everything. Ike wasn't encouraging you to wing it, nor was he giving you (and every other project planner) an excuse to toss aside detailed project plans and roadmaps. The point is that the *process* of planning is just as important as the artifacts that it spawns.

As you build the roadmap, you'll have to take a microscope to your needs and abilities, think through more than a few ideas and possibilities (to make sure you haven't "group-thought" yourself into one solution when another might be better for you), and make contact with people who can help you — both within your organization and without. Don't short-circuit the planning process by thinking that the roadmap document itself is the goal.

While you want to make your roadmap as complete as it can be, don't get stuck in the mud if you don't know with absolute certainty all the answers and have to leave some stub headings that have no attached content beneath them for the time being. That's an inevitable part of the planning process. For example, if you work for the International Widget Corporation and you know there's a chance the unprofitable Micro-Widget division will be sold, you may need to account for that variable in your roadmap by inserting an assumption stating how different outcomes could lead to different planning decisions. Above all, don't bring the project planning process to a halt while waiting to nail down every possible loose end.

Centralized Versus Decentralized Architecture

The roadmap's shape and form will hinge on the overall shape of the solution. And one of the biggest drivers of that is the question of whether to build out a centralized or decentralized system. The two architectures involve very different approaches to the implementation process. In this section we'll take a look at why the question is so important, and talk about ways to approach the answer. It's considered the biggest decision because it's the first. Everything you do in your BI implementation will be affected.

A couple question

Some BI specialists use the term *coupling* to describe the degree to which a BI system is centralized and consistently applied. A highly centralized system might make a common set of tools available to the entire company, share the most effective practices across the organization, and (usually) give a single entity or team the responsibility for making key BI decisions that affect everyone. In a system like that, one department's BI system is coupled to the central BI regime — both technologically and procedurally. It makes for easy management, but can stifle the effectiveness of a BI solution if the business situation calls for more versatility; everyone has to use one-size-fits-all tools.

On the other hand, a decentralized system allows some variations of policy and practice across different BI domains and functional areas. Departments and business units might use the same tools, but they aren't obligated to do so as they would be in a centralized system. This kind of system, where tools and practices are built up independently and *de-coupled* from a central decision-making power, is often appealing because it can put ideally suited BI tools in the everyone's hands. (Of course, it can also be a tad inefficient and hard to manage, what with everyone doing their own thing.)

Chapter 5 discusses departmental and enterprise BI arrangements, but that's a matter of scope. A BI system's scope isn't the same as how *coupled* it is. It's possible to have a highly decentralized departmental implementation of BI. For example, imagine an international conglomerate that wants to introduce BI for its sales team, but the sales team has sub-units that work on different products with wildly different sales dynamics. Perhaps they're in different countries and don't even speak the same language. In that case, a one-size-fits-all solution wouldn't work; you'd have to allow those sub-units to customize the BI solution as needed.

How to choose

So which one do you need? A centralized or decentralized architecture? Well, that depends on a handful of variables that can be summed up under two headings:

- ✔ **Organizational culture.** Most companies have one of two basic cultures:

  - **Autocratic:** Decisions are made from the top down, with little room for interpretation. Autocratic cultures lend themselves to centralized BI; the apparatus is already in place for centrally controlled strategy and application administration, and usually that's what their people are used to.

- **Entrepreneurial:** Business decisions are made throughout the company and innovation is encouraged. Where departments and teams have the authority to dictate the terms of how their supporting tools are built, decentralized BI systems are more likely to flourish.

✔ **Organizational structure.** In most cases, but not all, the organizational structure aligns with the company's culture. For example, if decisions are made at the top, the structure of power and communication radiate from a handful of top executives down to the rest of the organization in a rigid way, while entrepreneurial companies are likely to be matrix-managed rather than hierarchical.

It's important to be aware of organizational factors because they will dictate how data moves between business units and teams, and that will ultimately guide your centralized versus decentralized decision. Since BI typically needs to bring lots of disparate data together, a company where teams are not in the habit of sharing data or working together for the greater good could make it difficult to install a centralized BI solution.

You'll want to understand how the business units work together to perform common functions, as well as where they are geographically.

It's probable the answer lies somewhere in between centralized and decentralized BI architecture. That may seem contradictory, but the reality is that while large chunks of the organization may require tools and practices in common — and a rigid control system — pockets of decentralization may persist as well. For example, a company might install an enterprise-wide, centralized, homogeneous BI system, but allow one key team with a unique function — say, the corporate-strategy group or the sales-operations crew — to build their BI solution as they see fit.

Here the first key decision is setting policy to specify how coupled your BI environment should be; it's arguably as important as any decision you'll make throughout the life of your project. Answering it forces you to look closely at many aspects of your existing systems — and of your company as well. It's not a question you can expect to answer in one sitting.

When you answer this how-coupled-is-it question, you set the direction for the entire BI implementation. The degree of centralization you specify will cascade to the other steps in the plan; when you've decided on a coupling scheme, you're ready to move on to other major choices — such as what kind of tools you're going to use and how the data will be handled. And none of those questions can be tackled without answering the first question.

Bringing disparate data under a common umbrella in the form of a *data warehouse* (a dedicated repository for historical operational data) is a common choice made during the roadmap phase — but it may not be right for every situation. Integrating data into one big centralized melting pot is far easier said than done — and will inevitably occupy an enormous chunk of your project resources. A data warehouse may well be the answer you're looking for, but it's certainly not the only solution out there. Often alternatives are available that work just as well and spare you some heartburn along the way. We'll discuss data warehouses and other ways to bring information together in Chapter 16.

BI Architecture Alternatives

Once you've developed either a centralized or decentralized model, you can make the other general architecture choices. You'll need to consider a number of vital factors, such as these:

- ✔ How and where will the data be maintained?
- ✔ What will the integration schedule be?
- ✔ What tools will sit on which desktops — throughout the organization?

You won't lay out every single detail of all possible solutions until you get into detailed requirements and design (as discussed in the following chapters), but you'll want to get a broad perspective on the solutions available in the marketplace. In the beginning, you have a lot of questions and few answers, so you'll have to start by working through a list of all possible alternatives. After that, you narrow it down to a few good candidates.

Starting an architecture evaluation

So what factors are important when you're looking into possible solutions? You'll want to stick with the basics and view every alternative through the prism of your main business needs.

For BI implementations, your architecture choices will almost always start with three major categories of technology:

- ✔ Hardware
- ✔ Data management
- ✔ End-user tools

Of course, each of those main categories can be broken down into subcategories (even sub-sub-categories), but start with the big three.

Sure, there's more to an enterprise-wide BI solution than just hardware, databases, and front-end tools. For example, you'll probably have to consider the network infrastructure that acts as the conduit between system components, as well as a vast collection of *middleware* (software that acts as the connective tissue between network components, data sources, and applications). BI can affect all of it.

As you examine each architecture alternative, be sure to address each of the main three components. For example, you may be starting your evaluation with the constraint that the hardware environment can't be changed. That could happen for any number of reasons — budgetary, political, or otherwise. In that case, you'll be forced to use what's available; the project team will have to find data-handling and tools software that can be placed on existing infrastructure without affecting performance any more than absolutely necessary.

In general, every architecture solution involves three general components that mirror the "big three" technology categories:

✔ **Hardware:** A discussion of what, if any, hardware changes are required (for example, will you have to increase server processing horsepower to handle the complexity of the transactions expected?).

✔ **Data management:** A small list of data-management options (such as how the data will be transported and transformed, and what the target database will need to be able to do.)

✔ **End-user tools:** Recommendations of one or more tools that meet the system's general business needs directly (such as an advanced statistical package, or a managed reporting solution to meet the needs of the prospective user groups.)

Start with the end-user tools. If you have a rough idea of the requirements, then the tools are a good brass-tacks place to start. You can develop a list of available software that will meet your querying, reporting, and analysis needs, then work backward to expand the evaluation to identify compatible data handling technology that can support the tools. Then you'll look for what hardware is required to run it.

Proven techniques for narrowing down options

You're not the first person to have to make a solid choice from a complex array of options, but if you're the one ultimately on the hook for the decision, it can be a lonely position. Fortunately there are some tried and true techniques to narrowing down your architecture choices. Can any selection methodology guarantee you won't make a monumental error? Unfortunately no, but read on and you'll find there are some ways to approach the task.

So many choices

Laying out all plausible alternatives — and giving each its day in court — is a step in the process skipped by far too many organizations. This phase doesn't have to last long, but it's an important step because it opens you (and the team) up to technologies and techniques that may not be in the standard recipe.

You want to work through a wide variety of choices while keeping your project's basic constraints and objectives in mind. But feel free, at this stage, to be a little more open with your ideas; allow your team some latitude during your planning sessions.

You'll want to look at solution elements like these:

✔ Operating systems

✔ Network protocols

✔ Server hardware

✔ Primary database vendor

✔ Data Warehouse and Extract,Transform, and Load (ETL) processes

✔ The kinds of front-end BI tools you absolutely must have

✔ The kinds of front-end BI tools that would be nice to have

So little time

At the beginning of the project, the slate is almost completely clean. The possibilities stretch out before you — the software tools, hardware platforms, protocols, and processes that will comprise your BI implementation. The skies are blue, the fields are green; whatever you envision can become a reality.

Get real.

While you certainly want to have a free-flowing discussion about the possibilities and endless alternatives, you'll need to narrow down your options to a few main candidates pretty quickly.

The company's installed technology and on-the-record future direction will be a primary factor in deciding architecture. Are there internal standards that limit your choice of tools both today and in the future? For example, does your organization rely on one main vendor for its database-management system? If so, does that mean the BI system is similarly limited? Keeping such basic constraints in mind should yield a general idea of what your options really are.

The planning process is a notorious quicksand zone, where projects get bogged down as team leaders agonize over the initial choices, knowing their importance. You're not going to make the right call every time. Sometimes identified "best practices" aren't "best" for your organization. But don't get paralyzed by the fear of making a misstep. You have no choice but to get moving, and surround yourself with vendors, consultants, and team members you trust. Keep a close eye on what they're doing, but put your faith in their ability to perform due diligence and meet the priorities you've laid out. As the old saying goes, *trust but verify*.

During the planning phase you look at the architecture as a whole, as well as the individual pieces. The categories of questions you'll need to ask at this point:

✔ Which solution components work well together? And which don't?

✔ What infrastructure is currently in place and does it have spare capacity?

✔ Does the company have existing relationships with some of the target vendors?

During this phase, you'll also start to get a handle on which pieces of the puzzle have higher priority than others. That's important information; you'll need to put it to use very soon.

The short list

The goal is to produce a short list of architecture alternatives that satisfy all of your bare minimum requirements, and hopefully supply some nice-to-have features as well. The vetting process is far from over; you'll want to turn over the short list of alternatives to some key stakeholders and analysts on your team to pick apart and find reasons to narrow down the list.

Each short list will include the querying, reporting, analysis, and other front-end tools that the end-users throughout the company will be using. There will also be the underlying database technology — not just software, but configuration options and architectural considerations as well. Finally, be sure to put any hardware requirements on the short list. For example, if the short list includes a solution that involves creating a new centralized data-warehouse environment, the entry on the short list should include

✔ A basic analysis of existing processing and storage capacity (relative to the minimum amount needed)

✔ An ideal hardware configuration for maximum performance

Taking a second look at your short list

You're going to have to get your hands dirty now; it's time to stop looking at solutions in a vacuum. You'll want to judge their capabilities and constraints in the context of your infrastructure.

You may have already analyzed the gap between your existing systems' capabilities and the business requirements for the BI system; now it's necessary to put the solutions in context. You can do that by examining your short list solutions and visualizing how they'll actually *work* when they're installed in your company's environment. You're looking to identify compatibility issues, integration problems, and other potential roadblocks that might arise when you start introducing new hardware and software to your existing technology environment. Eventually you're going to have to chop the architecture alternatives that don't play well with the other kids in the sandbox.

At this point it makes sense to begin in-depth discussions with candidate vendors and consultants so you can get detailed information on their product capabilities, plus a full menu of their support options to go along with their wares. Invite them in for a discussion of your situation and take careful note of how they would approach the challenges you face.

This is a great time to have software vendors do live demonstrations of their products. You can put an application through the paces and see how it holds up. If it's an end-user tool, invite a few key end-users to the demo, and ask for their input on how appealing, usable, and useful the software actually is.

It helps if the vendors have an idea of what you're trying to do, so you should be prepared to share a little information with them about your project. Project details will help the third parties tailor their pitch toward what you actually need. Check with your legal team and see whether there is a standard Non-Disclosure Agreement that you should use.

For gigantic implementations, you might have a vendor do an extensive Proof of Concept (POC) implementation as a way to test a product's ability to meet your specific needs. For a business intelligence solution, POCs are particularly useful to demonstrate whether different brands of software work together in your environment without building out the entire solution. POCs move beyond the theoretical realm of PowerPoint presentations, white papers, and even canned product demonstrations and reveal something of the true nature of the software.

Examining costs for each alternative

So far, cost has not been a factor in the conversation — but that big green dollar sign is always lurking in the background (unless, of course, you're in another country and working in their currency). Bottom line: software licenses cost money. Servers and networking gear cost money, as does integration vendors' time. Evaluating possible solutions without considering your budget affords you a certain amount of freedom to isolate the best alternatives, and identify the most important components without constraint. But sooner or later the piper must be paid.

Costs can sneak into IT projects in a lot of ways. Keep your eyes open for the following expenses:

- **Software licenses:** Don't be haphazard in your approach to buying licenses. Many vendors have complex and confusing schemes that can lead you to pay for more seats than you end up needing. A software partner with simple and flexible licensing can be worth its weight in gold.

- **Hardware-acquisition costs:** Buying new gear for your BI solution can be an expensive proposition, especially where it concerns high-performance servers and networking gear. Having a scalable solution is a good way to save money; you can start small and work your way up to the hardware capacity you need, but not until you actually need it.

- **Service and maintenance costs:** Many vendors make their money not from the initial purchase of their product, but from ongoing fees exacted from customers for supporting their products. Make sure you account for all outlays over the life of the products you're buying for your BI system, not just the big check at the beginning.

- **Training and support costs:** Complex software means the end-users of your business-intelligence system will need help before they get full use out of it. It's important that quality education be made available for the user community, and that costs money.

Always remember the *business* in *business intelligence*. Your organization is trying to make money, and that can only happen if you increase revenues or reduce expenses. In most cases, a BI implementation is already a big investment for a company — but don't confuse executive approval of your project with license to go crazy with the company checkbook. With limited resources, you'll want to stretch your budget resources as far as you can.

As you examine the costs of each solution alternative, keep in mind that *the most expensive solution isn't always the best.* It's a common trap that has snared many a project manager. Price is clearly an important component, but make sure that money don't enter into your *qualitative* evaluation of products to meet your needs.

Looking at technology risks

To this point, you've taken your short list through the paces. You've performed an analysis of each solution's viability as a way to meet your business needs. You've examined the associated cost of each element of your solution as well. Now it's time to look at risk.

We're not talking about the risk that a huge meteorite could crash into the Earth and end all life as we know it. We're talking about specific risks that go hand-in-hand with technology — say, a *medium* meteorite that crashes into your data center but leaves the rest of the planet intact.

It's a scary word, but in essence, technology risk is nothing more than a *variable expense* that you don't see coming. It's impossible to predict with any certainty, but if you do your best to see it coming, it's possible to minimize its impact.

Fortunately, there are some common guidelines you can look to if you want to understand risk in an IT environment better because it can have a huge impact on your BI rollout. Every large, complex IT implementation has common risks associated with it — these, for example:

- Software has unknown bugs that pupate and hatch at inopportune times.
- Software doesn't perform as promised by the vendor.
- Products don't work together as well as projected.

Included in your architecture and solution assessment should be a risk analysis of each choice on your short-list. You should include a list of the most likely things that could go wrong with each solution. It's always a good idea to quantify the likelihood of a risk scenario coming to pass, and include a projected damage toll — including how it would affect your BI initiative.

Suppose, for example, you find that Application A has a large chance of causing minor performance issues with the system while the alternative, Application B, has a tiny chance of bringing the entire BI implementation to a halt. Depending on the values you assign for the likelihood of each outcome, you might actually decide Application B makes the most sense from a risk perspective.

When in doubt, go with proven solutions. And while you want to look at vendors with a track record of stability, you should avoid version 1.0 of just about any species of software. First-generation applications often have kinks that still need to be worked out, and they're a risky bet to build your environment around unless you're getting major concessions from the vendor to protect and compensate your company for any problems that might arise.

Making your decision

It's a great feeling when a single solution emerges as a winner. Your project is practically laid out before you on a silver platter when one candidate solution is the only choice that fits your needs and your constraints.

Unfortunately, that's a rarity. More often than not, a few solutions score very close to one another and you end up with a dead heat.

In spite of the temptation to flip a coin or end your planning meeting with a round of eenie-meanie-miny-moe, you should take this opportunity to do a fresh analysis of your candidate solutions. That will usually lead to finding a deeper set of criteria from which to judge each candidate solution, with the aim of selecting a winner.

These three steps can help you break any ties:

1. **Verify your information**. Make sure all your existing information is correct. That means re-working pricing numbers, compatibility issues, and functional capabilities. Go over the features of each product step by step; make sure the analysis you're reading is fair and unbiased (not to mention up-to-date, since software features can come and go from release to release).

2. **Revisit your criteria.** After you've verified your research data, make sure you haven't missed anything in terms of judging criteria. Are you basing your judgment on the *complete* set of business drivers? Or are there some considerations you initially left out because they seemed irrelevant to a particular architecture choice?

3. **Get a new perspective.** It's a great idea to get a fresh set of eyes on each solution. Sometimes you'll find if you stare at something long enough you lose all objectivity and perspective. An outside resource, even someone who has no direct expertise in the kind of system your building, might have an angle that you hadn't considered on why one solution is better or worse than another.

Developing a Phased, Incremental BI Roadmap

Like the project itself, the roadmap is something you build one iteration at a time. You take a first pass at the document with candidate solutions, then narrow those down to a few, and finally a winning architecture emerges. At each step of the way, the roadmap changes, becoming more focused, and providing a deeper level of detail.

With the architecture selection made, and the solution coming into tighter focus, it's time to start working through how you're going to make your vision a reality.

The goal is not to create a full project plan with step-by-step instructions; instead, the roadmap must include what you're going to deliver and when. The roadmap is where you lay out a strategy for building your business intelligence solution in a way that keeps momentum up, maintains support throughout the organization, doesn't use up resources too quickly, and tolerates occasional failures.

And oh, by the way, it's a good thing if it delivers on its promised business value as well. (But you knew that.)

Deciding where to start

Instead of starting with the first single step, you'll want to define what the entire first *phase* is going to look like.

It's almost always to your benefit to start with a limited solution that grows into a full BI implementation after several subsequent phases. Doing that ensures that any early failures are small and can be overcome quickly. If you spend several years on a comprehensive, enterprise-wide BI implementation, the audience anticipation grows with each passing month. When the big day comes and the spotlight is on you as it's time to hit the switch, you'll be in big trouble if the Christmas tree doesn't light up as planned.

So instead of shooting for the moon, you should look for objectives within your grasp for the early phases of the project. No IT book would be complete without the low-hanging fruit metaphor, so here it goes:

Your Phase I implementation should pluck the lowest-hanging, ripest, best-tasting fruit from the tree. That is, the initial goal should be to start building a solution at the intersection of the highest-value, least risky functions that are also the easiest to deliver:

- ✔ **Highest value:** If you have a system in place now that's already working, only at a level that requires eventual change, then skip that functional area for one where the user community is clamoring for anything to make their lives easier.

- ✔ **Least risky:** Don't roll out executive dashboards first, or any other function whose failure might lead to the bigwigs pulling the plug on the whole shebang. And we're not just talking about political risk; it's wise to avoid implementations that might interfere with systems that are functioning perfectly well.

✔ **Easy to deliver:** You should also avoid implementations that are highly technically complex as well. A simple solution establishes your team, lets you develop your internal processes, and build a tradition of success with the company.

Out of those three qualities, chances are you may only find two, but it can't hurt to be optimistic.

It's always best to do improvements to existing systems, rather than brand new systems. If (for example) you already have a sales analytics module up and running, it probably makes sense to make the early phases of your project include an upgrade to advanced sales analytics before building the HR function from the ground up.

Keeping score

It's easy to decide to go after the low-hanging fruit, but what if the fruit one branch up is extra-tasty? And what about the fruit that just fell off the tree and doesn't even require a ladder?

It's not always easy to decide where your priorities should be. A back-of-the-napkin scorecard system might make sense early on — where you lay out the key variables listed in the previous section, along with a few that are peculiar to your situation. Work through the possible first steps and grade them out based on how they fall in each category. From that scorecard, you'll get the optimal combination of functions for Phase I.

If you do a rough-and-ready scorecard of categories to evaluate, be sure you score each category the same way — even if that seems a little counterintuitive. Figure 11-2 shows a list of four possible Phase I initiatives for your BI system. On this scorecard, a higher score simply means "more advantageous to the company," so under Value a score of 4 means *more valuable* and a score of 1 means *less valuable*. For the Risk category a score of 4 means safer — that is, *less risky* (since less risk is more advantageous to the company, right?) and a score of 1 means the *most risky*. When all the individual scores are added, we find that the best Phase I solution is the upgrade to the reporting tool, whose score totaled 9. Sure, it's the least valuable — but because it's going to be easy and virtually risk-free to install, it makes the most sense.

The scorecard example in Figure 11-2 assumes all three criteria matter equally. You can always adjust the scorecard differently depending on what you're trying to accomplish, or if there are any special circumstances surrounding the choice you have to make. For example, if your company is especially risk-averse, you can rig the scorecard to be more sensitive to the risk category by multiplying each Risk score by 2 prior to totaling the sores for each choice. Just remember: A perfectly balanced and fair scorecard is not the goal here; it's just a tool to help illuminate your options.

Figure 11-2:
A sample score-card for determining sensible initial steps for your BI project.

Phase I Solution Choices Scorecard

↓ Project	Value	Risk	Easy	Overall
Sales Dashboard	2	2	3	7
Finance OLAP Conversion	3	1	2	6
Reporting Upgrade	1	4	4	9
Productivity Analytics	4	2	1	7

Deciding what comes next

The decisions you make about Phase I will determine how to proceed. If Phase I includes a Sales analytics implementation, you'll proceed like you would with any other IT project, beginning with an informational or discovery phase, followed by an architect phase where you design the solution, and on into a build and test phase.

Deciding what comes next, and next, and next . . .

Now you're on your way. You've got your roadmap in place with Phase I's deliverables. Rinse, lather, and repeat with Phase II. If you want, you can simply look at the next best item on your scorecard and pencil that in as the next priority on your roadmap. Or you might consider adjusting the score-card and adding the scores again; priorities may change after you have the first success under your belt.

Planning for contingencies

You know what they say about the best laid plans of mice and men. Whether you're rodent or human (or somewhere in between, like your boss), you'll need to get familiar with the practice of contingency planning, and build some emergency scenarios and decision points into your roadmap.

A contingency plan is little more than a carefully designed set of alternative branches in a project roadmap. Under certain conditions, the contingency plan gets activated. For the purposes of your roadmap, you'll need to flush out specific project risks that could hamper development, delay the release, or put the entire initiative in jeopardy. The simplest contingency plans are those that reduce the scope of the project in case something goes wrong. Or if a part of the release fails, your contingency plan could be as simple as preparing a pre-assembled trouble-shooting team that swings into action.

We'll talk more about identifying risks in Chapter 12, but for now, understand that like any large complex high-visibility project, a business intelligence implementation has dozens of inflection points where problems can appear and derail your initiative.

Some examples of project risks include these:

- ✔ Higher-than-expected project staff turnover
- ✔ Loss of project champion or sponsor
- ✔ Higher-than-expected — or unexpected — expenses that cause you to blow through your budget
- ✔ Technology-specific risks such as these:
  - Integration problems with existing software and hardware
  - Over-promised (or under-delivered) software functionality

A good contingency-planning process identifies risks like these and creates alternate pathways into the roadmap, and later, the project plan itself. In some cases, best practices can show you the way to a safe harbor in the event of a storm. But for certain problems — including those unique to your team, your implementation, or your company — you'll need to be ready to toss out the book and improvise.

If you read the transcript of the radio chatter between the spacecraft and Mission Control during the failed Apollo XIII lunar-landing mission, you'd think they were dealing with a backed-up space toilet rather than the grave problems the astronauts actually faced. That's because NASA emphasized contingency planning in the early days of the space program, and does so even today. The transcript shows only the slightest hints of concern from the astronauts and Mission Control — even after discovering the crew's oxygen was leaking into space.

Your BI project is like a space mission — a large, complex system where pieces can fail unexpectedly. The better you can anticipate problems — and work out solutions and plans ahead of time to deal with them — the more likely your project won't be lost in space when something goes wrong.

Dealing with moving targets

It would be nice if you could freeze the world in place as you build out your BI system. That way you wouldn't have to worry that while you were off solving one problem, another problem on the other side of the company changed shape without you knowing about it.

Unfortunately, BI implementations don't happen in a vacuum; there are all kinds of dependencies and vital connections with resources in various parts of your organization. Given the fact that planning and design takes time, it's always possible that things will change in an unexpected way.

It's not always easy to do, but as you build your roadmap, it's incumbent upon you and your team to account and plan for as many external variables as possible. Suppose, for example, your data-warehouse system is designed to use a state-of-the-art storage network that you've been told will be launched only a month before the data warehouse comes online. It's probably a good idea to have a contingency plan available in case the new storage system *isn't* available.

And it's not just major IT systems that can change, either. Tiny changes to the data schema that feeds your data warehouse (or perhaps an adjustment to the network addressing scheme) may happen without you being any the wiser. Seemingly insignificant updates can have a big impact on your project.

Open a line of communication with other project managers in your company who are working on IT-related initiatives parallel to yours. Be aware of their roadmaps; work with them to coordinate the dates on your project plan with theirs. Reach out to technology-governance boards wherever possible to ensure you're up to date on scheduled system and process changes. And most of all (again), do some good contingency planning.

Leaving time for periodic "architectural tune-ups"

In spite of what you might have heard about the Pyramids in Egypt, not all architectures are designed to last forever. And the time to face your BI architecture's mortality is now, rather than after it becomes obsolete, useless, or just aggravating to the users and administrators.

A BI system is a constantly-evolving organism; there will be regular upgrades and tweaks to functionality. The applications might be rolled out to a new team one month, and a software patch might be rolled out the next month. In such an environment, it's easy for changes to pile up without paying attention to their combined effect on system performance.

One way to avoid problems is to plan for occasional code freezes in your project plan. During these periods (a good standard is *one quarter out of every two years*), the system gets tuned from time to time, but that's about the extent of the changes. The code freeze gives you an opportunity to replace servers, tune your databases, upgrade your front-end user tools, and perform other tasks necessary to keep your system in shape. It's also a good time to make an honest evaluation of the state of the system.

As you examine the various elements of your system for how effectively they're performing their tasks, you'll want to ask yourself some key questions not just about raw quantitative performance issues, but also about softer, more qualitative issues — for example, how user-friendly the system is, whether it's time to upgrade the training program, and so forth.

It makes sense to have some "meta-metrics" (metrics that keep track of the metrics) for your BI architecture; they're essentially performance indicators for the system itself. Build some universal benchmark tasks that you can execute every so often to get a glimpse of the system's health and allow you to compare performance over time. Keep track of system uptime and throughput. And it's always important to have a standard user-satisfaction survey that gets distributed on a regular basis. This will provide you a good heads-up when issues start to crop up.

It can't hurt to stay in touch with the state of the marketplace for the main cogs in your system — the data warehouse, the ETL software, the querying and reporting tools, and so on. The goal is not to create a killer case of buyer's remorse for you, but rather to keep an eye open for new pieces to your puzzle that might improve your performance, extend your existing functionality, or allow you to extend BI's reach to a new set of users within your organization.

Part IV
Implementing BI

The 5th Wave   By Rich Tennant

"I think the BI app. has found a lot of opportunities for improvement."

In this part . . .

Okay, Mr. or Ms. Lemonade maker. You've dreamed the impossible dream for too long now. It's time to turn those dreams into reality, to put those plans into effect.

This is where the BI rubber hits the BI road. You'll start off with a chapter about the project plan you'll need to assemble that takes the best parts of your strategy and architecture ideas and codifies them, breaking them into tasks assigned to resources.

Is there a business analyst in the house? You're going to need a good one to manage the requirements elicitation process for your BI project. That means working through the users to find out what they really want, then analyzing it to discover if it's what they really need.

Then you have no choice but to put it into a pot, mix it together and come up with a reasonable design that fits into the constraints of your business while meeting all of your goals. After that it's the glory of a successful launch, followed by long days of maintaining and enhancing the system you so successfully installed.

Chapter 12

Building the BI Project Plan

*T*he BI *project plan* is the primary tracking and control mechanism for your business intelligence implementation. It's where you list and organize every single task required to make your BI project a reality. That doesn't necessarily mean you list "reading this book", or other early-stage day-dreaming . . . er . . . research tasks.

The project plan is there to help you choreograph every move the project team members will have to make. All the tasks, milestones, and deliverables are there so that each moment of implementation planning, designing, coding, and testing is accounted for and scheduled properly. But project plans are more than mere task lists; they include resources, constraints, risks, and budget issues; wrapping it all around a calendar (or multiple calendars) to show the impact of changing the resources working on the project or deviating from the schedule.

The project plan is really a dual-purpose document:

✔ It's the high-level blueprint that maps, *ahead of time*, which tasks have to be done, in what order, and by whom.

✔ It's the central organizing tool for the project team — and for many of the stakeholders as well. The plan keeps everybody marching to the beat of the same drum.

Prior to beginning work on the project, the approved project plan communicated throughout the organization is a kind of promise to stakeholders. It says the BI implementation team will do *these* specific tasks in *this* specific way.

After the project kicks off, the plan's tracking function comes into play. As the days roll by, tasks are begun and completed, issues arise, resources come and go, and these events ultimately affect the project delivery date. The project manager monitors everything that happens on the project and updates the plan so resources are utilized efficiently and the rest of the organization knows the expected completion date.

The project plan is a full-fledged communication tool that project managers use to set expectations both inside and outside the team. It offers everyone a glimpse of how each piece fits into the big picture, so it's bound to foster teamwork and cooperation.

A project plan is never really *complete* in the traditional sense of the word. It's a snapshot of the current state of the project, combined with your best estimate about what's going to happen in the future. As the renowned management guru Alan Lakein once said, "Planning is bringing the future into the present so that you can do something about it now." The project plan — including the process of building it — shows one possible future scenario for the business intelligence initiative.

If you wait until you know every little detail about the project plan, you'll never get your BI venture off the ground. Be thorough when you're creating your project plan, but not so much so that it brings the entire process to a halt. It's true that the finer a level of detail you can define in the project plan, the more likely you are to spot potential bottlenecks and risks to the implementation. But at some point you have to actually get to work.

Planning the Plan

When you're ready to build a project plan, start with an inventory of the information you're already working with, which many not be all that much. Chances are you have done some research and have produced a project mission statement. Then there will be official communiqués from executive sponsors. It doesn't seem like much, but you should be able to glean some important information from these items. Then it's time to think about how you're going to record it in a project plan.

Revisiting the vision

Start the process of developing your project plan with the basic goals of the project:

- ✔ Why is the organization undertaking this venture?
- ✔ What are they expecting to get from it?

▮ ✔ Who needs to know the project plan?

Most of these answers should be available to you in the project artifacts you've already created.

✔ **Project vision and roadmap:** An approved description of the overall purpose and direction of the BI initiative. The roadmap will list sets of features and group them together into releases.

✔ **Project architecture:** The architecture is the overall technology approach you're going to take, as well as specifics about what hardware and software you're shooting for with this release. It's also the guide for which application delivers which functionality.

Project plan format

The plan can take whatever form is appropriate for your company. Most project managers build their project plans with a mainstream tool like Microsoft Project.

Dedicated project-management tools like MS Project are helpful because they link related tasks so that changing one task or date will result in other appropriate changes being reflected through the rest of the project plan.

Project Resources

With a technology architecture in mind and a list of major applications to build, the project manager works with his project team to begin working out the major tasks of the project. A list of required skills must accompany each step so the project manager can assign a role (or roles) to cover the task. Eventually the generic role will become a specific resource.

Early on you should assemble a general list of roles required for the project. A *role* is a standard combination of abilities and sets of skills that commonly go together.

Think of a role as a job associated with a single verb — say, "tester" or "documenter" or "network analyzer." It describes someone who has all the skills necessary to perform that one more general function in a project environment. Of course, some of those titles sound a little silly, so use the commonly accepted industry terminology — in the case of the roles listed in this paragraph, that would be (respectively) "Quality-Assurance Analyst," "Technical Writer," and "Network Engineer".

Roles versus resources

Once the project-management team determines all the roles, it's time to match them up with your available resources. Figure 12-1 represents a typical chart that matches roles with resources; in this case, the role-to-resource relationship is (in database terms) many-to-many. That's because you may find that some team members can play more than one role — and in some cases, you must have multiple people playing a single role.

Project management software

Microsoft Project is the most common integrated project-management software on the market, but hundreds of project-support applications are available to project managers. They range from general project-planning-and-management systems to time and expense software, business-graphics packages, and other applications. Many of these are designed for specific types of projects or have specific features.

Every organization has its own standards for — and approach to — project management. Those differences vary by company, and mean more (or less) analysis and rigor at particular stages of the process. What's customary for your shop will probably determine the kind of software you use in your process.

For example, you might be required to undertake in-depth risk assessments at every phase of the project, both quantitative and qualitative. Specialty project-management software can help you produce a comprehensive list of risk events and plan a response in light of these two elements:

✔ Pre-defined risk-assessment templates adjusted to match your project's circumstances

✔ Your company's aversion to certain kinds of risk

Such functions might be covered in your integrated application. Along with risk assessment, your project package should be able to cover — at a minimum — the following activities:

✔ Hierarchical organization of project activities and tasks

✔ Task calendar that includes basic scheduling information, as well as dependencies among tasks and appropriate constraint calculations

✔ Progress tracking — such as percentage-completed dates for specific tasks

✔ Lists and descriptions of resources you can assign to tasks (eventually)

✔ Basic budgeting functionality that tracks the cost of resources and overhead for the project

✔ Multiple project views (such as pert charts and Gantt charts), as well as reports and various ways to summarize information

If the BI project is integrated with other IT projects, you may be asked to use *a portfolio-management solution.* That helps you track multiple projects that share a single resource pool.

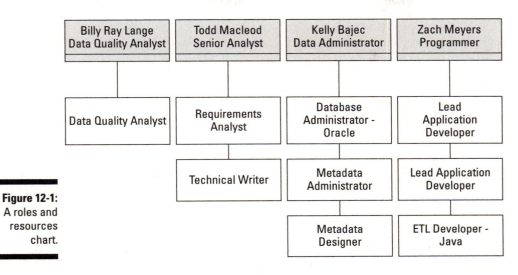

Figure 12-1:
A roles and
resources
chart.

If you're tempted to start with people and fill in the roles underneath them, beware: Don't count on stretching a person's abilities to cover a role they're not equipped to handle.

If you start with project roles instead, and then do your best to match them to the people available in the resource pool, you have a better chance of fitting the right person to the job, as well as identifying skills missing from your team. It's best to understand exactly what you need first — without considering what resources you have available. Only when the roles are defined should you start adding real live people into your plans.

The project budget and timetable both play a big role during this process. In an ideal world, you'd put seasoned experts at in every role, but in reality, you may have to make some sacrifices to meet the demands of the schedule and still come in under budget. If you can't spend the money it takes to hire a seasoned BI/ETL developer (for example), your regular application developers may have to play that part and just do the best they can.

Roles are not people. A role is not necessarily equivalent to a specific resource. Think of a role as a part that has to be played in your little BI drama. It can usually be summed up as a set of skills and a series of tasks, and will eventually be quantified into an amount of work required.

BI project roles

The roles on a BI team are as diverse as the applications and tools that make up your solution.

Team members

Most business intelligence projects include the following professionals who are each experts in one or another key area of the project. You should get familiar with the titles and responsibilities of these roles:

- **Project manager:** This person coordinates and manages all project activities.

- **Business analysts:** This person is tasked with working closely with all stakeholders to codify the requirements for the project. BA's also manage the requirements documentation and oversee the change control process.

- **BI developers:** Often these are experts in particular domains of technology. They manage the end-user environment — whether in terms of reporting, analysis, visualization, or some other tool. This group might include application developers, data-mining experts, or report developers.

- **Database administrator:** This person designs and maintains the target data repository that is the destination for operational data feeds.

- **Data administrator:** The person in this role plays an important part in any BI project: identifying and analyzing operational data sources throughout an organization, and developing a process to bring the data together.

- **ETL developers:** Various people can fill this role (unique to BI projects): *e*xtracting, *t*ransforming, and *l*oading data. This domain of responsibility includes all processes that affect the data as it moves from the operational sources to one of two destinations:

    - The BI data repository

    - The end-user environment

- **Testers:** With so many diverse elements in a BI application environment, there could be a considerable variety of quality-assurance roles.

    For example, some projects may require all of these specialty testers:

    - Front-end testers for the user-facing software

    - A data-quality analyst who can monitor the data itself to ensure that it's performing as advertised

    - Integration testers who will make sure that applications are working together properly, and that all the pieces have come together as designed

If you're on a budget, or even if you're not, a jack-of-all-trades can be a revelation to any project manager. In this day and age, it's not unusual for professionals to have a second (or third) skill set — say, some one filling the Business Analyst role who also has a Q/A background, or someone serving as ETL Developer who has a DBA background. It can save you some money, and it always helps to have human resources who can take a broad perspective on the project.

Other players

When you're developing the project plan you'll need to account for people who serve as quasi-resources — folks outside the project team who aren't under your control, but whose time is required to complete the project. Some examples of these roles are

- ✔ **End-users:** These people will ultimately be relying on the BI environment to perform their daily tasks. Their perspective should guide the requirements process early on in the project; they should have a role in evaluating the tools at various points in the development cycle.

- ✔ **Network infrastructure:** Because all that BI data will flow over the corporate network, and the data repository and applications will probably reside in the company data center, you'll need the cooperation of the infrastructure team to get the environment's hardware and connectivity in place.

- ✔ **Risk-management and security experts:** These people help your team comply with corporate standards for handling data and recording your organization's processes.

- ✔ **Subject-matter experts:** Interpreting the data (and the kinds of insights the users are seeking) may require an outside expert who understands the nature of the business. For example, a large retailer might invite a store manager or the point-of-sale application administrator to consult on building a BI tool — even though they won't be using it, nor will they have a direct stake in the outcome of the project. Nevertheless, without their expertise, the BI data administrator might not fully understand the information that the systems are storing.

Project Tasks

After you have the BI project's roles developed and its resources designated, you can begin listing the major tasks in the project plan. Creating a project plan is a naturally a process of iterations; it's common to start out at a high level, jotting down the major components, go through the plan again to add more detail . . . and go through it again to add even more detail. After several passes, the project plan will contain a list of specific tasks broken down into sub-tasks and sub-sub-tasks.

The project plan is a navigation aid — both a map that helps you plan prior to embarking *and* a compass that lets you know when you've lost your way. Take care with how you insert tasks and milestones.

During the project-construction phase, every task must be accounted for in terms of its current state, the availability of resources associated with it, and other diagnostic snapshots that help measure the health of the project. For now, however, the goal is just to list and connect the tasks in a logical order.

First pass: Project milestones

When you have your broad project outline in place, the development leads, senior architects, and most experienced analysts will play a major role in populating the project plan with details. But the first thing the project manager must do is to insert milestones.

Milestones are broad targets that large swathes of the project team work towards. In a large, multi-faceted project like a BI initiative, reaching each milestone indicates the completion of a discrete goal or task.

 A milestone event is like a state of being, usually described in such a way to make sure the length of time listed is 0. It's an intermediate goal, not a set of steps to reach the goal. A milestone indicates an important step in the project, like the start or finish of a phase.

For example, some amount of time and effort has to go into completing the tasks "mix dough," "put dough balls onto baking sheet," and "put baking sheet in the oven." "Cookies done!" is, however, a milestone — a checkpoint that tells you a particular phase of activity has drawn to a close. You could add any number of descriptive milestones to this project, but normally they're just used as summary descriptions of the status of a project.

The first iteration of the project plan will include major project milestones that indicate the completion of the various phases of the project. For example, the following milestones are common in a BI project (go ahead — capitalize 'em, they're important):

- ✔ Stakeholder Interviews Complete
- ✔ Begin BI Pilot Project Design
- ✔ BI Pilot Design Complete
- ✔ Begin Pilot Development
- ✔ Pilot Development Complete
- ✔ Begin Pilot Test Phase
- ✔ Pilot Testing Complete
- ✔ Pilot Launch
- ✔ National Rollout Go/No-Go Decision
- ✔ Begin BI National Rollout Phase I
- ✔ National Rollout Phase II Complete
- ✔ Begin BI Project Phase II
- ✔ End Project Phase II

The preceding list includes no actual tasks. You put specific tasks and activities under such headings as "Testing Complete," but the headings themselves are *status markers only.* Milestones don't describe what you're doing, they describe where you are on the road to completion of the project.

The milestones should be aligned with the overall strategy and architecture of the project. That means they aren't always technology-focused. Often the important milestones for a project include business decisions and anything else that might affect the project schedule. Think of milestones as inflection points on the calendar, watershed moments, or important forks in the road that show progress toward the strategic goals.

Sometimes it's not always clear what the specific project activities will be well into the future, but milestones are a different story. They can be anticipated months, even years, in advance. Even if you don't know how you're going to get to a given destination, you know that's where you've got to go.

Next to those milestones put in any hard dates that you know have to be met. For example, if your pilot implementation has to be up and running by the end of the fiscal year, insert that date next to that milestone. Those milestone listings become the immovable bedrock on which you build your project plan. From there, when you go through and start adding tasks (in the next section of this chapter), they will all be bound to the hard dates of the milestones.

Don't force dates into a project plan unless you absolutely have to. Project software is designed to calculate realistic completion dates for you based on the amount of estimated combined effort for all the tasks.

Second pass: High-level tasks

After the project manager consults with the team about the milestones, you'll need to start in on the second iteration of your project plan creation. In this loop, it's time to start adding the high-level tasks required to reach each milestone. Don't panic if you don't know them all now, or if you aren't sure about the order they should be accomplished in. Just enter them in to the best of your ability.

Figure 12-2 shows how indentation works in project-management software.

Microsoft Project organizes tasks automatically by creating a hierarchy based on how the user indents entries. A good place to start a project plan is the first entry at indentation level 1 (i.e. all the way to the left) which usually contains the overall name of the project. Then task 2 would be one indentation level to the right and would be the first major activity area of the main event, such as "Project Research" or, if the project is to happen in multiple releases, "Release 1: This or That Function" or something similar.

ID	Task Name	Start	Finish
1	**Milestone: Begin Project Phase**	**7/31/2007**	**8/27/2007**
2	**Major Task 1**	**7/31/2007**	**8/10/2007**
3	Sub-task A	7/31/2007	8/6/2007
4	Sub-task B	8/7/2007	8/10/2007
5	**Major Task 2**	**8/13/2007**	**8/27/2007**
6	Sub-task C	8/13/2007	8/17/2007
7	Sub-task D	8/20/2007	8/27/2007
8	**Milestone: End Project Phase**	8/28/2007	8/28/2007

Figure 12-2:
Project plans display hierarchies of tasks through indentation.

If you maintain all milestones on the same indentation level — and put only the milestones at that level — you can always roll up the outline at will when you want to reduce your project plan to a simple, straightforward list of milestones.

Regardless of whether it's a task or a milestone, all entries directly below and indented to the right of a given task will be considered its *child tasks*. So the task that says "Database Development" might show five or six activities beneath it (and indented one level to the right) that represent the core tasks of developing the database. By using a hierarchy in the central task list, Project show the user exactly which sub-tasks are grouped together into broader activity categories.

As you fill in high-level development tasks, you rely on your technical leads much more than you did with the milestones. After all, the project manager isn't expected to know exactly what the technology effort will be (otherwise the project manager would be a developer or database administrator!) But it's important to record the most important system development activities and their larger subtasks, even if you aren't sure what it all means. When it comes time to actually manage the project, you can reference those high-level technical activities — such as writing code modules, installing software packages, performing necessary analyses, regression testing — to assess the development team's progress..

The original project roadmap should provide a number of major tasks. For example, the roadmap may produce high-level goals like these:

- ✔ Gather requirements for querying and reporting software
- ✔ Design solution
- ✔ Identify data sources
- ✔ Develop ETL processes

  ✔ Build data warehouse

  ✔ Feed live data into the data warehouse

  ✔ Test the solution with live data, using dummy queries

  ✔ Perform user-acceptance testing

It won't be a perfect match, but you can take advantage of the technology roadmap to fill in the initial project plan.

Linkages and constraints

For larger tasks, you'll need to begin thinking about linkages and constraints. These two factors, when combined with other information, will eventually lead to milestone dates:

  ✔ **Linkages:** This is one of the most important concepts in the entire project plan. When tasks are *linked*, it means they can be completed *only in a given order*. Usually that means a first task must be completed before starting a second task — for example, the code must be complete before integration testing can begin. However, there are other types of linkages as well, such as start/start linkages where a second task can't begin until a first task begins also.

  Defining linkages is also called creating predecessor and successor tasks. These task-level dependencies will ultimately determine the completion path for your project — that is, what order things get worked on.

  ✔ **Constraints:** These are external factors that affect the completion dates of certain tasks. For example, maybe a system you've planned on updating for the BI project is on a code freeze until a certain date. That means your development work on that system can't begin sooner than that date. Or perhaps a key resource has a vacation planned a few months after the project begins. Constraints usually come in the form of dates, but can include any external factor that will impede work on your project.

Don't languish over linkages just yet. Determining predecessor events is not always an obvious or easy task. Just insert those that you know. The key is continuing your iteration through the project plan and assembling the major tasks and task groups.

Third pass: Break it down

For each main task, you'll need to begin listing the more detailed sub-tasks that lead up to it and draw the same conclusions about dependencies and constraints as you did before.

Task dependencies depend on whether you can work in parallel. *If you can, no linkage exists.* If, however, you have to wait for one task to reach a certain point before you can begin another, you should insert a dependency into your project plan at that point.

Gantt Charts

The main type of visual for a project plan is the Gantt Chart. These useful charts contain a lot of information about a project.

First and foremost, it's a list of tasks. But beyond that, it shows how tasks link together in dependencies and extend over a calendar.

Figure 12-3 is an example of a task list with an associated Gantt Chart out to the side. When the task list is populated with major and minor tasks, the project manager fills in task durations and dependencies. The idea is to represent whether effort can be done in parallel; here each bar on the Gantt chart represents a discrete task.

Duration estimates

After the sub-tasks are listed and as many dependencies as possible listed, you must add duration estimates to each sub-task. Your resource team should be able to provide rough estimates in either hours or days for how long the individual tasks will take.

Other than the start date for the project — and any constrained dates — you should not enter specific dates into your project plan. The combination of task durations and dependencies will get processed by the project-management software to produce start and end dates next to each task.

Make each iteration of the project plan as complete as possible. Don't assume that you can break it into functional pieces and assess any one section completely before you move on to the other sections. The best route is to start with high-level tasks for the entire project, then move down to mid-level tasks for each area of the project. Then you can dig into the details. With each iteration, your plan gains visibility into successively finer points into the project.

Once the project begins, you'll continue to revise the list of tasks, the dependencies, the time estimates, and just about everything else. There's no such thing as a completed project plan; it's always just a snapshot of your best guess about what the project looks like now and how it will look in the future.

Roles and skills

By the time you get to this point, you'll have a general idea of the team roles required for the project. Only after you build the detailed plan will you understand the precise level of effort required from each participant.

After the tasks are broken down into their component elements, you'll need to assign project team members to them.

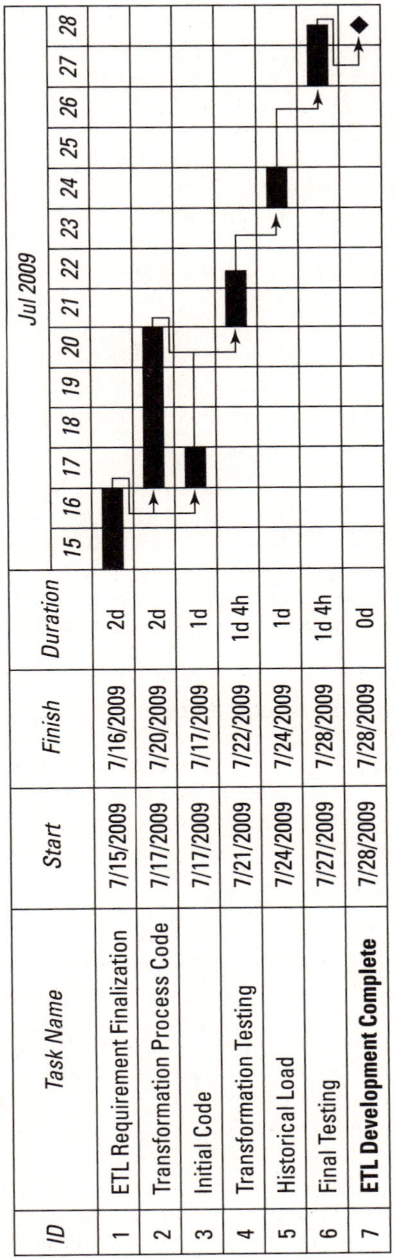

ID	Task Name	Start	Finish	Duration
1	ETL Requirement Finalization	7/15/2009	7/16/2009	2d
2	Transformation Process Code	7/17/2009	7/20/2009	2d
3	Initial Code	7/17/2009	7/17/2009	1d
4	Transformation Testing	7/21/2009	7/22/2009	1d 4h
5	Historical Load	7/24/2009	7/24/2009	1d
6	Final Testing	7/27/2009	7/28/2009	1d 4h
7	**ETL Development Complete**	7/28/2009	7/28/2009	0d

Figure 12-3:
Task list with associated Gantt Chart.

Most project-planning software allows the project manager to add resources to tasks, reducing the duration of each task in proportion. For example, if you estimate it will take 40 hours to code a certain piece of the ETL process, the project manager will need to decide whether to assign one developer to that task for 5 days, or to assign 5 developers for one day. You probably see a problem with this right away: Project software often assumes an hour of work is an hour of the *same* work, but the reality is it's not always so easy to stack more people on a task to get it finished faster.

As a general rule, beware of how your project software handles extra workers on the same task. If the second worker won't perform at the same level of efficiency as the first, you'll need to account for that. For your 40-hour project, one programmer may be able to do it in 5 days, but adding 4 programmers may only shave off a day or two because of reduced efficiency.

There are literally thousands of project plan formats that offer general models for running all kinds of IT projects, including BI implementations. Don't try to re-invent the wheel; use a template for one that's worked successfully for you or someone else in your company, then change only the elements you need to.

Risk Management and Mitigation

During the planning phases of a project, the scenario that inevitably gets the most attention is the *happy path* — what happens when everything goes right and all deliverables are completed on time.

It's only natural that this course gets most of the project detail. But when things go wrong, a well-planned project can turn into the Wild West if no contingency plans are in place.

Contingency planning

There's plenty of good advice for running a project when everything is going well. Fewer project management professionals want to talk about it when things go wrong.

Contingency planning is a lost art in some organizations, but its value is unmistakable. When a project gets derailed, it can turn into the Wild West very quickly. A contingency plan is a branch off the main sequence of tasks and events, designed to get the project back on track and performing as it should.

Treat a contingency plan as you would any other piece of the project plan: List major milestones, tasks, and sub-tasks. Work out details and timelines with your lead technology team, and then define what conditions must exist for you to implement that plan.

Checkpoints

A good project manager stays abreast of the general health of the project, but it's easy to get lost in the day-to-day tasks. That's why it's important to insert pre-arranged status-checking tasks into the plan ahead of time at regular intervals. No matter how busy it gets, you and your project leaders will pause to take a breath and evaluate how things are going. It helps to have a pre-set list of metrics that indicate the wellness of a project — for example, how many man-days of work you're either ahead or behind, or the current budget status.

If you reach a checkpoint and everything seems fine, good for you; continue as you were. And if there are a few items that seem a little off-balance or out of whack, you can quickly work to correct them before they become bigger headaches.

But what if *all* indications are red lights? The best project managers have mitigation strategies worked out ahead of time in case specific problems emerge for the project. Prepare a mitigation module for your project plan — a remedy for fixing whatever the problem is — and be ready to activate it if necessary. For example, if all the code checks out and is functioning properly, but the system performance is inadequate, be prepared to lead the team down a specific fork in the project plan that focuses on repairing any damage done.

Keeping Your BI Project Plan Up to Date

A project plan is designed to be a living, breathing document. It's not meant to be an unchanging blueprint to be hung on a wall in a frame.

Project plans are *management* tools as well as planning tools. Even if everything goes as expected on a project, the project managers have to be able to track the progress of tasks, assign new tasks, manage resources, and so on. Not only that, but the project plan acts as a *de facto* reporting mechanism because it lays out milestones and dependencies, resource lists, utilization rates, on-time metrics, and a pile of other information — all in a way that makes it easy for people inside and outside the project to understand.

Managing to the plan

Ensuring that the project as a whole is delivered on time involves making sure individual tasks are completed on time.

Project management is an ongoing activity, day by day and hour by hour, from the beginning of a project to the very end. A good project manager spends most of his or her time working between the resources and the plan, relying on each resource to provide updates on progress (and expected completion dates) for the tasks. In addition, individual contributors to the project have to inform the project manager of any changes in the list of activities, the schedule, or the order of tasks.

The project manager then compiles the resulting information into a list of changes for the project plan. For example, if the team identifies a new activity or deliverable, the project manager must undertake a thorough assessment of what's being called for. That entails breaking the target into its component tasks, assigning each task an owner from the resource pool, gathering estimate data for level of effort and duration, and (finally) easing that set of tasks into the project plan in a way that minimizes disruption on the rest of the project.

Working through issues

A common problem on projects is task delays or other changes in the schedule. When tasks are completed late, the effect cascades to any subsequent task. The first order effect is that any secondary or subsequent tasks that can't begin until the primary task is completed becomes late as well. But there are other effects: resources may be tightly scheduled to move between tasks at specific times. So if a task is late, not only can you *not* begin dependent tasks, you also have to delay any tasks that expect to have use of the resource assigned to the first task.

Sound confusing? Try expanding that to dozens of simultaneous activities, resources, and milestones, all interconnected and interdependent in ways that make your project plan look like a jigsaw puzzle. On a BI initiative, project managers earn their money.

Daily updates

The moral of the story is that the project plan must be updated every single day. BI projects are notoriously complex because they often touch so many different departments and teams of all disciplines across the company, even extending to third parties. A plan that doesn't get updated with the latest realistic outlook for the project ceases to be a useful central management tool for a fast-moving effort. Worse, an obsolete project plan causes tasks and resources to fall out of alignment, leading to waste and confusion among different groups.

Maintaining the project plan is an entire project unto itself. The project manager will often hire a *project controller* or *project administrator* who handles the administrative functions of the project, and that includes being master and commander of the project plan. A good rule is that for projects involving at least ten full-time technology professionals, the project manager should focus on actually managing the *project* — interacting with the resources, solving problems, making contingency plans, and communicating with the stakeholders and sponsors — and not the project *plan*.

Keeping task data up-to-date

Regardless of who does it, updating the project plan boils down to maintaining the list of tasks — keeping the tasks up-to-date relative to each other, and the information associated with each task current.

For each task, the project manager should monitor

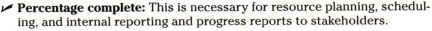 **Percentage complete:** This is necessary for resource planning, scheduling, and internal reporting and progress reports to stakeholders.

The percentage complete affects the task's completion date, and that can have ramifications on subsequent activities. It will also affect the estimated delivery dates displayed for all dependent tasks.

✔ **Resources associated with the task:** Are the same members of the team working on the task that were originally slated to do so? Is the political mix correct between groups working together? If we need to complete a task sooner, what resources could we call in to help in a pinch?

Microsoft Project includes financial tracking information for project managers to maintain. In the Advanced tab for every individual task's Information dialog box, you'll find so-called Earned Value information. This data keeps you on track to ensure you've actually earned what you're billing the client (whether internal or external).

Back to the Ol' Drawing Board

Nobody wants to have to do it, but sometimes no matter how well you've planned, no matter how well you've kept your project documentation up to date, and no matter what level of detail and forethought you've put into the project, sometimes situations arise that force you to completely reevaluate the plan. If several factors conspire to throw your current working plan out of whack, it may be too complicated to try to simply repair it.

At those moments, some project managers have invoked the dreaded "nuclear option" of project planning: They throw out the current plan, go back to the drawing board, start from scratch, and rebuild the project plan from the ground up.

The potential reasons for such drastic measures are manifold. Here are some typical examples:

✔ A key source application you were counting on had a delayed release or was canceled at the last minute.

✔ The company is going through layoffs or some other major economic event, forcing you to change the shape of your team and re-evaluate who will be left to use your application.

✔ A new executive enters the picture and dramatically alters the scope of your BI project.

Tectonic shifts don't have to doom the project, but you have to be realistic about the validity of your existing plan. If any of the following elements change, invoking the nuclear option might make sense:

✔ **Project budget:** When funds get slashed, it's your job to rework the plan in an attempt to achieve the same goals with a reduced resource pool or with a different (read: less expensive) set of tools.

✔ **Project goals:** The broad strategic objectives of the project exist independent of the implementation, and they can shift over time as the company evolves. A change in direction often forces a change in implementation; if that's what you're facing, it might be time to build a new project plan that supports the new goals.

✔ **Technology constraints:** Having to conform to external systems or standards can shape your project in profound ways. If these requirements change, they could affect the entire BI initiative.

✔ **Team resources:** Layoffs are not uncommon in the IT industry, and you wouldn't be the first project manager asked to do more with less. But if the shape of your team changes today, don't expect yesterday's project plan to continue to work.

BI initiatives are best designed as incremental implementations, and if that's the case, they are also funded that way as well. There are often stoplight milestones along the way, where the executive sponsor or technology committee will evaluate progress and make one of three decisions:

✔ **Green-light (Go):** Progress justifies "full speed ahead."

✔ **Red-light (No-Go):** The project comes to a screeching halt.

✔ **Yellow-light (Slow Down):** The team is directed to proceed, but with reduced or changed objectives, or down an adjusted path.

To make this decision-making process smoother, the project plan should include evaluation-and-approval tasks as well as decision points for funding.

Project plans aren't just for technology tasks

Most project plans are focused squarely on the technology tasks and milestones that must be completed in order to meet the goals of the project. Hardware staging, setup, and configuration time — as well as troubleshooting, application installs, and testing — are all common tasks that appear in the plan.

But while the technology tasks may represent the critical path of the project, there are always as many administrative tasks that must be considered as well. They may not be a part of the implementation itself, but if they aren't completed, the project will fail.

Remember, the goal of the project plan is to identify every task that has to be completed, define how its completion affects other tasks, and then assign resources and deadlines to those tasks. That means weaving an administrative thread into the plan in addition to your core technology tasks and milestones.

The first thing you should consider is *budgeting* milestones and tasks. Money makes the world go around, as they say, and it is the fuel that drives your BI project. The BI project manager may need to make a case in front of the finance committee for the budgetary needs of the project.

Even if you personally don't have anything to do with the money-related tasks, they still have to be completed before the BI project can begin. You probably won't have direct control over the completion of the tasks. But because the entire project depends on their completion, be sure financial tasks appear in the project plan.

The administrative thread goes beyond the dollars and cents of the project. There are always personnel tasks to deal with — such as developing a staffing plan and allowing interview time for the developers and other resources for the project. If the project is to take longer than a few months, plan on periodic one-on-one performance reviews for your key team members — to say nothing of the time you'll spend working through unforeseen human resources issues. (Of course, unforeseen issues are by definition difficult to quantify for the sake of a project plan, but estimate some time for them anyway).

There's more: What about working with the facilities department to make sure there's a workspace for your team? It's a bit recursive but bears repeating: You'll need to include time on the project plan for basic planning functions, and those include updating the project plan itself.

It's easy to dismiss these activities, but if you stop to consider all the work that goes into a complex project, you'll find that there's much more to it than its core technical tasks. The more comprehensive your project plan is, the better prepared you'll be to tackle the unknown.

Creating a project plan happens in iterations. You can't know everything about everything during the first pass through the plan, so it's advisable to start with the high-level items first, and then work your way into the details. List the things you know first; you can dig into the shadows for the details a little bit deeper with each pass.

Chapter 13

Collecting User Requirements

. . . .

In This Chapter

▶ Figuring out whom to invite to your requirements session

▶ Making an agenda for your requirements session

▶ Knowing how to run a requirements session

▶ Working with requirements once you've collected them

. . . .

*W*hen all the software has been installed, when all the cable has been laid, the servers have been slid into their racks, and the switch is flipped for your BI solution, one group above all will determine the success of failure of your project: the users. And if they haven't been involved from the get-go, more often than not the project will end in failure.

The users are what it's all about. Whether your business intelligence tools are designed for corner-office folks who haven't flown on a commercial flight in years, or whether it's clerks in the accounting or shipping department, their satisfaction with how well the tools work is going to define the outcome.

For that reason, the user community has to be involved in the development process. Now, of course the accounting clerk or CFO who logs in to work with your BI tools may not be able to tell you one thing about whether to use a service-oriented architecture or how often to refresh the metadata. But what they *can* tell you is how things are *supposed* to work, what features would make their life easier, and how the BI tools fit into their daily processes.

Users tell designers what they need the software to do, and how it needs to look to support their activities. This role can't be thrown out for the sake of convenience. When developers or database administrators are left to divine how the applications are supposed to perform, they are more likely than not to get it wrong. That's why gathering business requirements *directly from users* deserves its own chapter in this book; it's often overlooked or done incorrectly, and the end result for the BI project can be catastrophic.

In this chapter, we take a look at the process of gathering requirements from top to bottom. It's primarily a people process where two or more professionals directly interact to solve a problem; you'll have to get the right people on your team, and you'll need to identify the right people to engage in the user community. Another important focus of this chapter is the documentation process. The requirements document is your blueprint moving forward, so you'd better get it right.

It's Business, Not Technical

The user community needs to be involved in the early phases of the specification of any business intelligence implementation and can best determine the overall needs of the system. Users have a great vantage point on what constitutes a solution to a particular business problem — and what doesn't. They know how to prioritize different functions and sub-functions in a business system.

Documenting business requirements

Different companies — even different teams in the same company — have different names for this process. But whether you call it a Business Requirements Document (BRD), a System Requirements Specification (SRS), Needs Analysis (NA), or any one of what seems like a million other stuffy names with two- or three-letter acronyms, you need a master document that tracks all the functional information about your system. And your BI team has to build it.

There are entire books written on how to best capture application requirements. Whether your master repository of requirements is a document, spreadsheet, report, or searchable database doesn't really matter, so long as you *have* one. Whether you use a requirements-management tool such as Rational RequisitePro or create your own format and process isn't terribly important either, so long as it works. What matters is that the requirements document must have all the information the developers need to build their technical solution.

Specifically, a *requirements document* should contain some or all of the following general features:

- ✔ **Project assumptions:** Elements either fully or partially outside your control that must be in place for the project to succeed.

- ✔ **Project features:** A quick overview of the main deliverables.

- ✔ **Requirements:** The meat of the document — a numbered, organized list of specifications to be built into the system.

- ✔ **Process flows:** How the main components of the project will interact, and how the users will work with the system.

- **Requirement priority:** The subjective level of importance assigned to a requirement or group of requirements.

- **Traceability and change information:** Links that show requirements' origins and interdependencies.

- **Prototypes and screen shots:** Mock-ups of key user interfaces.

- **Use cases:** Step-by-step narratives outlining how *actors* (users or external systems) interact with the system in question.

As long as the resulting document addresses these two main concerns, you're in good shape:

- Specifies the functional requirements of the application being designed

- Describes the business processes that the application will address

Most project artifacts (that is, documents, spreadsheets, templates, and anything else that describes some part of the project) are in a constant state of flux as information is added, removed or edited. You'll hear team members describe them as "living and breathing" documents in that they are constantly evolving throughout the life of the project. A requirements document can't afford to be so flexible. Instead, it needs a well-defined lifespan during which it can be in flux — but after which it's frozen into final form. At that point, any other changes must go through a predefined, tightly controlled change-management process.

Document size and structure

As a general rule, the structure of the requirements document should mirror the application itself. Every system function should have its own sections or sub-documents. The more extensive and complex the business function, the longer the section of the requirements document, and the more detail is required.

There's no way around it: The requirements document is likely to grow — and become more complex as it gets bigger. That's natural; the requirements document is to become the central repository for *all* functional specifications. After all, BI implementations usually address a variety of different business problems and touch multiple entities within the organization. The system will affect many pre-existing processes and will (of course) create new ones as well. Every feature will have to be accounted for in the document. Don't be too shocked if it goes through several revisions and eventually fills several hundred (or even thousand) pages.

This and subsequent steps in the design process spotlight the need for a requirements elicitation and capture process. Why? Because (more than likely) you'll need to have a look at *existing* documentation to get a handle on the current functions of the systems you expect to interface with your BI implementation. Often you'll need to know the exact capabilities and limitations of the existing software before you move forward with new features or extensions.

A little help from your friends (and enemies)

You'll need to hone your political skills; this phase of the implementation requires the services of many people in your company, most of them coming from outside the project team. Two groups in particular can offer key perspectives on how the application has to work, and on how business problems should be resolved:

- ✔ **Stakeholders:** This broad term refers to just about anyone in your company who will be affected by the BI implementation. Specifically, stakeholders include managers and decision-makers from teams that rely on the particular business process your BI implementation addresses. They can also be interested executives looking out for an entire business unit, or the whole company. A stakeholder naturally views decisions about the implementation through the lens of his or her particular team and area of responsibility, and they usually have the power to influence others either for or (hopefully not) against your project. Getting key stakeholders involved and on-board is one of the toughest challenges you'll face.

- ✔ **Users:** This group comprises the individual workers who will actually be using the applications that sit on the front end of the BI implementation. The user community must be heavily represented in the requirements gathering process to offer their perspectives on the underlying business process being improved, how the applications can best suit their needs, and how they'd like to see the front-end applications assembled.

Notice who's missing from this list of essential personnel: technology folks. The focus during this phase is on the people who actually have to use and rely on the BI system. Database administrators, data designers, and developers will have to take a back seat (at least for a day or two).

Requirements-Gathering Techniques

The task before you is simple: Get the best ideas that currently reside in the minds of dozens (maybe hundreds) of employees out into the open, then manipulate and prioritize those ideas to reach a consensus design that maintains the integrity of the project plan, and meets the budget and timeline.

Got all that? Good. Now, before you charge right into it, you should under-stand that there are some tried-and-true methods that can help you get the most out of the requirements phase of the project. The usual methods include the following:

- ✔ **Group meetings:** Get a bunch of stakeholders in a room and hash out the requirements.

- ✔ **Individual interviews:** Talk one-on-one with representatives from the user community.

- ✔ **Questionnaires:** Ask stakeholders what their needs are via e-mail.

- ✔ **Prototypes and pilot storyboarding:** Show folks the possible scenarios of how the application might look — and ask for feedback.

Just keep in mind that (as with every other hard-and-fast rule in the world of BI) there are no hard-and-fast rules. You can't expect an approach that worked for the company down the street (or even another department in your company) to work for you. Nor can you expect to copy the techniques that worked for previous teams when they gathered requirements for a big technology implementation; those approaches might not work for the current project. That's just the way it works; you'll have to find the best methods to work into your circumstances.

The data difference

Requirements-gathering activities for a BI implementation is different from that of other technology implementations in one key respect: the data. With business intelligence projects, you're not conducting any transactions that create new data; you're simply using data that already exists in the system. That means you have to work with the user groups to determine what data they need to do their jobs well, what data they'd *like to have* to do their jobs better, and how best BI tools can deliver that data to them.

On the flip side of that, you'll be working with data providers — teams who control historical data in various databases throughout the organization — to determine what information your BI tools can access and make available for the users. Your team will need to carefully research and specify both data supply and data demand in the project requirements; how you match the two will determine the success or failure of your project.

User focus

The people who actually operate the application (and consume the informa-tion it produces) are at the core of any requirements-gathering process. More than likely they have experience with the existing business problems you're trying to solve, so their contributions should be taken seriously.

For example, if your company is building an advanced customer-relationship management (CRM) and sales-data system, your user community will consist of several groups — say, account managers, inside sales staff, and support personnel. But you should also include other stakeholders (such as the whole Sales Management hierarchy) who make strategic decisions around the business insights produced by the BI implementation. Users may be able to tell you how they'd like to use the BI system, but their managers set policy and are the ultimate arbiters of the project's functional needs.

Any project that fails to include the end-users in the process is almost certain to fail. It's tempting to try a shortcut and let BI techies act as proxies to the user community — and infer requirements from their general knowledge of business processes and report layouts — but don't do it! Reach out to the people who really know what the business problems are, even if the requirements seem obvious. That detail you miss could mean the difference between success and failure for your project.

Requirements-gathering activities

No way around it: Gathering requirements means holding meetings — but not just any old meeting. This section offers a closer look at your main options for gathering BI requirements: group sessions, JADs, one-on-one meetings, small-group meetings and virtual design sessions.

Group sessions

By far the most common requirements-gathering technique is the *group session*. Sometimes it's called a *design session*; if you want to get really fancy, your Business Analyst might talk you into calling it a Joint Application Development (JAD) session. The *Joint* in that name means you get all the stakeholders into one room (instead of interviewing individuals separately) and develop a consensus about the final application function and form.

So who should attend a group session? Anyone with a vested interest in the outcome of the application. That doesn't mean you have to (or should) invite hundreds of people to a single meeting, but it does mean your attendees should represent the diversity of the user community. For example, if you're building a big BI financial suite, you'll want to get representation from anyone who'll be running reports off the system, as well as folks who are actually making decisions based on those reports (where possible).

Sometimes it's hard to tell the difference between someone with a business interest in the application and someone with a technology perspective. When in doubt, invite them all. And if the meeting grows too big, divide the group and schedule a second meeting, a third, a fourth . . . whatever it takes to get everyone involved while limiting the meeting to a reasonable size. Usually you want no more than 10 to 15 people in a single meeting, with a duration for each "chunk" lasting anywhere from 90 minutes to about three quarters of a workday. You certainly can — and should — schedule multiple "chunks" over multiple days for the same group if you have a lot to cover. If you need to bring folks in from out of town to hold a single marathon session, just make sure you schedule plenty of breaks to keep participants sharp.

The *Complete MBA For Dummies* by Kathleen Allen and Peter Economy lays out the following universal rules for a meeting:

> Be prepared
>
> Use an agenda
>
> Fewer meetings, better results
>
> Include more people
>
> Maintain focus
>
> Assign action items
>
> Get feedback

JAD sessions

No, a JAD isn't a military acronym or an ancient throwing weapon. The Joint Application Development meeting evolved from best practices for eliciting and documenting software requirements.

The hallmark of a JAD session is that *everyone in the room plays specific roles.* And the roles themselves have fun, gimmicky names. For example, instead of everyone taking notes, there is a designated Scribe. People aren't just attendees; they are *specialists* and *experts.* At the core of the JAD session is one or more *facilitators* to act as the emcee of the event, as well as the *arbiter* and *interviewer.* Typically the facilitator is a senior-level business analyst with a knack for asking probing questions (and not putting meeting attendees to sleep).

JAD sessions usually follow a very strict agenda, developed from extensive pre-session work done by the project team and business analyst. The business analyst assembles and presents any prior decisions and existing knowledge about the project — as well as what the constraints and assumptions are. With those facts in mind, the BA forms an agenda that roughly mirrors the main application features relevant to the attendees for that session.

At the beginning of the JAD session, the goals are laid out for the attendees. In most meetings, that means the facilitator explains what's known about the project up to this point, introduces the room, and defines the scope of the day's work for this meeting. Depending on how the sessions are divided up, that might mean tackling only one or two business problems — or it might mean taking on the entire application in one session. Either way, the entire room should be aware that nobody gets out alive until the agenda is complete and the deliverables for the day have been created.

During the actual meat of the meeting, the facilitator encourages participation from everyone in the room — and urges wallflowers out of their silence. There's a good reason for that; you don't want the most vocal people to decide every feature. The quiet types should be heard from too; their ideas are likely just as good. Once ideas start getting tossed around, it's not the facilitator's job to decide which is the best, but rather, to guide the meeting participants to a *consensus* on the best approach.

By the end of the JAD session, there should be pages full of notes on the meeting, and all the decisions taken therein. An array of to-dos and next-steps should be distributed to the participants of the meeting in case there were any issues that couldn't be resolved due to lack of information.

In the end, the combined notes from the JADs are the foundation on which you build the formal requirements document — and from there, the technical design and build can begin.

Individual meetings

Sometimes it makes sense to meet one-on-one with certain stakeholders involved in your project for logistical reasons (say, scheduling conflicts) or even because of office politics. For example, if the C-level executives (the Chiefs of This and That) want to be involved in the requirements-gathering process for your new Sales Information System, they may have very specific ideas about how they want to contribute. And since their titles start with *Chief*, you don't have much choice but to accommodate them.

With only one other person in the room, consensus should be easy to find (for the moment, at least). But what happens if you go to your next one-on-one session and find the second stakeholder disagrees with the first? People who don't have to face each other in a meeting are far less likely to be agreeable, and far more willing to place blame and point fingers. Keep in mind that individual meetings have limits in terms of producing good requirements information.

In a one-on-one meeting, make sure you add some rigor to the reasoning process. You'll need to play the role of devil's advocate during an individual session, essentially representing the possible range of opinions you'd get in a full group-design meeting. The people you plan on meeting with one-on-one should be warned in advance that you're not going to just accept opinions without question; you'll offer counterpoints and opposing views and ask them to defend themselves. That process ultimately helps build a more robust, well-thought-out system.

Small-group meetings

Sometimes it's not necessary to have a full-blown JAD session with 10 to 20 people in it — sometimes it doesn't even make sense to. When the subject matter is complex it might make sense to have fewer people in the room. That might seem counterintuitive, but it's not uncommon for people to tune out in larger meetings, or to lose touch with the course of a complicated discussion and get left behind. That's especially true when you're working through minutiae of a complicated application and only a few attendees have sufficient expertise to hammer out specifications. If there's not a lot of downstream implications in the problem you're solving, spare the rest of the crowd the boring detour; invite the two or three experts to join you in an offline discussion, and move on to the next agenda item to keep the meeting flowing along.

Contentious subject matter also lends itself to smaller settings. Sometimes having too many people in a design session can expose hidden political rifts that can cause a meeting to spiral out of control in a hurry. Smaller meetings — with fewer attendees — are a good way to avoid any extra drama.

Virtual design sessions

While face-to-face is the ideal format, sometimes it's simply not possible. Technology exists today to get folks in the same *virtual* room, either by teleconference or by audio conference call. If you're pressed for time or in a budget crunch, these solutions can make a lot of sense. But be aware: Virtual meetings can fall prey to the same logistics hassles as real meetings.

If there's no other way, of course, the business-analysis team can distribute e-mails to stakeholders and users to get their feedback — but this should be a fallback position only. Outside the group setting, there's no interplay for an e-mail respondent to work with — and without a live interview it's impossible to have a dynamic, reactive conversation. Even if the e-mail, questionnaire, or other content is very well done, it's always hard-put to hold its readers' attention.

What, Exactly, Is a Requirement?

Retaining skillful business analysts and data modelers who are experts at eliciting requirements saves you from extreme heartburn later on in the process. Most basic application issues have poorly written or marginally understood requirements at their source.

At this stage in the process, you're going to capture the essential functional and data needs of your end-users. That starts with some basic questions to the users about what business functions they're trying to perform, and what questions they need to be able to answer in order to do their jobs.

Along the way you'll encounter adjunct requirements that aren't at the heart of the business functions but are, nevertheless, important to explore and record. For example, you'll need to understand the security and compliance constraints that govern the processes and data handling. It's important to understand what historical data must be kept, and who the ultimate decision-makers are that can change such policies.

Reporting and analytical functionality

Most business intelligence systems revolve around reporting in some form or another, so it's a good place to start gathering requirements.

Start with a list of standard, regular reports that the user community's known to need. For example, in a sales system, an array of broad-based, general-information reports gets distributed among the management team — such as weekly and monthly performance reports, client roles, pipeline reports, and so on.

For a sales department, those standard reports are the low-hanging fruit — after all, every sales department from every business in the world looks at the same basic information. The challenge is to move beyond the easy stuff and to get the business users and stakeholders to start talking about requirements for reports they'd *like* to see, the high-value data that's been unavailable prior to the BI implementation. As you gather requirements, part of that process is opening users' eyes to the enormous possibilities a business intelligence solution can provide.

For example, suppose a networking-gear manufacturer has several hundred enterprise customers who, combined, make hundreds of purchases every day of the year, all around the world. The sales force is fragmented; each of its units operates with a lot of autonomy, and the cost structure is Byzantine. Up until now, the only perspective on profitability has been in the aggregate, along product lines and sales regions. The new BI implementation will make it possible to see up-to-the-second profitability reports for each customer. So, as you gather requirements, ask users what they *want* to be able to do, not just what they're currently able to do.

At this stage, you're not actually designing the full reports yet. The goal is not to get an exact view of what heading appears over every column; it's to get a general idea of the major classes of information that will be needed. You're working with buckets at this point, understanding general data requirements and categories of analytical features. The precision work of designing reports comes later during the design process.

Gathering requirements for the reporting process should always be informed with the high standards of business intelligence. So if you've forgotten the magic words, it's time for a refresher: The reports should reflect information that's timely, accurate, high-value, and actionable.

Data needed to support your desired functionality

At the heart of the business intelligence process is the information stored by your system (or systems) that will ultimately feed the applications and lead to insights. When it comes to data, you have a few basic questions to ask:

- ✔ What data do we need to work with?
- ✔ Where is it currently stored?
- ✔ How important is it to the users (that is, how often is it used)?

The answers to those questions, taken in aggregate over the entire system, will point to several fundamental choices you'll need to make in the technical design process, covered in subsequent chapters.

Unlike transactional applications, business intelligence systems never actually *create* data. Your system will read information from existing systems, manipulate it, and perhaps even derive some temporary data to work with, but it's a one-way street; your BI system won't create data that will be permanently stored. That means all the data you're going to work with already exists somewhere in your company. One of the big challenges of BI is deciding whether to pull the data into a data warehouse, or access it where it sits.

Know-it-alls

Gathering data requirements can be one of the more overwhelming tasks in a BI implementation, especially when you're talking about an enterprise-wide solution that may cover several different functional areas.

Fortunately, there are some requirements-gathering strategies that can be utilized to make the process a little bit simpler. After all, if you just ask users what data they need, they'll inevitably answer, "Everything."

Investigative reports

In addition to looking at the business processes, another good way to analyze the data needs of a department or team is to look at their existing reporting processes and the reports themselves. You'll want to see how data is used, how often it appears, and — most important — how information gets grouped together.

Reports are the most common end-point for data, but the reality is you want to look at any existing systems that play a role in one of the key business functions that will be touched by the BI implementation.

Break it down — divide and conquer

In a complex system, analysts should break down larger functions into their component elements before querying users about business requirements. For example, if the BI implementation is going to include a human resources (HR) module, a good place to start would be to separate the main HR disciplines — such as recruiting and retention, payroll, benefits, performance measurement, and so on. Each of those functions contains elemental business processes and reports that make the company go.

Breaking down the requirements into more manageable functional groups will reveal some data elements common to all the company's processes; keep an eye out for data that's repeated. Of course, repetition isn't always obvious; sometimes data appears in different forms. In the HR example just given (for example), the payroll system might handle employee salaries as a bi-weekly figure while the other systems store essentially the same data in its annual form.

Matchup maker

You'll need to go into your requirements session(s) fully understanding where all the data lives — and where it's going to live when the implementation is complete. For example, will a data warehouse change the kind of data that's accessible? Will it improve performance to such an extent that it makes advanced functionality possible that wasn't before?

The *matchup* process is where you outline relationships between the functional needs of the user community and the data that currently exists in the system. This happens in two general stages:

1. **Get the data requirements from individual users.** You're not just asking whether you'll need the data, you're also asking users how important it is, how often they'll need to access it, what the security requirements are, and so forth.

2. **Link everybody's data needs together.** This is where you draw the big picture of the combined data needs of the entire company. It will give you a broader perspective on the data requirements for the entire system.

The "look and feel" for how information should be delivered to users

The requirements sessions are a good opportunity for you to go beyond plain-grid reports and start taking requests for the best presentation format to apply to the data being accessed by the users. Typically the available formats include these types:

✔ **Reports:** This means, primarily, tabular and grid reports. Through the requirements process you'll learn how dynamic these reports need to be, whether they need to be accessible via the web, what the security demands are, and so on.

✔ **Visualizations:** Do your users need to go beyond the numbers and see data represented in charts, graphs, or more complex graphics? Use the requirements-gathering time to find out what visualization techniques work best for users, which graphical elements are required, and the priorities attached to each.

✔ **Dashboards:** Depending on your audience, a dashboard solution might make sense. The key question is what kinds of decisions and actions are being made from the dashboard tool? In addition, you need to know who the primary users are. Is it being built for executives to monitor corporate key performance indicators (KPIs)? Is it being used by managers to make daily decisions? That will determine what kind of data needs to be displayed, how it should be displayed, how often it should be refreshed, and what backup information should be made available to the user.

✔ **Custom formats:** Users might well need a hybrid solution or a customized front end that presents data in a unique — and unforeseen — way.

Finally the BA will want to gather look-and-feel requirements from the stakeholders and users. There are a lot of different options depending on the tool the team is going to be using. This might seem a bit much, but don't be fooled; stylistic concerns can mean the difference between a satisfied user group and a dissatisfied one. Doing it right and at least giving the appearance of concern for the users' desires can go a long way in terms of goodwill.

Users know best when it comes to how they need their data presented. If they're clamoring for a dashboard approach, don't stick them with some boring tabular report. Asking questions can bring to light some surprises, so make every attempt to keep an open mind as you start eliciting requirements.

Validating BI Requirements You've Collected

It's not uncommon to wrap up a series of JADs (or other requirements sessions) and realize that one or more features are working at cross purposes. The purpose of the next step — *validating* your requirements — is to ensure that the requirements all make sense when viewed together, and in the context of the underlying business processes. This stage is about laying out all requirements, finding commonalities, building a list of unknowns and questions (and ultimately seeking answers for them), and mapping out the data needs of the project to make sure they're feasible.

Conducting the initial double-checking

When requirements don't agree with each other, or don't appear to correspond correctly to the reality of existing business processes, it's an issue that will have to be flagged and noted. After the initial double-checking is complete, it's the business analyst's job to return to the original stakeholders and research the issue. Sometimes it's simply that a requirement needs further explanation, or perhaps the notes are incorrect. If there's a legitimate dispute though, the BA will have to explain the circumstances of the conflicting notes, and (if necessary) make a recommendation about how to move forward based on the project constraints.

In a large BI implementation you might (for example) run across two groups that claim to use two different canned reports for an identical process. The requirements were recorded correctly, but when this business function is represented in the design, only one version will represent the truth about the process. Who's right? And if they're both right, should one report win out while the other one goes away?

The validation step can easily take as long as gathering the initial requirements. Don't skimp, and don't take shortcuts. You must document all disputes and questions very thoroughly, along with any resolution that was decided on. No requirements are correct or final until they've been validated.

Prioritizing Your BI Requirements

In the process of collecting business requirements, the focus will always be on the details of the project itself — but don't let that distract you from an equally important concern: requirement *priorities*.

There's always a chance you won't be able to fit everything into a single release. Too many features, too few resources, or too little time means something has to give — and that usually means you'll have to go with a phased approach, releasing one set of features first, then following it up with a second release of additional functions and tools. The inevitable question is: *what gets pushed to later releases?* Easy: the less important requirements!

Judging how important requirements are relative to each other is the task of prioritization, and it's a part of the overall requirements management process to be performed by analysts with input from stakeholders. Even if you're not planning on a phased approach, you should still take the time to assign priorities that make sense to major requirements and functions. You never know when you'll be asked to cut the scope of the project; it happens more often than anyone would like.

Identifying "must-have-or-else" requirements

If you don't prioritize the requirements now, it's inevitable that you'll have to circle back later and gauge their relative importance after the fact. That's bad because decisions made in requirements sessions are probably the most valid way of coming to a consensus; everyone's in the room, you're working through the flow of the system, all the information is on the table. Suffice to say, the participants are well-informed about the topic at hand. Going back to them later means you've lost that moment and the decisions may not be as good.

The most common technique for prioritizing requirements is to divide them into categories ranked by how necessary they are to the project. Sometimes it's as simple as a binary question, where each feature or function is judged to be a *nice-to-have* or a *must-have*. More commonly there are three classifications:

- ✔ **Must:** These features are deal-killers — if they're not in there, the solution doesn't work. The application should not be rolled out unless these features are present and working.

- ✔ **Should:** Requirements listed as *Shoulds* should have a solid business case for including them in the system. However, if circumstances change and you have to leave out one or two, it shouldn't hold up the scheduled release of the application suite.

- ✔ **Could:** These requirements are nice-to-haves. If the development team can fit them in, all the better. But under no circumstances should the project be delayed just to include a Could feature.

Some Must features have nothing to do with what the users want or what the stakeholders may think makes sense. Every application has external constraints — such as regulatory requirements or companywide standards — that shackle them with a few extra features that normally wouldn't be considered essential. Make sure you do your due diligence and get input from the appropriate governance boards and central planning bodies within your organization *before* you assume the application is yours to do with as you please.

Getting the final buy-in

After the requirements are vetted, it always pays to run the completed requirements documentation by the group of high-level stakeholders. The goal of this step is to take one final look at the business needs to make sure that what came out of the requirements elicitation sessions were what you said you needed going in. Were all the areas covered? Do the requirements actually represent a solution to the original problem? Have the needs been prioritized?

Don't get caught in an analysis-paralysis loop where you can't stop refining the requirements. Sooner or later, you have to stop analyzing and take the next step: The design process, where you take the requirements and actually begin making technical decisions on how to implement them. Sometimes it's best just to move forward and let the questions be answered down the road rather than halting the process in its tracks.

Stepping on the baseline

The final critical step in the requirements-gathering cycle is to get final sign-off on the requirements document from the client organizations, stakeholders, or project sponsors. It may be a symbolic "signature" but it has a very real meaning: from this point forward the project requirements cease being a moving target. Even if a stakeholder dreams up a new feature for the BI environment, the requirements document cannot be altered.

The goal is to create a requirements baseline, just as you would a project plan, so the entire team has a single point of reference for what the project is supposed to entail and how it's supposed to be built. Once baselined, the requirements documentation can be distributed to the development teams and they can begin work in earnest on the design and construction, comfortable in the knowledge that the requirements are now stable.

Using requirements scorecards

It's not always easy to decide what goes into a project and what gets left out, at least during the first phase. Sometimes things are a little bit more complicated than Must, Should, and Could.

If the choice is still not clear after validating and doing an initial prioritization of requirements, a scorecard could help alleviate a lot of the stress of choosing features. Scorecards at least offer the appearance of impartiality by comparing choices with a set of pre-selected criteria. Scorecards also invite engagement from the stakeholders, force the debate forward, and ultimately help flush out a function's true priority that much faster.

Considering features in a BI implementation with a scorecard is simple. You build a spreadsheet that lists all the potential choices down the page. In corresponding columns, you score each function according to a list of pre-determined priorities. In some cases, you might be judging two features to determine which one is really necessary for the project — and even if they both scored highly, it wouldn't be necessary to implement them both. For scoring criteria, use factors that are important to your particular project. For example, you might list "ease of integration" or "level of technology risk" or even "cost" as scoring factors.

Evaluating features with a scorecard in the context of a group meeting can actually be an enlightening and engaging experience for the team. People can act as advocates for one or more features and stand up and state their case. It gets the project team thinking about things with a broader perspective, and it can turn your meetings into something like a game show, which is always more fun than a lecture.

The downside of scorecards is that they are only as impartial as you make them. If you're the one deciding on the criteria, you could slant them so that your own priorities are served, or you could leave certain criteria out altogether. But in the end, the goal of the scorecard is to not to create a final decision per se; it's simply to spur healthy debate and provide a basis for comparison.

Changing Requirements

In an ideal world, system requirements would be fully defined during the early stages of the implementation and would never change. But the reality is that change is inevitable with requirements. First of all, BI projects can go on for months or even years, so it's possible (often likely) that a company's business needs will change during that time. But most likely the cause of changes in the requirements is a part of the design process: As the design matures, certain needs are flushed out that weren't obvious during the requirements sessions.

A certain amount of change is to be expected. In fact, some project managers say that changing requirements are actually a good sign because they show that your stakeholders are actively engaged.

But don't let your guard down. Shifting sands under a project have caused many well-conceived and perfectly planned projects to fail. It's absolutely essential that you have a plan to deal with changes in requirements. Specifically, you'll need a process to manage change requests so they can be tracked and prioritized. Additionally, you'll have to do an impact assessment to see how the suggested (or demanded) change affects the rest of the project requirements and, ultimately, the overall implementation schedule. Changing requirements during development is expensive, and a good change management process quantifies just how high that bill will run. After that, the stakeholder can judge whether their change is worth throwing the project plan off track, or if it's a requirement that can wait for the next release.

Chapter 14

BI Design and Development

. . . .

In This Chapter

▶ Thinking about your users first

▶ Designing a sound data environment

▶ Assembling quality front-end systems

▶ Testing the BI application

▶ Getting feedback from the users

. . . .

*E*ven the best-laid plans can (and often will) go awry, so the development process is an interactive phase where your most talented team members reveal themselves — where the true problem-solvers and can-do types bubble to the surface. The development process requires almost constant interaction between the technology team and the business-facing team.

Between design and deployment comes an intense testing phase that challenges all the ideas of the previous months. That leads into the deployment circus, where your new systems go into production, the old ones are phased out, users are trained, and the rubber hits the road.

Successful BI

There's no guarantee that flipping the switch will bring success and accolades for your business intelligence solution. In fact, rave reviews shouldn't necessarily even be a goal when you're starting out. The best BI deployments are compact, well-conceived, and work as expected. That gives your team an early success and a platform to build upon.

At the risk of sounding ridiculously tautological, a successful BI solution is one that . . . well . . . succeeds. If the system meets its business objectives — whatever those may be in your company's situation — that's all that matters. And there are certain things you can do to increase your chances of success. In fact, most successful BI projects usually share similar characteristics.

Be realistic

That means shoot for reachable goals, such as a finite domain of reports, or a single analysis tool. Realism means grounded in reality, but it also implies well-defined. The business headaches you're addressing may not be sexy, but you know exactly what they are and what their negative impact is on the organization.

Think in terms of six-month timelines. The first six months may include the task of assembling a data-collection point — say, a data warehouse with some simple reporting tools on top of it. But after the six-month iterations that follow, your solutions should all be bite-sized chunks. Don't get greedy for results until you've got some skins on the wall.

Follow demand

There's nothing worse than an IT team forcing a solution on a team that's satisfied with the applications they're already using. Wherever possible, your BI solution should aim to solve a problem that's dying to be solved — one that's been neglected for years, really important to the company, or both.

Sometimes the sorest tooth has the hardest cavity to fill. Rule #1 — *set realistic goals* — has priority. Don't get yourself in over your head; you'll find that the hot potato isn't so easy to pass along once it's in your hands.

On the other hand, you'll often get a lot of help if you're trying to crack a tough nut. And you'll need that cooperation from the business groups you're working with.

Act now, but think ahead

Your implementation strategy is built to solve an existing problem, but the steps should be additive; each piece of the solution contributing to the success of the next.

A perfect example is building related data marts that cover related subject matter while keeping an eye on creating a grand solution down the road; that's a holistic, data-centric view of the truth about your sales organization. In the interim, you're solving an important problem such as determining the success of marketing campaigns, or defining characteristics about your customers. Those short-term, small-scale successes fuel the team to do bigger and better things. And the tools they build — along with the experience they gain — from those data-mart implementations will make later success that much more likely.

Design with Users in Mind

Business intelligence is about getting the right information into the hands of the right people. No doubt you've spent a lot of time worrying about what the right information is. But what about the people?

A successful BI design is akin to any good product-marketing effort. You define and segment your customers according to what they know about your product, what motivates them to buy (or use) it, and what onboard conditions are present that will affect how they use it, such as any preconceived notions about the information they're receiving, experience with similar products, and broad-based skills they can apply to using it.

Not every knowledge worker can take advantage of the advanced features you roll out. Some can slice and dice the data; others shouldn't be allowed near sharp objects.

The best design treats the users of business intelligence tools as customers. And because customers of the same product might have very different needs, designers should prepare for varying usage patterns among user groups such as these. . . .

Power users

These are the analysts who will utilize your tools to their fullest capabilities, taking advantage of advanced features that even the manufacturers forgot about long ago. The following is often true of power users:

- ✔ They study the data architecture and know where to find key nuggets of data. That might be because they've worked with it before, or simply because they're motivated to take full advantage of the integrated information and blaze their own path through the database until they get what they need.

- ✔ They go beyond simply reading reports; they develop and administer their own, using report-design tools fed by advanced queries. They use reports for analysis — to make decisions — not just as a way to transport data from one set of eyes to another.

- ✔ They can be more demanding, in some ways, because they have high expectations about the BI solution's robustness, thoroughness, and usability. On the other hand, making this group happy is what often leads to the greatest positive impact on the business; they're the ones who find innovative approaches to finding BI insights and applying them to business problems.

Take advantage of power users' expertise by getting their input on advanced features during design. In all likelihood, they have a mental wish list of high-end BI functionality they'd like to be able to use when the system is complete. Ask them what kind of tools they'd like to see for exploring the data and building their own reporting-and-analysis tools. And get a clear understanding of each feature's importance; that will help you prioritize the development effort according to what the experts really want.

Business users

This crowd toils at the opposite end of the user spectrum from the power users. Business users are a broad class of information consumers — up to two thirds of the user base in most companies — who are using the BI tools as a means to an end. They're unlikely to create custom queries or reports, or use the advanced features of front-end tools.

In case you get the wrong idea, the business users' lack of expertise is not indicative of their importance to the success of the BI initiative, or in their ability to create business value from BI insights. Most of the time, they're viewing reports and using the data they find there to make decisions, but they're less likely to be digging through the minutiae of the metadata model.

- They work in the business units and teams that you're designing the BI solution for in the first place; they're accountants, salesmen, or perhaps marketing analysts who need data to make regular decisions.

- They rely on canned output. Business users expect the scheduled reports to take care of their needs

- They're not tasked with building new ways to look at the data, or finding new insights in the data model; they're simply going to retrieve what they already know to be there. If they find they need different information than what the pre-fabricated reports provide, they'll have to rely on somebody else to retrieve it for them.

During design, use the input from your business users to help you create your standard reports. It's what they know best, and what the broad spectrum of users will be handling from day to day. Don't focus on technical details; ask about accessibility, appearance, and seek advice on how to make the basic features more user-friendly.

The middle class

In addition to power users and business users, there's a middle class of knowledge workers who (under normal circumstances) behave like business users, consuming standard reports and utilizing only the standard features of the front-end tools. If they take advantage of parameterized reports, for example, they rarely go beyond adding some basic inputs to customize the final results.

Occasionally, however, middle-class types may surprise you — designing queries and reports or doing analyses beyond their comfort zone. This is where good, flexible design can make an enormous impact.

The middle class are the hardest to design for, because normally they don't venture beyond the skills of business users. But this crowd has latent BI user skills that can be brought to the surface by applying good application requirements-gathering and design principles. When advanced features are more accessible and user-friendly, they fall within the comfort zone of a wider audience of users — to the company's advantage.

During design time, run some "What would it take for you to use this . . . ?" types of questions by your user representatives to get information on how to make expert features easier for non-experts to master. If clever design and packaging can transform a basic report consumer into a user comfortable with complex guided-analysis pathways and drill-down exploration of data, you've created a more powerful user.

Best Practices for BI Design

There's no need to reinvent the wheel in the design phase of your BI project. Although BI is a relatively new discipline, the principles of good, sound IT design remain the same. The most important steps will be blueprinting and building a target data environment with the appropriate structure, horse-power, and quality control.

One dirty little secret of designing a BI environment is that you can't always follow an established methodology. The book you bought may tell you to start with business needs, then do a technology assessment, followed by data modeling — but that book doesn't work at your company. Often the only option is to start with what you know and work outward from there on your plan.

That's easier said than done. With so many undefined variables, a BI project has precious little solid ground in its early stages. It's natural to gravitate to those few pieces that *are* nailed down and build from there, even though you had planned on starting somewhere else.. For example, if your company is committed to a certain software vendor, causing the procurement team to balk at buying the competing BI software you want, that's your starting point (such as it is). Hey, at least you know *something* about what your environment will look like. Sure, the tool that you're stuck with will have certain features and limitations you weren't counting on, but you have to press forward. Your path through the maze is governed by where the walls are.

Designing the data environment

The business intelligence front-end system has to feed on the collected, aggregated operational data you prepare and assemble for it. For most BI environments, this collection of data to be used by the front-end tools is a data warehouse or a data mart (which we discuss further in Chapter 16).

Business intelligence is the delivery of insights that are timely, accurate, high-value, and actionable. As long as those business revelations have those characteristics, you've got yourself a BI environment, whether it's operating against a data warehouse, a data mart, or something else entirely.

The target database

For purposes of this discussion, we'll simply call the data environment the *target database*, and its conception and design will be largely a function of several factors:

- ✔ **Data sources:** What information do they contain and what condition is that data in? How accessible is it to the BI system?

- ✔ **Query requirements:** What kind of questions are your users expecting to be able to start with to begin their analysis? Are there specific reporting patterns that need to be considered?

- ✔ **Performance requirements:** How fast will your users expect their answers?

The answers to those questions will determine how the data analysts on your team will decide the data environment that best suits the needs of the BI tools.

Database tradeoffs

Getting to a BI-friendly data environment means balancing the needs of two distinct but related functions: the ETL design (which determines how and when the source data moves) and how the users of the target database actually interact with that data.

ETL design

The *ETL (Extract, Transform, and Load)* processes are the steps that the system takes to move information from the source data systems to the target database. That may seem like grunt-work; it may not be glamorous, but the design of your ETL process is one of the most important factors (if not *the* most important) in the making your BI environment function successfully.

Database design has a longer history (and a large literature built up around it), but as BI becomes more important, ETL has grown in stature. Its challenges have attracted some of the most talented minds in the industry over the last 10 years.

Extracting and loading are simply moving data, but transforming it is where the complexity lies — and where the magic happens.

Transforming in this sense means effecting any change on the individual data elements required to create a single, useful, correct body of data to be used by the BI front-end applications. For example: your ETL software may be required to convert several tables from avoirdupois measurement units (you know: feet, pounds, or gallons) to metric measurements (meters, grams, or liters). The ETL software will be responsible for reading the original avoirdupois data element from the source database, performing the calculation to change the number into a metric unit, and finally writing the metric conversion number to the correct location of the target database.

Source databases are the Wild West of your company; there's no telling how each local Sherriff is storing and treating the operational data you'll need for your BI system. A lot can *be* wrong with the data, and a lot can *go* wrong with the transformation process. The 'Transformation' part of ETL is what makes that data usable. If data fields need to be validated against complex business logic, then changed or erased, it's the ETL software that makes that happen. And if multiple data sources feed the same target database, the ETL product must recognize overlapping data and pick the correct value in case they're different.

Your business insights are a function of how reliable and useful the information in your BI target database is. And your target database is a function of how well the ETL package has performed on the data sources. If data gets loaded in an unrecognized format, or if the values themselves are inaccurate, then that data is worthless to the user.

Figure 14-1 shows a simplified rendition of what an ETL process might do. Phone lists in the systems data sources have been maintained with no universal formatting or information standards. In order for the lists to be combined and used together, useless data must be stripped out, duplicate entries have to be removed, and the information put into a common format.

It's easy to think of ETL as a magic wand of transformation that cures data of all its ills as it passes through a wonderful cleansing doorway. The reality is it's a multilayered, complicated process that involves several steps:

1. Harvesting the data from the source systems. The tools must be able to operate on a specific schedule, and be prepared to interact with many different types of source databases and communications protocols. Extraction also sometimes involves gigantic swathes of data moving around the company network, so the ETL tool should be able to deal with high volumes efficiently.

2. Moving the data to a staging area where it can be cleansed and rearranged according to the business rules of the ETL process.

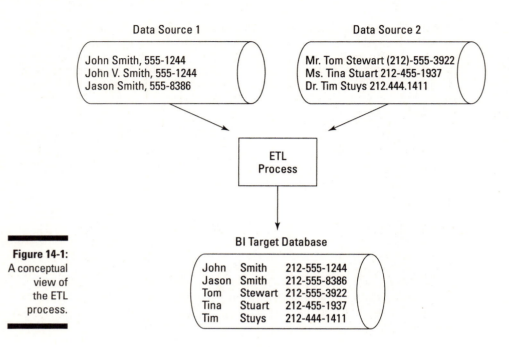

John Smith, 555-1244
John V. Smith, 555-1244
Jason Smith, 555-8386

Data Source 2

Mr. Tom Stewart (212)-555-3922
Ms. Tina Stuart 212-455-1937
Dr. Tim Stuys 212.444.1411

ETL
Process

BI Target Database

John	Smith	212-555-1244
Jason	Smith	212-555-8386
Tom	Stewart	212-555-3922
Tina	Stuart	212-455-1937
Tim	Stuys	212-444-1411

Figure 14-1:
A conceptual
view of
the ETL
process.

3. Reordering and rebuilding the data, slowly and carefully, so its new
   shape fits the model of the target BI database.

The state of the data sources will ultimately determine the design of the ETL
(Extract, Transform, and Load) process that harvests the data on a set schedule, cleanses it, transforms it into a single format the front-end systems can
use, and loads it into the final data environment. There are scores of ETL
tools on the market today to help your data developers create an process
that feeds your target database what it needs.

Put your team's top talent on the task of designing sound ETL processes —
for now and for the future. It's too important to leave to people who don't
know or aren't sure how to approach the problem, how to deal with common
pitfalls, and how to test their work.

Target tradeoffs

When the data gets to its target environment, your BI system faces another
balancing act: What the user base does with your data will ultimately determine the kind of data environment that gets built.

Best practices dictate that your users' needs must influence the design of the
data environment at least as heavily as ETL technicalities do. Here are two
typical scenarios:

✔ If your users are looking for the flexibility to create queries on any piece of the data in any way, shape, or form, then your target database will have to be a relatively normalized environment. That means less redundancy and only limited summary data. Queries in such an environment take a long time to run, but your users will get what they want.

✔ If users follow some standard patterns of viewing data — for example, looking at reports along thematic lines like sales or product information — then the target database is likely to be a multidimensional design. This type of database is perfect for slice-and-dice activities that highlight various aspects of the data, but you also get more redundancy and a less efficient use of space.

Designing the front-end environment

There's no rest for the weary after your basic design work on the back-end environment is complete. The ETL process ensures the source data flows into the target data environment, but once it's there you'll need to design ways for your users to access the stored data. In most BI environments the front-end systems include the reporting, querying, and all levels of general and custom analysis packages.

Reports

For any business intelligence solution, the core of the front end is the reporting environment.

Standard report design

Your developers will design and develop a family of standard, pre-fabricated reports for the BI front end. These reports form the backbone of the business intelligence environment. They usually consist of core business information, divided into lines of business (or subject areas) and presented in a tabular format. The idea is to help the reader grasp what's happening with the business — as quickly as possible.

Reports require data, and it takes one or more queries to populate a report with data. So the first step in the creation of any standard report is to define the set of queries that request the appropriate data from the target database.

In some cases, the report may require multiple datasets. For example, you may have revenue data in one fact table and costs in another. To show product contribution, you may need two separate queries to combine these two sources. Your front-end tool will have to join the two result sets that come back from the queries so you can calculate revenue minus costs.

The metadata layer

Database developers and BI architects will likely spend a good deal of time developing the *metadata:* the set of definitions and relationships that describe the information stored in every component in the system. Metadata is field- and table-level information that allows all data-handling applications to interact with each other including the source and target database systems, the ETL toolkit, online analytical processing (OLAP) applications, and even data-administration tools.

In the old days metadata was called a *data dictionary*, a resource used by developers and users alike when they took any action that touched the data. Rather than leaving data properties and associations open for interpretation, metadata gives a single reference point for everyone: users, analysts, developers, and administrators. Because the actual schema of the target database is likely to be very confusing (and unlikely to supply much useful context about the data), users turn to the metadata.

How metadata is stored and accessed is a hot topic among designers these days. Metadata is often brought together in a centralized repository, either custom-built or purchased from a vendor. This repository can be a single facility that provides universal metadata to all applications in the company, or it can be decentralized to serve the unique needs of individual applications. Each approach has its advantages and disadvantages, but a centralized approach is more common.

Your development process for that report will include coding the queries to retrieve the two datasets, manipulating the information to create the product contribution figures, and the code that assembles the viewable report. That means deciding what goes into the rows and columns, what calculations take place in the report, and how the report should be formatted.

Additionally, the development team might have to work out other details for this report, like figuring out the best data source and managing administration details (such as how the report may be accessed and altered).

Central to the creation of effective report formatting is the idea that they should be as easily understood as possible with no need for outside explanation or reference documentation. BI teams commonly face the challenge of striking the correct balance between report clarity and the relative utility of displaying data in more complex patterns.

Although many people are competent at creating reports, doing it *well* requires a combination of talents well-grounded in information architecture, business understanding, and even graphic design. Report writers are specialists; a good one can add a great deal of value to the BI process. This is especially true when you're building the basic templates on which all future standardized reports will be based. If you short-change that effort now, it will come back to haunt you.

Effective communication via reporting requires that you produce a solid set of standard templates to house information. In addition, those templates should adhere to a set of information standards that make the reports more valuable and user-friendly.

Standard reports have a fixed (or mostly fixed) format, driven by well-understood standardized parameters (such as time periods or product lines). Whether template-driven or not, every report should contain standard data such as the following elements:

✔ Report name

✔ Report category or family

✔ Date and time the report was created

✔ Source system name

✔ Reference source or help desk

In addition, the following standard features should be set and adhered to for all reports:

✔ Legal disclaimers and privacy policies

✔ Font type and size for headings and data fields

✔ Justification details for columns

✔ Color and corporate logo information

✔ Number formatting for currency, dates, and so on, including level of precision

✔ Inclusion or exclusion of data sources and query names (or entire query strings) in the report

Figure 14-2 represents a standard report template that might be created and published for use by the information consumers in your BI environment. It contains a set of standardized elements that reflect the list just given.

In all likelihood, your team will look at the most common reports currently produced, and create a family of report templates to be shared by the community. In addition, basic reports will also be built and scheduled to be run on a regular basis, or as needed by the user community.

The standard reporting system consists of several technology components:

✔ A tool for defining and building reports, which the report designer (either someone in IT or a skilled business user) uses.

✔ Management services for report storage, execution, and security.

✔ A portal through which end-users can select and view the reports (often a browser-based system).

Prymus Widget Company							System Logo

Product Line Margin and Share Report
<Division Name>
<Quarter_First> to <Quarter_Last>

<Quarter 1>	<Quarter 2>	<Quarter 3>				{Data Dictionary Link}

Product Line	Sales (Units)	Sales ($)	COGS ($)	Burdened COGS ($)	Net Margin (%)	Share (%)	Previous Share (%)
Xxxxxxxxxxx	#,###	$#,###	$#,###	$#,###	##.##	##.##	##.##
Xxxxxxxxxxx	#,###	$#,###	$#,###	$#,###	##.##	##.##	##.##
Xxxxxxxxxxx	#,###	$#,###	$#,###	$#,###	##.##	##.##	##.##
Xxxxxxxxxxx	#,###	$#,###	$#,###	$#,###	##.##	##.##	##.##
Xxxxxxxxxxx	#,###	$#,###	$#,###	$#,###	##.##	##.##	##.##
Xxxxxxxxxxx	#,###	$#,###	$#,###	$#,###	##.##	##.##	##.##
Xxxxxxxxxxx	#,###	$#,###	$#,###	$#,###	##.##	##.##	##.##
Xxxxxxxxxxx	#,###	$#,###	$#,###	$#,###	##.##	##.##	##.##

Report Category: {Sales Analysis} {Standard Report}	Report Compile Date: {mm.dd.yyyy hh:mm} By: {Domain}/{Username}
Report Name: {Product Line Margin and Share Report}	
Source: {System Name} {Data Source Name}	

Figure 14-2:
Layout of
a typical
report.

Here's a question worth asking: Before your newfangled BI system came along, how did the company ever survive without reports? The answer, of course, is that they didn't; there are plenty of existing reports floating around from the old environment. You won't be breaking new ground by *delivering* reports so much as by delivering a new *kind* of report — based on the wider breadth of data you'll be bringing together. BI tools also give you the power to control distribution and maintenance of your reports with far greater precision.

It may be tempting to copy a set of these old reports and just use them in the new environment, but beware the risks of doing so. There may be embedded business logic or data that won't translate to the new environment. The data might not make sense in its new context, or it might not be displayed at all. By all means, take the best elements of the legacy system — but to make the most of the new system you'll want to design the new reporting environment from scratch.

Figure 14-3 is a simple rendering of a reporting environment that runs off of the target BI database. The team that designs the reports also provides access to the reports; those who consume the reports use a controlled portal to view and use the ones they need as allowed by their security-clearance levels.

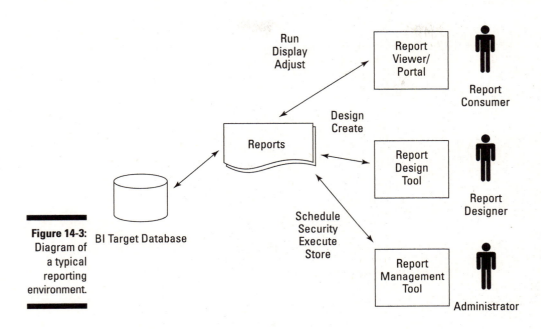

Figure 14-3:
Diagram of
a typical
reporting
environment.

As a best practice for BI implementation, the report developers are responsible for using the business requirements gathered from users and stakeholders to create a prioritized list of reports. The reports on that list will be released with the first launch of the system.

The best way to create the prioritized list of reports is to start with a full list of candidates created while you were eliciting requirements. Each report should be scored in terms of its business value and how difficult it is to build. Then your team will need to decide which reports can be built for this release, and which reports will have to wait until later.

Many reporting environments have several components — including developer tools, report viewers, an administrator tool, and a report server. Installation and configuration of a front-end reporting tool can take more work than you might expect.

Ad-hoc information access design

If your environment is to support users who want more than standard reports, you'll need to create a robust ad-hoc reporting environment.

Ad-hoc reports are extremely valuable for information consumers; they allow workers to operate outside the information contained in standard, canned reports. An ad-hoc reporting environment exposes the key entities of the database to the user, who can then pick and choose among them to create a custom report.

To be an effective report creator, a user must understand the underlying data model in the BI target database. Therefore a company that relies on ad-hoc reporting tools must design a logical data model that makes sense to its information consumers. That means the entities should match real business elements; the hierarchies used to describe the data should add up, both figuratively and literally. For example, a user should be able to write one query for the total sales for October, November, and December and get the same total as if the report were run against the Fourth Quarter of the same year.

There are a number of BI front-end tools that specialize in ad-hoc reporting — for example, Microsoft's Report Builder product (which comes with SQL Server).

For users who like standard reports, but need the flexibility to make changes, some ad-hoc reporting tools offer an "in-between" solution. The user starts with a standard report template, then fills in the data variables they need to see. In more flexible and abstract environments, the user starts from a blank slate, literally able to design a report from scratch.

OLAP design

Online analytical processing (OLAP) is a highly specialized implementation of the ad-hoc reporting environment. Instead of static reports, an OLAP front-end tool gives users a multidimensional view of the underlying data, where information can be rearranged on the fly to support fast-moving business needs.

In an OLAP environment, data is stored along central facts, such as individual sales transactions, and can be queried along any combination of dimensions connected to those facts. Instead of re-writing complex queries and waiting for the system to return the dataset, users can manipulate the dataset instantaneously, re-ordering, navigating through different dimensions, and using "drilling" methods (drill-down, drill-up, drill-through) to find just the information angle they're looking for .

OLAP front-end tools offer flexible analysis and reporting that can feed many different areas of the business — from the strategies in the corner office to tactical decision support. There are a number of OLAP tools on the market, and the specific implementations can vary from one product to the next.

In general, designing an OLAP front-end solution involves four main steps:

1. Identify the variables to be tracked, measured, or described.

2. Group the variables together in logical domains of association.

3. Define the relationships between the major entities.

   Consulting an OLAP expert can help your team define the dimension members, hierarchies, measures, and attributes.

4. Define the formulas and derivations that serve to aggregate and combine the measures in a useful way for the end-users.

Entity-relationship diagrams

The *entity-relationship (ER) diagram* is a common tool in database design. It models both the entities in a database and the relationships between them, showing snapshots of exactly how data is organized logically in a database. Basic symbols represent the information's main components.

Think of an *entity* as a logical class of data — in effect, any important element of information, at whatever level is important to the data being represented. A table in a database (for example) can usually be represented as an entity.

Attributes, on the other hand, are what describe entities. For example, if you are tracking information elements such as `vehicle owner`, `vehicle manufacturer`, `vehicle identification number`, and `vehicle license plate`, the entity in this case would be `vehicle`, since that's what each of those fields seem to describe. The attributes associated with `vehicle` would be `owner`, `manufacturer`, `identification number`, and `license plate`.

The figure in this sidebar is a very simple entity-relationship (ER) diagram. This type of model is essential in database design of any kind; it's particularly useful in the design of BI systems, where multiple data environments share the same concepts and ideas.

The real value of the ER diagram is that it forces the database designer to completely deconstruct the information to be stored. When you have a good understanding of how data entities and relationships map to each other, you can use them to assemble a low-level data model that can help shape the actual creation of the database, its table structure, and fields.

Building an ER diagram can be a challenge, especially in an enterprise environment that has a large, complex table structure. A data-warehouse environment gets even more complicated because two different data sources may store overlapping information. For example, two systems at a hospital might have one table called `Customers` and another table called `Patients`. The treatment of these two entities by their respective parent data sources is an important difference to investigate; modeling can help that process, as well as the process that combines the two into a unified entity.

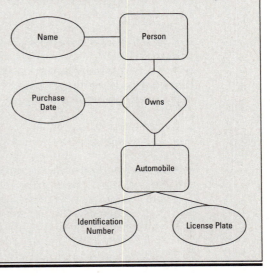

Sometimes dimension data can be hidden. If you're converting tabular data into a dimensional model and you're not sure what's a fact and what's a dimension, a good starting place is to assume that keyed attributes are the dimensions and attributes that aren't keyed are facts. For spreadsheet data, look for the way the data is separated into groups. If (for example) your master product sales performance spreadsheet has 15 different worksheets representing the 15 divisions of the company, then *division* is an important dimension that users will want to differentiate when they're analyzing reports.

Analytics and data-mining applications

These applications are at the top of the complexity ladder — but in essence, they serve the same purpose as any other BI front-end system: to supply business insights to users in whatever form is most useful to them. Some of the most advanced analytics applications are designed to predict rather than merely describe, building a model of the past that can be used to envision future events, project available choices, and allow analysts to game out (as in "game theory", not as in Monopoly) the possibilities.

Analytics applications focus on a particular aspect of the business process — such as sales, inventory, or manufacturing — and attempt to spot useful trends by using pre-loaded algorithms. Analytics software is built not only to spot trends from the past, but to forecast the future. For example, if you collect a huge volume of customer sales data for a large retail chain, an analytics application can create a complex model of your market's buying behavior. The application spots trends that would take human eyes eons to recognize. Best of all, you can use that customer model to predict how customers might react to price changes or promotions.

In terms of design and development, the approach is largely the same. Starting with the overall business goals, the analysts and designers should derive what-if scenarios and questions that can't be answered simply by looking at a summary of yesterday's data. The patterns being sought are codified into broader analytic goals.

In the pursuit of those goals, however, analytics applications suffer from the common pitfalls of all front-end BI applications:

- ✔ **Analytics programs are only as good as the data that feeds them.** That means data sources must be checked and monitored for data quality and consistency. It's not unusual for companies to spend a fortune on high-end analysis tools, only to find that the conclusions and forecasts produced are worthless for the simple reason that the underlying data is unsound or inaccessible.

- ✔ **High-intelligence reporting and forecasting software is only as good as the data model used to populate the analysis engines.** If the real world doesn't match up to what the software *thinks* is the real world, the forecast and analysis will be off. Analytics applications built by the major software companies normally ride atop the same target database that other BI applications use. Provided that model is sound, the insights gained from the analytics applications should at least be quantifiably correct. Whether you have the right people to *interpret* that information is another matter.

✔ **For analytics to work, the reports must be usable and relevant to the business.** That means you need individual contributors who can get the most out of the analytics applications to produce regular insights. But more than that, the business must be ready to react to what the data-mining and analytics applications have to say. That's more likely to happen if the application is correctly interlocked with the other systems in the BI environment. The analysis engine must be synced up with the data model, and it must take full advantage of the reporting environment to present and distribute findings.

Getting Users On Board

The best way to ensure that the user community is happy with the work you're doing is to keep them involved in the design process. That's easier said than done for brand-new applications for which users have little or no frame of reference.

Reporting review

But for a reporting environment, you're dealing with familiar ground for the users. They're used to seeing information in a certain format at certain times. Your new reporting environment should be rolled out to a select group of expert users who are open to the new system, but who are *also* willing to give you honest feedback.

Have the user group review and validate the following information:

✔ Review your list of high-priority standard reports; make sure any gaps can be filled in with the ad-hoc environment or by tweaking one of the existing templates.

- Review the reports to ensure they are displaying data correctly.
- Ensure that the reports are readable and that the titles, headings, and extra information (like instructions) are correct.

✔ Work with the report developers on the run-and-release calendar; the schedule should ensure that the data is getting to the necessary targets on time.

✔ Show the user community how to navigate the reporting tool. The way you've organized the standard reports and explanatory information should make sense to everyday consumers of that information.

✔ Give a walk-through demonstration of the new environment's capabilities — particularly new features that differentiate it from the legacy system (say, a slick new browser-based interface or advanced tools that are available for the first time).

✔ Try out any drill-down or drill-through reports to ensure that the information is linking correctly, and that the drill links are logically placed and visible.

✔ Distribute the library of report templates and ensure that the information displayed on every report adheres to company and project standards.

Testing, 1-2-3 . . .

The quality-assurance process in a BI environment will probably resemble that of other major technology projects: Unfortunately, that implies that it's often done haphazardly, without any kind of real plan, if it's even done at all. You can't afford the usual testing chaos in a BI project.

Testing is an essential part of the design-and-deployment process for BI because mistakes caught at this point are far cheaper and easier to fix than they would be after the systems are in production. Testing comes in several different phases and flavors:

✔ **Unit testing:** This is the lowest level of testing that the developers complete. Do the code libraries compile into binaries? Do the applications load successfully?

✔ **Integration testing:** At this stage, you're testing to see whether the components are speaking to each other. Can the ETL application communicate with the source data systems? Are the front-end applications working together as designed?

✔ **Quality-assurance (QA) testing:** This is the point where professional testers get involved. If all goes as planned, your QA analysts write test scripts that check the function of every component in the system against the original specifications. That means testing everything from the quality of the data in the reports to the appearance of the reports themselves — along with any qualitative measures of performance such as return time, error rates, or latency.

✔ **User-acceptance testing:** Here the end-user group finally gets its hands on the application, puts it through its paces, and reports back issues.

Maintain tight control of user acceptance testing or it can spiral out of control quickly. Choreograph the testing process for the guinea pig users by supplying them with test scripts, expected results, and a firm schedule for reporting issues and comments. It's common for users to have a change of heart about an application specification (or to simply not remember what they asked for) and report it as an issue. And it's possible some of the testers weren't involved in the requirements process to begin with, and will ask for extra functionality to be added to the project at this late date.

Document your testing just as you would document system specifications. Have QA professionals create a test plan and test cases while the developers are still building and coding the system. Document the outcome of every test and log the results for future reference. The reason for that is simple: when you upgrade the system later on, you'll need to do regression testing to ensure that the improvement or upgrade hasn't broken anything. Without documentation from the original testing phase, you'll have to re-invent what could be a fairly complex wheel.

ETL testing

Testing the extract-transform-load process is one of the most critical QA efforts of the BI project, because mistakes can lie hidden like needles in haystacks. There may be an error in your transformation process that only manifests itself once in every thousand records processed.

Testing the ETL process is a matter of deconstructing each step of the flow through the system. As the data moves from one state to the next, your testers are there to ensure every validation step and manipulation is working correctly. Once you're sure every step works by itself, it's time to do integration testing with the ETL process; making sure that every step leads smoothly into the next.

It's not necessary to employ end-users for testing the entire ETL process, but you must find experts in the appropriate business subject matter to validate the data cleansing and transformation processes. Business users and stakeholders will have been a part of specifying the requirements when the ETL process was designed, and they must play a part here, too: ensuring that the data that comes out of the ETL chain is correct.

Front-end testing

After the ETL process has been through a full QA cycle, you have to focus on the front end. Make sure the queries are populating the reports as expected, and that the analysis tools are being fed the appropriate data.

To test your reports and front-end tools, start with the presentation of the report itself. Does it appear correct? Are the calculations producing accurate results?

Then the QA testers turn their attention to the parameterized data in the reports. They will likely throw various permutations and combinations of parameters — legal and illegal — at the reporting tool to ensure that it responds properly.

Now in limited release

Doing a full release without any interim steps comes with significant risk. For one thing, you're committed to a certain direction without knowing if the technology you're interested in using is even feasible, or if the opportunity area makes sense for applying BI concepts.

Pilot projects

For business intelligence applications, a *pilot project* is more than a dry run; it's essentially a small-scale demonstration designed to show that BI can add value in a certain domain of the business. A pilot focuses on one functional silo, such as supply chain management or human resources, and builds a limited-capability system that includes only the core functions of all the main BI components. Some characteristics of a pilot project:

- ✔ Time to launch is measured in months.
- ✔ Software is not licensed for permanent use.
- ✔ Budget is significantly lower than it would be for a full iteration of the project.
- ✔ BI functionality is limited.

Pilot projects have limitations, to be sure. But they put the main concepts of a BI initiative to the test, just with limited complexity and scale. The pilot project would include identifying source data, constructing an ETL process (including developing capabilities for standardizing and cleansing data), and developing a target database environment.

You will connect front-end tools to the target data environment, but advanced functionality will be kept to a minimum. The goal here is not to produce high-impact insights immediately, but rather show that all the moving parts can work together. The lessons learned (and, potentially, internal allies gained) from a successful pilot program can be parlayed into a full project cycle with a permanent release.

Proof of concept

A *proof of concept* is different from a pilot project in terms of its goal: to apply a particular solution to a business problem to see how well the proposed system can withstand the accompanying demands.

A common use of the proof-of-concept project is to build a prototype, using an untested BI component (such as a front-end analysis and reporting tool or an OLAP engine). The results of the test (which could last for as little as a few weeks) determine which direction the project team will go concerning a particular technology.

Chapter 15

The Day After: Maintenance and Enhancement

Research data say that most business intelligence projects don't live up to their expectations. That means they're not meeting their return-on-investment (ROI) goals — and the users don't think they're worth much, either.

Avoiding that fate is easier said than done. Hopefully you went through a careful planning process and kept the business goals front-and-center while you developed your BI platform. And if all went well, you listened to the user community, gathered good requirements, and designed a sound system.

After the team has successfully launched the first iteration of the platform, the real work begins. Before you fluff up the bed of laurels to rest upon, however, it's time to start thinking about how you're going to keep this environment running smoothly — and how you can make it even better.

It's a common misconception that says businesses need only install BI software, and then they're "finished" with the job; they can check it off the list and move on to the next IT project. The reality is that BI is not a project — it's a *process* that's driven by the business and supported by technology professionals. BI is a way of thinking about and utilizing information in the day-to-day and year-to-year processes that guide organizations.

BI = Constant Improvement

The BI process manifests itself in two main forms: software implementation projects and the accompanying business process changes that work in concert with the software.

An extended example demonstrates this point: imagine a company installs a comprehensive BI solution connecting detailed financial information with sales activity. The system brings a previously-unheard-of level of insight into the sales process. With the new system, sales managers can attach precise margin data with individual sales transactions and sales representatives.

Suddenly the sales management team can hold both the field and inside sales teams accountable for the deals they make — and demand that each transaction meet certain margin requirements. To ensure the sales teams can meet the new margin thresholds, the business might implement a change to the sales process; adding a BI system-guided approval process when creating quotes for deals. Without the new system, there would be no mechanism available to add this step, leaving the sales teams in the dark about margins. But in this case, BI is driving the business process — enabling the sales team to improve how it handles its core functions.

BI creates a cascading evolutionary process within organizations, where technology not only demands process changes, but permits new ways of thinking and encourages better, more innovative methods for tackling problems.

That's why BI practitioners have to be prepared to think about system enhancements. A business intelligence system should be built to solve problems and offer insights, but it should also entail a certain amount of planning for the future.

Post-Implementation Evaluations

First things first after launch: You need to understand how you did. An often-overlooked — but extremely important — part of any business intelligence project comes after the applications have been put into production and it's time to pause and look back at how well the project was executed. At the same time, you should survey the landscape to see what impact the new tools are having on the business.

Make sure your evaluation isn't perceived as just another testing period where users expect their feedback to be registered and acted upon — from this point on, they're going to have to do some adapting. Users don't always know what they want until Day 2 (that is, the day *after* you've delivered their new reporting-and-analysis application.) They finally get a look at the new system and only then they realize what their needs are. That's what phase 2 is for.

Overall project review

After it's been put into the production environment and the end-users are getting full use from it (as designed), it's time for a post-implementation review. Call it a post-mortem, a health-check, or whatever you want, but the purpose is always the same:

- **Recap:** Review the highlights of the entire development narrative, from the idea stage all the way to launch.

- **Qualitative analysis:** Identify which business goals were met or exceeded, and which ones, if any, the effort fell short of attaining.

- **Quantitative analysis:** Evaluate the project against standard performance metrics: Did we meet the budget and schedule requirements?

- **Lessons learned:** These should cover both the good and the bad. What went well? What areas of the development process needed smoothing over?

Technology review

The overall project review brings into clear relief the elements of your BI environment that are working as expected — and those that aren't. During the technology review, your team should take a closer look at the root cause of certain successes and failures. The examination shouldn't stop at the application level; it should get as detailed as necessary: Why haven't certain application features worked as expected? In most cases, the problem can be correlated with the main steps of the implementation process:

- Was the software installed and configured correctly?

- If it's working as planned, was there a flaw in the requirements process? Was there an unanticipated problem that should have been identified in the design phase?

- If it the application was specified properly, maybe the problem is broader: Did the feature, element, or report in question align with the business goals of the BI program?

These questions are valuable not only for fixing current deficiencies with the BI system as it is today, but also in planning for enhancements and the next release. The technology review should provide a reference for requirements or specific functionality considerations that must be accounted for in the subsequent release.

Document what you find; technology lessons learned are only worthwhile if you can remember them. A common problem with BI projects is that mistakes are repeated. A poorly conceived user interface or a poorly designed report shouldn't be allowed to serve as the model for subsequent releases and enhancements.

Business-impact review

While it's certainly important to examine how well the implementation went, if BI is to become woven into the fabric of the business, you'll need to look at more than the efficiency of your project team. You're going to have to understand — and, if possible, quantify — the actual business value of the new BI tools, and the contribution the new applications are making to the functioning of the enterprise.

That's easier said than done, of course. Not only is a meaningful assessment a time-consuming process to conduct, it can't even begin until the new processes and tools have taken root. Start looking for results too early and you may not get a representative sample of data.

To conduct a business-impact review, return to the planning artifacts you created early on in the project (Chapters 10 and 11 cover the early steps in a project). In all likelihood, you and your team conducted extensive research — put together roadmaps, strategy briefs and papers, as well as capability assessments and gap analyses. That documentation adds up to your baseline business case — the original justification for creating (or, later, extending) the BI program.

In some cases, you may have created metrics early on in the program. Not just broad goals for what the organization was hoping to achieve, but specific measurements that indicated organizational improvements, along with precise methodologies for taking those readings. It's a good idea to stick with the original metrics built into the program — say, reducing processing time for reports or improving access to information. Filling in the blanks on measurements like these is a good way to close the loop in a BI project.

After that, it's necessary to investigate the impact on the users. You'll want to collect and analyze information from the knowledge workers who come in contact with the new BI tools. Typically the improvements will fall into one of several standard categories, which the next subsections describe.

Reducing the time per task

This measurement might apply to how long it takes to produce a given report, develop a specific analysis, or complete some other activity assigned to your knowledge workers. Reductions in the amount of time incurred by the company can be measured by multiplying the amount of time saved by a standardized hourly rate for the personnel involved.

Another way to approach this measurement is to attach a specific value to the completion of a given task, and then multiply the extra tasks that can be completed thanks to the BI implementation by that rate.

Reducing the cost per task

A BI end-user tool is likely to reduce the number of people involved in the research-and-analysis process — and that means cost savings for the company.

These reductions don't necessarily mean laying off all the people no longer necessary to the task; it just means their time is freed up for different, potentially *more valuable* tasks.

Improving core competencies

The core goal of many BI systems is more than just making the reporting process more efficient. It's about the insights that come from those reports — the ideas and information that, in the right hands, actually have a positive impact on how the business is run.

A BI environment might enable a business to identify efficiencies throughout the core business activities, whether it's the supply chain, manufacturing process, marketing and sales efforts, or any other main task performed by the company with the aim of making money. For example, BI might make possible better, more efficient use of direct mail by identifying customer buying patterns and connecting those patterns with geographic regions. That connection might allow the same direct-mail budget to be used to reach a more receptive audience and improve the ROI for each campaign.

Refining business direction

Ultimately, the insights gained from integrating a BI environment, and the entire business intelligence mindset, into its strategic planning process may pay dividends in the long term by leading the company into new, more fruitful markets and activities.

Maintaining Your BI Environment

No system can really run itself. In exchange for the advantages BI brings, the organization has to pony up with ongoing maintenance — in particular, these three activities:

- ✔ Assessing the health of your BI system (how well it performs its designed functions).
- ✔ Evaluating how relevant the system is to your evolving business needs.
- ✔ Checking the extent to which the system improves communication within the organization.

System health

The most basic (though not at all simple) BI maintenance tasks revolve around keeping the core systems up and running for your users.

Data health

In theory, if you test adequately, your data should remain in good health as it moves between the source systems, through the ETL process, and into the target database. A disruption in the chain of events that feeds information to your users could be disastrous to the organization. If people use information that doesn't actually reflect reality, reports will be inaccurate, decisions will be off-kilter, and forecasts will have no relationship to the actual future. That's why constantly monitoring the data flowing into your BI environment is of the utmost importance.

One way to ensure good data is with a discovery-and-profiling process: The project team gets access to statistical analyses on the information flowing through your system. This can be a manual process — data experts on the team can create their own queries to check on the data's characteristics before and after it's loaded into the target system. Better yet is an automated tool that analyzes the range and distribution of field values, relationships between tables, and other facts that can provide a complete profile on the information in your BI environment.

Don't wait till you hear complaints from users to check to see whether your data's in good shape. The outward symptoms of this disease won't appear until the patient is already on life-support. Keep an eye on incomplete or corrupted data as part of your normal maintenance process.

Response time

Monitoring data load and query-response times is essential to maintaining a useful and usable BI environment. And success has its own price for a BI system: A more useful tool means more users will want access to the data; in the long run, more business domains will be included in the BI system.

As the number of users grows, the strain on the system will naturally increase.

It's equally true that the target data systems will fill with more data over time, and the nature of the queries and usage patterns will evolve (often in the direction of more complexity), slowly but surely eroding performance. Add to that the possibility that sometimes things just break, and you have the makings of trouble right here in River City. It's imperative to have one eye on BI system performance *at all times*.

Most database applications have built-in diagnostic tools for monitoring performance, and BI vendors often have add-on utilities that provide more visibility into how the system handles complex queries and peak loads. High-end monitoring tools can even detect slowdowns by sniffing out increases in response times, and then triggering diagnostic processes to isolate the source of the problem.

In a BI environment, *recognizing* and *fixing* a performance problem are usually two relatively simple tasks sandwiched around a much more difficult one: *identifying the root cause*. With so many systems intertwined in a digital tango that may stretch across the company, isolating the weak link in the chain can be a real challenge. That's what makes active performance monitoring so critical; it buys you more time to locate and fix the problem.

Waiting until users complain about response times is a recipe for trouble. Chances are, by the time word gets back to the project team, lots of people have been affected by the reduced performance.

By measuring elapsed times for regular processes and requests, and then watching the trend lines for those response times, you can anticipate when it's time to upgrade the system to handle more capacity. You'll be able to spot trouble before it arrives.

During the design process, define the response time needed for every piece of data — keeping in mind that not all of it has to be refreshed in real time. For example, if you're monitoring sales performance for a growing chain of coffee bars, you'll want to refresh the actual sales data as often as possible. But reference information (such as store locations and employee data) doesn't change all that often; you only need refresh it once a week or once a month. Reloading that relatively static data once an *hour* would only bog down the system unnecessarily.

Tuning the target database

All databases require regular tuning to maintain performance, and BI target data systems are no different. The database administrator will need to perform regular diagnostics and tuning procedures to ensure that the database-management system (DBMS) remains optimized for the kinds of queries it's required to do, that it's making the best use of storage, and that the database is staying aligned with the applications it supports.

Updating the application

As is the case with any complex application, vendors are constantly releasing bug-fixes and updates to address users' complaints and demands for improvements. A good BI team will have a systematic way to keep track of these upgrades and to apply them to the environment efficiently and with minimum disruption.

System relevance — Keeping up with business changes

A successful BI system will constantly acquire more data. That's inherent in a data-warehousing environment where the information being stored is based on historical operations. But it's also true that as more detailed business data is stored and more subject areas are tracked than before; the demands on the system increase and become more complex. The BI system must constantly be tweaked to ensure that it's capturing relevant information, in the right timeframe, and at the right level of detail.

Lots of factors can affect the health of a business intelligence system. The following tasks highlight the challenge of keeping up a BI system in a dynamic business environment:

- **New information:** Whether it's a new category of data, a new business unit, or a new source system, the environment must be flexible enough to be able to take in and process new data.

- **Source data changes or goes away:** The opposite of the preceding concern is true as well: Source data systems won't stay the same forever. They'll upgrade, get rolled up into consolidated systems, or sometimes go away altogether.

- **New leadership and sponsor changes:** The strategic importance of the system is a function of how the leadership views it. Be aware that changes in the corner offices or changes in the organization of the company can affect how the system is used, both on a day-to-day level and as a long-term strategy tool.

Maintaining lines of communication

Communication is the key to supporting the business intelligence environment. Keeping users trained, informed, and in touch with helpful resources goes a long way toward maintaining a healthy system and happy user community.

Figure 15-1 shows the communication links, both direct and indirect, that must exist between the project team and the various stakeholders in the company.

The project team is tasked with keeping several different channels of communication open after they launch the system, each with its own predefined needs:

- **Providing immediate support:** This is helpdesk support that provides basic aid for users who run into trouble with operating the applications or performing basic tasks. Larger companies often create a shared help-center function; in smaller organizations, the project team is responsible for this Level-1 support.

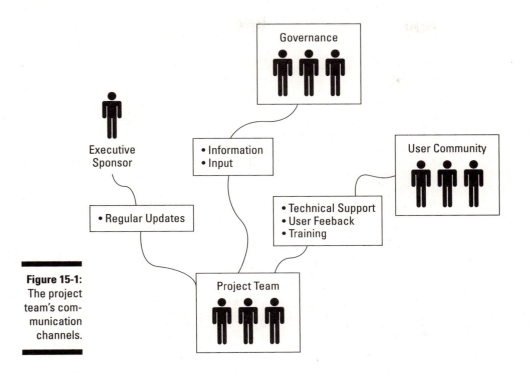

Governance

Executive Sponsor

• Information
• Input

User Community

• Regular Updates

• Technical Support
• User Feeback
• Training

Figure 15-1:
The project team's communication channels.

Project Team

✔ **Providing a feedback mechanism:** It's not all about fixing bugs and getting users online. You'll also want to provide the stakeholders and application users with a way to offer complaints, comments, and criticism. And in case you were thinking about routing those comment cards straight to the trash can, take a moment and consider that the user is golden in the BI environment. As is the case with BI as a whole, the information in your users' comments provides the basis for your rational decisions about the system's future. (Who knows? Somebody may even say something nice.)

✔ **Ongoing training for users:** This isn't just helping users get through basic tasks over the phone via live chat; this communication pathway is designed to *upgrade* user skills. One of the biggest problems in BI systems is that he applications are often complex, and the project team assumes the users can pick up on how to use them right away. Establishing a training program is a great way to ensure that users get what they need from the system.

✔ **Participation in standards and governance committees:** The BI project team should stay directly involved in any corporate-wide oversight committees. When the data stewards act, the BI team needs to know about it right away to apply the appropriate system updates. Not only that, but by maintaining a presence in governance committees, the BI project team has an opportunity to spread the word about the proper role of business intelligence in a company like yours.

> ✔ **Regular contact with executive sponsors:** These people went out on a limb for you, so the least you can do is keep the bigwigs apprised of the system's status. Share good news, bad news, and everything in between. They'll hear it all anyway.

Extending Your Capabilities

With business intelligence touching more and more areas of the enterprise these days, there are expansion opportunities everywhere. It's important to maintain your system, but the glory is in expanding it — bringing new features and applications to your user community to make the system work better than it did before.

As always, the business users and stakeholders should be driving the BI project. And the project team must always keep in mind the underlying business objectives so they remain lined up with the technology activities.

Follow the same basic procedures as your original installation — except in miniature, and from a slightly different perspective. With a particular business need in hand, decide the best technology path to support it.

Expanding existing applications

The first — and easiest — enhancements to make are those where you take what you already have and make it marginally better. It's not uncommon for BI vendors to ship BI tools with a limited feature set turned on (often under a particular licensing scheme). And because those features are already there in your system, turning them on is minimally disruptive to the environment.

Start simple. During the first few enhancement and expansion phases, don't bite off more than you can chew until you get a feel for the strategic and operational challenges of upgrading the system.

Picking up leftovers

Here's where you revisit the prioritization exercise used during the requirements-elicitation phase of the project (see Chapter 13). That exercise reflects the reality that you rarely have time to do everything you plan to do during the initial implementation of the BI system. So the high-priority items got installed and the lower-priority items had to wait.

The first system enhancement is the perfect opportunity to revisit those initial drafts of the project plan and requirement documentation. See whether you have any leftover old priorities you can deal with right away. The requirements you didn't get to in your last BI implementation often are the simplest to complete.

The beauty of the initial-implementation rejects is that their specs are usually already defined and vetted for business validity. You've already talked them over with the users and determined they were important in an absolute sense. They just didn't make the cut.

Moving up the complexity chain

Sometimes it makes sense to upgrade users from simpler software to more complex applications. If users have mastered the basic features of an interface, they may become more productive if you expose advanced functionality to them, or install new applications that naturally build on the existing features.

A typical BI system evolves in certain predictable ways because of the way features of one application are similar to, or build towards, features of a different application. Figure 15-2 shows an initial BI installation on the left, connected to a few potential evolutionary paths on the right. For example, experts at the managed reporting tools may want to expand their capabilities and move into report authoring and building their own ad-hoc queries. Others from that user group may ask for visualization software to turn their reports into graphics-laden masterpieces.

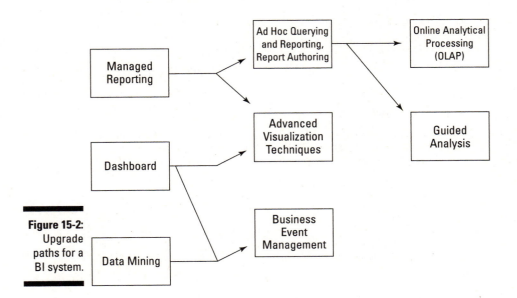

Figure 15-2:
Upgrade paths for a BI system.

As your system grows in capability and reach, it's likely you'll follow these common growth patterns:

- ✔ **Cater to power users:** Create opportunities for power users to do even more detailed and in-depth analysis than before.

- ✔ **Move BI toward real-time decision support:** Your initial BI implementation was aimed at helping you do a slow-motion analysis of business problems. With your first enhancement project, consider applications that can support users making day-to-day decisions based on the analyses they do.

- ✔ **Move BI into the realm of the strategic:** Applications that support broad strategic planning are at the end of a long BI software continuum. Your enhancements should be pushing in that general direction — to make BI part of the forecasting and planning function.

- ✔ **Expand from ad-hoc to managed environments and back again:** Both these types of reporting environments can be extraordinarily valuable if deployed to the right people with the right training. Move to a managed environment if you have more users with limited ability and there's a need to author custom reports. Introduce an ad-hoc environment if folks are asking for more flexibility in running queries.

Don't do it just because you can. It may be technically possible to deliver real-time cash register data to the sales analytics application, but come on, do you really need that kind of information overload? If all the analysis is being done with week-to-date reports, you don't need to invest the time and hassle in establishing a real-time data feed. That's a common pitfall in BI; there are so many little ways to improve at the margins, you'd better pick and choose where to dedicate effort — carefully — or you'll wind up with features you don't actually need.

More advanced work within existing versions

This kind of BI expansion doesn't require any new licenses. Enhancements don't have to involve applications, and they don't necessarily mean adding gobs of computing or storage capacity. Sometimes it's about pausing to make a report better, or to improve the usability of a component.

Usability is an important aspect of your BI environment — as is the look and feel of the day-to-day tools. Take these factors into account when you're considering system enhancements. Applications that are hard to use or unpleasant to deal with will eventually fall into disuse. And the visual, aesthetic qualities of the software are often the first things a user notices — and complains about.

Adding new users to your BI environment

Sometimes an enhancement is less about adding new functionality and more about adding a new user group. Adjust the system to handle more users by upgrading for capacity. The goal is to allow the new users to access the data without imposing any noticeable lag in application performance, query lag-time, and the like.

If the new user group has a different skill level (or comes from a different part of the business), you may also have to deploy a different application apropos the new, wider target audience. Giving the sales management team access to the BI system, for example, may mean providing a tightly controlled, managed reporting environment in place of the ad-hoc environment that used to work fine for a smaller, more skilled user group.

Installing advanced upgrades

On certain occasions, you really can't do any more with what you have. You can't expand or enhance the existing BI tools. All the low-hanging fruit has been eaten. Now it's time to branch out and expand into tools that aren't already in place.

Is your new enhancement going to endanger your existing system in any way? Will it make it harder to use? Will it be slower? Make sure you don't break something in the process. To protect your system from potential bugs an upgrade may bring, any good QA professional would tell you to make sure you engage in full-system *regression testing* as you add new enhancements.

Here's the short list of key questions to ask for any system upgrade:

✔ Who will implement the enhancements? Is it the same team that did the first project, or a whole new team?

✔ Do you have executive support for the upgrade?

✔ Have you fully specified the requirements for the new system — according to the same methodology as before?

✔ Which current BI users will use this application? What training will they need?

✔ Does the new functionality distract from or disrupt existing functionality?

Business intelligence projects in particular have special concerns that the project team should take into account. Because BI is a transformative approach to business and technology, there is always the concern that business processes haven't had a chance to catch up with the technology. In other words, the technology tools are indeed supplying insights to the users — but they're not being adequately used. Stacking shiny new applications on top of existing applications can lead to trouble. If the users aren't making the most of the *simpler* BI install, what makes you think they'll get the most from the new software? They might, but there's no guarantee.

Also, because there are so many puzzle pieces that have to fit together, compatibility is always an issue. Most vendors today offer a standards-based approach. But sometimes two pieces of software simply don't work (or at least don't work *well*) together.

With any enhancement or expansion, it's critical to keep expectations in line. Are we fixing something? If so, what was broken, and how do we know for sure? Is this a new tool with new functionality? If so, what is its purpose and where is it documented?

The Olympic Approach

Every 18 to 24 months, review the entire business intelligence system, soup to nuts, top to bottom. Set sacred cows aside. Subject every piece of your environment to scrutiny as if you were buying a used automobile.

The squeakiest wheel gets the grease first. That's why a complete review is imperative. It gives you a chance to cast a critical eye at the pieces of the environment that may not be causing acute headaches, but are acting as a silent drag on the system.

In your evaluation, consider what's working well for users of all stripes — from executive skimmers to power users to peon information consumers stuck in the corporate dungeons. Do the same kind of analysis discussed when developing the initial BI approach. Think about these five levels of questions:

1. Are people using the tools they're supposed to be using?

2. Are they using the tools correctly?

3. Are the tools performing as expected?

4. Do the users perceive that the tools are adding value to their process?

5. Do the users have any needs that aren't being met?

The answers you get may or may not point you in the direction of an overhaul. It's possible you just need a round of retraining, or to refocus the company culture on the BI process. But don't ignore legitimate complaints from the user community, and don't interpret their commentary as trashing your initial design. Remember, change is inevitable. It's the sign of a healthy, dynamic system.

Don't stop at the users. Ask administrators and BI support personnel to participate in a subjective evaluation of the environment as well. It's not uncommon to have a system that's humming along for the user community but is a major resource drain backstage. An upgrade or overhaul may not matter much to users, but it can be a godsend for the BI team.

Thinking long term with a roadmap

The Olympic approach, or planning major upgrades every few years, means developing a keen sense of where the BI environment is going. That product vision and calendar should be codified, documented, and kept up-to-date.

The product vision should list approximate release dates and functionality groups or application types. For example, your goal may be to deliver a data-mining-and-forecasting tool to the sales team in a year's time. That goal should be recorded, along with the specific need it will meet. The project team can then use the product vision to guide the planning process.

Not sure where to start on your product vision? For BI projects, the best practice is to deliver basic functionality with the first release, then with the second release wrap up the loose ends of the first release. Only later, when the target data system is stable and the kinks are long gone do you go back and add new user groups and the exciting enhancements and new tools.

Remember, things change. Do some basic contingency planning, even for unlikely future events, provided they could have a big impact on the BI environment. For example, say there's talk of reorganizing the company from a shared services model into a divisional model — how will that affect your plans? Have two different branches of the long-term roadmap if necessary.

What's the difference between an enhancement and a planned release? Nothing, really, except the name — any time you change the configuration of your BI environment, it's an enhancement. Just remember that enhancements are not the same as *maintenance*. You don't have to do enhancements to keep your system humming. But maintenance activities, hardware, software, network, storage, and even process updates will keep your system healthy regardless of the enhancement schedule.

Evolvability

Business intelligence is more than a set of applications working together, it's a way of life for the company, and the tools you put in place to serve that way will inevitably change over time. In some domains this is known as planned obsolescence, but I prefer to call it planned evolution.

You'll likely have several integrated tools working in concert to deliver business insights to your BI users. Just as the pieces of a car give out or need to be replaced over time, you'll have to plan on swapping out or upgrading individual BI components. You have to weigh the advantages and disadvantages of the smaller disruptions involved in swapping out parts piecemeal versus doing a top-to-bottom overhaul of the entire system all at once.

There might be any number of reasons it's time for a change with one of your system components:

- ✔ **User needs change.** This is the obvious one. Your system can't do what you need it to do. Maybe there's a new product on the market that has piqued your interest, or maybe performance requirements have changed. Either way, it's time to upgrade.

- ✔ **Software standards change.** In this case, it's not that what you're using doesn't work, it's simply incompatible with the future state of the system.

- ✔ **External compliance needs change.** Perhaps there's an outside vendor?

- ✔ **An upgrade is available.**

- ✔ **Functionality can be combined.** There's always the chance that efficiencies can be gained by unifying applications. Remember, every piece of software that handles information is a potential weak link in the chain — and the same is true of the handshakes between components. Bringing two or more functions under one roof can make administration easier and improve performance.

The One Question

Whether a piece of software, or a given function fits into your long-term plans or not is certainly a question to ponder. But at the core, you have to ask yourself the one basic question:

Is it providing value today?

Some pieces of your architecture may be dead ends, planned obsolescence may be kicking in, or the long-term usefulness of the component may be obscured by a weird, hazy future. That's okay — as long as the piece is providing value right now.

Off-roading

Assemble your system according to the long-term plan. That means enhancements and upgrades should happen on schedule as you planned them, and as they appear on the roadmap. But sometimes it's clear that external events are going to lead to a change in business conditions — and that leads to a change in the needs of the BI system.

For large corporate events — such as reorganizations, buyouts, or changes at the top of the company — you have to know when it's time to take a turn off the pavement and leave your roadmap behind.

Part V
BI and Technology

"He won't use our BI app. Says he has a knack for trends."

In this part . . .

Since you're learning about business intelligence, you might as well learn about data warehouses, data marts, and other kinds of target databases that act as a central repository for your operational data. What a coincidence! That's what's covered in this part of the book.

In addition, it's time you started learning about the BI marketplace, and the vendors that peddle their wares to lemonade stand owners and managers just like you.

Chapter 16

BI Target Databases: Data Warehouses, Marts, and Stores

Data — the information that quantifies and describes your organization's activities — is the wellspring of any business insights that come from your BI environment. Developing a sound strategy to seek it out, clean it, marshal it, corral it, and move it into a useful posture is one of the most important steps in the entire process.

In order for users — by way of the software they use — to have easy access to your data, you'll need to place it into a target data environment. Once in this setting (which may take on a number of different forms), the data is available to BI user applications that can harvest and use it to produce the key strategic and operational insights that make the entire BI effort worthwhile.

The BI target database, no matter what form it takes, must be optimized for "data out" procedures — queries that feed reporting-and-analysis tools.

The target database must be built to withstand the pressures peculiar to BI usage. Normally the BI target database is geared to storing massive amounts of historical data, at all levels of summarization and aggregation. In addition, the BI target database may be designed to feed a diverse array of large, complex queries and reports — in addition to feeding high-end analysis tools.

This chapter discusses the most common BI target data environments: data warehouses, data marts, operational data stores, and hybrid models. As we go along, we consider these important questions:

- ✔ Where does the data that we need currently reside?
- ✔ How in the world are we going to collect it all?
- ✔ What efforts must go into its maintenance and cleansing?
- ✔ How can we make sure the data is standardized so we're dealing with apples-to-apples comparisons?
- ✔ How should we arrange the data to best serve the particular array of user-facing applications we've deployed?
- ✔ Where and how are we going to store the data? We need to make decisions on the storage architecture, protocols, and standards.

There are implementation strategies to fit every kind of environment. If you're involved in a BI implementation, what you're looking for is pretty familiar: timely, accurate, high-value, actionable insights. Answering these questions will help determine which data architecture is the best way to reach that goal.

Data Warehouses and BI

BI is built on the premise that the important operational data — the stuff you really need to look at — is stored in varying platforms and locations around the company. Bringing that information together under one umbrella is usually known as *data warehousing*.

Specific definitions may vary across vendors and experts, but in general, a *data warehouse* is a data-storage system designed and built to gather historical operational data together — for the purpose of creating reports and analyses based on it. Performing those tasks on your operational databases would be complicated and costly, to say nothing of the fact that it might slow your business down to a crawl. Data warehousing is a way to separate operations from reporting and analysis.

A data warehouse doesn't necessarily mean one *single* database full of data ready to be reported on and analyzed. Sometimes it makes more sense to bring data together in several related systems rather than one big system.

Data warehouses are often designed to bridge the gap across multiple functional areas of an organization, bringing related historical data together in a useful way. The finance and accounting departments (for example) may use one data storage system, while the HR and sales teams use their own data-collection mechanisms. Many of the objects and information nuggets contained in these different systems will be the same. The data warehouse provides the logical — and, in most cases, physical — link that connects those objects together across departmental (or even state) lines.

Part of the reason to create a data warehouse is because it creates a flexible environment from which you can perform enterprise analysis on your business as a whole. Developers, database analysts, and managers can build more complex queries, reports, and perform higher value analysis when all the company information is under one roof than they would be able to if it remained isolated within each business unit or team. When somebody asks a new question about the business, the information needed to answer it is already available in the warehouse; there's no need to find and integrate the data all over again. With all the data sitting in one place, the developers are freed to do higher-value work rather than create one-use tables for every business query that comes down the pike.

A note about terminology is probably warranted here. Some authorities give the term *data repository* more specific meaning than we have in this book; here it's been used as generic term for any place that stores data. In some circles, a data *repository* is considered an active operational system but a data *warehouse* is a storehouse of historical business information (that's the more stable and common definition). So the usual distinction looks like this:

- ✔ A data *warehouse* represents all the transactional events that make up the past, on which the parent company performs read-only activities such as running reports and statistical analyses.

- ✔ A data *repository* is a snapshot of the *present* (and perhaps the recent past); the company's transactional systems regularly update the data in the repository for specific tactical decision-support tasks.

An extended example

Sometimes a full example can help bring a business situation into sharper relief.

Wheels Automotive, Inc.

Imagine that Wheels Automotive is a car dealership that sells new and used cars to the public. You're the General Manager of Wheels; you need a better understanding of customer behavior, with the hope that you can identify your most profitable customers, and come up with some new sales and marketing strategies. You ask your IT department for a list of customers — and when they respond by asking you, "which list?"

With several parallel systems at Wheels containing customer and sales data, seemingly simple questions are hard to answer.

Let's imagine that the fictional dealership, like most companies in the real world, has evolved quite a bit in its 20-year history — first only offering new car sales, but eventually expanding into used cars, parts, service, and automotive financing. With the addition of each new line of business, the company added new information systems to support it. In addition to that, the salesmen use a shared Microsoft Access database to track sales prospects as they walk into the showroom or call to express interest in purchasing an automobile.

Figure 16-1 shows the multiple overlapping operational databases that track customer and/or sales information. They operate independently of one another, on a variety of platforms. A lot of the same information appears in more than one system; for example, nearly every database maintains information on customers for that line of business. But no single database has a complete view of the customer. If you wanted to see a list of a customer's entire transaction history with Wheels, you'd have to run several different reports (one or more in each system), then combine the results manually.

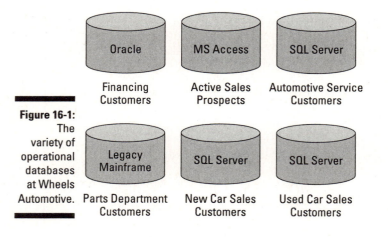

Figure 16-1:
The variety of operational databases at Wheels Automotive.

Oracle — Financing Customers

MS Access — Active Sales Prospects

SQL Server — Automotive Service Customers

Legacy Mainframe — Parts Department Customers

SQL Server — New Car Sales Customers

SQL Server — Used Car Sales Customers

Implementing a data warehouse at Wheels would take the operational information maintained on the dealership's six operational systems, and store it in one place, in a unified format, building a single historical record of the company's business history. That would give Wheels employees a single view of the activities across the entire company to work from in order to perform reporting and analysis tasks.

Figure 16-2 shows the desired configuration of the Wheels Automotive data warehouse: Each separate database feeds its relevant customer and sales information into a central data warehouse.

By moving the data from its different homes into a single repository we've achieved one single view of the customer base. Now, rather than making us scour through six different systems, the data warehouse shows every interaction with a particular customer by executing *one* query or compiling *one* report.

Now, if you look up a given customer of Wheels Automotive, the application would access the data warehouse to display the customer's profile information along with a list of every sales transaction involving that customer regardless of the department.

What you see in Figure 16-3 is a simplified version of the real data that would appear, and be stored, in a data warehouse. To keep complexity at bay while explaining the concepts, I've had to distill the customer and sales information into a basic format. A real car dealership would track detailed customer information (as would any business) — for example, e-mail, phone, census data, preferences, and other details, in addition to a mailing address. The sales transactions would also contain a far greater level of detail. But even without all the detail, the utility of a consolidated view of the customer should be clear:

- ✔ It allows for better operational decisions by the sales people when a customer walks in the door.

- ✔ Storing it in a data warehouse that's customized for reporting purposes, managers can build meaningful customer and sales reports in a fraction of the time it would take if anyone attempted to bridge the six operational systems for the same purpose.

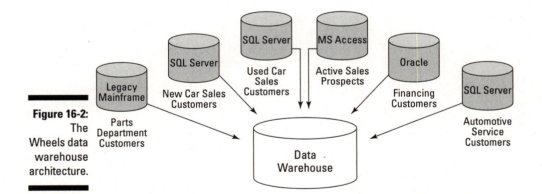

Figure 16-2:
The Wheels data warehouse architecture.

Figure 16-3:
A Wheels customer record in the data warehouse.

Eric Smith	909 Axton Ct.	Dallas	Texas	75022

Customer Sales Transactions

12/02/2004	Sales Project	2005 Ultimo LS	N/A
01/16/2005	New Car Sale	2005 Ultimo LS	$31,788.40
01/16/2005	Service	Ultimo-Extended Warranty	$1,125.00
04/01/2006	Parts	Wiper Blades	$19.94
09/21/2007	Service	30,000 Mile Checkup	$299.99
09/21/2009	Used Car Service	2007 Slider GT	$9,705.93

The challenge of unifying data

The data warehouse sounds good in theory, but in practice it's a little harder. For every live person who has ever transacted with Wheels Automotive, you want to eliminate duplication and store a single customer record. So part of building the data warehouse involves identifying situations where that single person is stored in more than one operational system.

To accomplish unification in the Wheels data warehouse, you have to compare the customer records in each database, combining those where you're sure the duplicate data relates to a single person. To start with, you have to sort the records into categories:

- Two or more identical records, where each of the data fields are exactly alike and likely relate to a single customer.

- Records where you can make an educated guess (or apply certain rules to come to a conclusion) that they relate to the same customer.

- Records that share a few characteristics and *might* be the same, but you can't be sure without further investigation.

Figure 16-4 shows the challenges of trying to match up information from disparate data sources to get to one version of the truth. Identical records can be treated as one person, but business rules must be thought through and then implemented on how to handle records that are not perfect matches.

This exercise is an example of what a data warehouse project team must do when it implements a single repository of customer data. If there are 100,000 duplicated names, your IT team will need to program the system with rules on how to combine them, since it would be too time-consuming to join the records manually. Note there are two records in the same database that *appear* to refer to the same customer: Gerald Z. Juarez. The person's name is unique enough to draw that conclusion, but how would you program a computer to make that judgment? The different addresses could simply mean the customer moved between visits to Wheels Automotive, that Mr. Juarez has two valid addresses, or that there are indeed two customers, each named Gerald Z. Juarez.

How does data get so confused in one small car dealership? It can happen in a number of ways. Wheels Automotive might have purchased the used-car business down the street and inherited their sales system. As business needs evolved over time and new systems were installed or upgraded, it's likely that the developers simply redefined data for each successive system. For example, when Wheels branched into the automotive-finance business, they had a vendor come in and build the supporting system from scratch, ignoring the existing database. Before long, the systems are completely fragmented and impossible to bring together. When you consider how a large enterprise faces similar choices with even greater volumes of data, you begin to see the value of the data-warehouse concept — and the challenges in implementing it.

Identical Records

Financial Database - Customer Record

Tedd Duncan	101 Marsh Avenue	Colleyville	Texas	76034

New Car Sales Database - Customer Record

Tedd Duncan	101 Marsh Avenue	Colleyville	Texas	76034

Closely Matching Records

New Car Sales Database - Customer Record

Christopher M Shope	7911 Windswept Ln	Dallas	Texas	75225

Parts Department Database - Customer Record

Chris Shope	7911 Windswept	Dallas	TX	75225

Questionably Matching Records

Parts Department Database - Customer Record

Gerald Z. Juarez	91801 W 30th Street	Boerne	TX	72009

Parts Department Database - Customer Record

Gerald Z. Juarez	615 Agincourt Drive	Berne	TX	72017

Figure 16-4: Challenges of unifying the Wheels Automotive customer data.

And if you're still not convinced, what we've reviewed so far is the simplest kind of data-standardization problem. Think about how complicated it can get with quantifiable information (say, sales and financial figures) when two different systems measure the same thing differently — or when two entire companies merge, each with entirely different data standards, definitions, and classification schemes for product and sales data.

The enormous complexity of wrangling corporate data is why the field of data analysis has grown so dramatically. If wringing insights out of historical data is important, you'll need someone on the team who knows exactly how to get the most out of disparate operational data. And since BI is a garbage-in garbage-out environment, bringing the data together correctly is the necessary inbound step to ensure the outbound results are (everyone) accurate, timely, high-value, and actionable.

Consolidating information across silos

Business intelligence requires a series of steps to crossreference the available data.

Data-analysis activities

Digging through the data from each individual source system to try to understand what information it contains and how it's stored and presented is the major design task associated with building a data warehouse. This is not the kind of analysis you'll do at the end of the BI chain, where the valuable insights start issuing forth from the front-end software. This analysis is the step that precedes *data integration* — standardizing and integrating data from different source systems.

In any scheme that involves a central collection point for data, you always run the risk that the owners of the source data will feel an acute loss of control and may offer resistance to scrutiny, if not outright hostility at the thought of changes to their system. That's where it helps to have strong *data governance* in an organization — a central authority that acts (in theory, at least) as a central data steward. With data governance in place, everyone in the company has to submit to the wishes of a central authority, a group (or person or set of standards) watching out for best interests of the company as a whole, and not one team or business unit.

To perform data integration, your analysts and architects have to reconcile data from across different operational silos of the business, make business decisions on how best to merge that data, then codify those decisions into hard and fast rules that can be applied to the data warehouse to deliver a unified view of the important objects of the business, such as sales transactions, customers, vendors, and just about anything else under the sun.

Integration of a company's master data often involves hub technologies that can access, cleanse, standardize, match, integrate, and propagate master data. Knowledge of master data management, the vendor options, and the architectures that support them are essential to enabling customer data integration (CDI).

The goal here is to develop a data-management strategy that gets the right knowledge into the hands of the right people. It has to be done securely and in a timely fashion. Oh, and the people who receive that data have to know what to do with it when they get their hands on it. In theory, their decisions will be better with a more complete vision of "the truth" (whatever that may be).

Data profiling

Before designing a consolidation plan, assemble a data profile of each source system. This usually involves a description of the relevant table structures, definitions of each field, and some statistical properties of the data (such as the record counts, the range of values found in each field, and other metrics the designers of the data warehouse use to develop a standardization process).

Common data-profile information includes the following characteristics as a starting point to cataloguing data:

- ✔ **Name and description:** Every element in every table should have a unique name in your data profile that relates to the specific field name used in system code. The data profile will also include a definition of the data's function and role — in non-technical language if possible and applicable.

- ✔ **Data type and validation rules:** Every value of a field must follow certain patterns and belong to a general domain of information. For example, the field NAME_F, which contains the first name of a person, will be a text field with a specific character limit.

- ✔ **Ownership and origin:** All data fields belong to a certain hierarchy that leads up through the table structure, the database, and application of origin. The key information here is understanding who sets policy on how the data is handled at the operational level — whether single manager or governance committee.

- ✔ **Relationships and business rules:** This important information comprises how the data fields and tables relate to one another in a business context, and what policies affect their values.

There's more information that can be captured, such as physical location of the data, security policies surrounding the information, usage details, and others that can be listed about source data. But there's no guarantee all or any of it will be available, so the data analyst is charged with doing the best he or she can.

For a large system with several operational data sources, profiling and analyzing the data can be a huge job. But it's an important one for a successful data-warehouse effort. This knowledge about existing operational data will provide guidance to the designers of the transformation and loading processes that come later.

The data analysts have to bridge the gap between the technical and the business worlds when they go through the integration process. They'll be connecting the two domains together with every decision they make. For example, when two customer records are being integrated, the data analyst must research and understand how company employees have input customer data historically. What process did they follow? Were there business rules that affected what information they recorded? Once they have a full understanding of the real-world processes, they can make a determination about the technical specifics for integrating the records.

These questions aren't as easy as they may first appear. What constitutes a customer anyway? If you restrict it to visitors to your store or website who have made at least one purchase over their lifetime, what happens to people

that are listed as prospects but who've never actually consummated a purchase? What if two otherwise identical records have different phone numbers?
In that case, the data analyst must make a determination about which one
"survives" (in that case the analyst would probably set up a rule to take the
phone number of the record that was edited most recently, assuming that
information exists in the system.) These are important questions and can
have far-reaching consequences for the business.

Structuring data to enable BI

If your data analysts do a good job for you, the data profile will provide a
complete picture of the state of your system's origin data. Now it's time to
get that data into a format that's usable for BI user applications.

You can't dump all the data you've just profiled into a data warehouse willy-
nilly. Once you know what you're dealing with in terms of source data, it's
time to work through the steps of cleansing and arranging it, then working
out how and where to store it, and in what form.

The user-facing systems that rely on the target data system will likely use some
combination of high-impact querying and reporting applications, statistical
packages, and possibly analysis and visualization software. The intended
uses for the data will actually go a long way to determining how you should
organize the data. You know where the data is coming from, and have a good
idea of the kinds of applications that will access it on the front end. These
applications will all have slightly different data-consumption needs, but
there are some standard parameters to keep in mind, as outlined in the
upcoming subsections.

The BI target data

The BI target database will have to be built for one-way performance — not
for storage efficiency. While operational databases work to normalize records
for rapid read/write operations, the data warehouse is there to feed queries
from front-end tools. Other than when operational data gets fed into it, the
data warehouse is a data *provider*, not a data *consumer*.

BI users will request information in formats that make sense to them, logically modeled on the business itself. So, rather than storing data in a way that
requires complicated queries for access, a data warehouse stores company
information in the same way knowledge workers actually think about the
business.

To perform advanced analyses, users will be thinking in terms of the familiar
business events and objects they're comfortable with: sales, products, customers, and stores. Users won't be thinking about confusing database

terminology like primary keys, cross-references, or the complicated `JOIN` statements required in SQL queries. Data must be made accessible to people who aren't database experts.

Designing an information hierarchy

When you think about the most important measurements to evaluate with your front-end systems, you'll probably focus on a series of simple facts and measurements. Good examples might be financial metrics — such as sales or gross margin — or utilization rates for resources, length of wait time for a customer-service center, or some other quantifiable metric that your company is trying to optimize.

Storing data in terms of *dimensions* makes it easier to retrieve for rapid querying and analysis for BI purposes; it allows users to search for facts according to their dimensions. For example, you can query the system for all sales transactions (facts) that included a certain product type (dimension) in a certain zip code (dimension). Storing data by dimensions is actually a closer approximation of the way people usually *think* about company data.

Each dimension is an aspect of an individual business event that describes or categorizes it in some way. Dimensions give events context and meaning. Combining facts with dimensions tells you what happened in the company under the exact conditions you specify.

As an example, consider a hypothetical railroad: passenger-carrying businesses typically measure their efficiency through a metric unique to their industry, known as passenger-miles (P/M). One P/M is a single paying passenger traveling one mile aboard a train operated by the company. So a train with 100 people on board that traveled 50 miles gets entered into the system as 5000 P/M. Normally the railroad would then use that figure as a denominator for some other measurement, such as revenue for the trip, the cost of operating the train, or the amount of fuel used. Each calculation gives some insight into the operating efficiency of the railroad.

At the most granular level, the railroad would look at a particular train trip between two cities, take the number of paying passengers, and multiply it by the number of miles to come up with the P/M for that trip.

The railroad might then want to measure P/M by several different aspects of its operations, starting with that same level of detail — these, for example:

- ✔ **By time:** Total P/M for the day, which adds up to P/M for the week, and on up to the month and the year.

- ✔ **By geography:** P/M between any two cities within a region, all combinations of which add up to the regional P/M figure. All regional P/M figures add up to the national P/M measurement.

✔ **By locomotive type:** P/M for a specific locomotive, PM for locomotives of the same type, PM for locomotives of the same family: electric versus diesel or, perhaps, steam (just for fun).

The list of "By" measurements is only limited by the number of dimensions you store. And any dimension could have a hierarchical quality to it — like the three dimensions shown here, where individual measurements can be grouped into successively more general ones.

Arranging data hierarchically in the data-storage environment makes it much faster and easier to get more meaningful chunks of information for users. In an operational environment, these hierarchies have to be calculated manually, and put through complex, costly (in terms of processing speed) database commands.

Aggregation is the general term that describes how data can be summarized at different levels of hierarchical detail. A data warehouse should support "rolled-up" calculations for a hierarchy of values for every dimension. In the preceding example, that capability would allow the user to query the data warehouse for broad swathes of data, such as the P/M in the East Region, for the entire month of June. Even though the you could see P/M measurements in much finer detail if you wanted to, aggregation and summarization capabilities provide quick response time for more general queries.

A word about Master Data Management

A host of buzzwords float around the concept of enterprise-wide data-management practices. One of the more common ones you'll see is *Master Data Management (MDM)*.

MDM is a concept that involves an enterprise-wide approach to ensuring consistency of meaning and quality of all company data. While that idea is consonant with data warehousing and BI target databases, it goes beyond simply integrating a few domains of data for reporting and analysis. MDM efforts are aimed at creating one version of "the truth" across all systems — not just in the data warehouse, but also in the operational environments, the Enterprise Resource Planning (ERP) modules, and anywhere else in the company where information is being handled.

MDM is meant to touch systems and environments that have nothing to do with your BI project, or the data warehouse you're creating to support it. What happens, in many cases, is the BI team adopts the MDM cause because BI projects require a level of data standardization across the enterprise. Once the team has gone through the various obstacles and created a single picture of company information for the data warehouse, other entities in the company begin asking about going through the same standardization process in *their* areas. The assumption is that the mantle of responsibility for MDM rests with the BI or data warehousing team. In theory, though, MDM should come first as a broad company goal, the achievement of which would make data warehousing — and BI — much easier.

Data derivation is another feature of data warehouses. It's certainly not a unique concept to BI target systems, but it's still an important one. A *derived* fact is an atomic (indivisible, highly specific) piece of data that doesn't exist per se in the source data. The data warehouse creates it with a prearranged formula based on a combination of original data elements.

As an example, a large computer-hardware manufacturer may not track gross margin on every component transaction in any of its individual source systems. But a developer may be able to derive that important measurement from existing data. The developer might create a formula based on figures from two different systems:

- ✔ sale price from the CRM system
- ✔ cost-of-goods-sold figures from the supply-chain database

Subtracting one from the other yields the required margin-by-component measurement. The data warehouse would be programmed to perform the calculation to derive that margin figure and store it in a pre-arranged table, where it would then be available for analysts to see in reports and analyses.

If the BI target database were a rock group, it would play nothing but cover tunes. No original songs would be on the set list. The BI target database is a repository for information that exists in other systems. Sure, there may be derived data, and some fields might be transformed to make the underlying information easier to understand or more accessible. But at the most basic level, there should be *no new facts or events* recorded in a BI target system that aren't already in an operational database somewhere else.

Data quality

Poor data quality undermines the value of information and causes users and stakeholders to distrust the applications that rely on it. Part of preparing the data for use by a BI application is going through checks to ensure the data's quality.

It's logical to demand stringent data-entry standards as protection against poor data quality. For example, if customers are being entered into the system without Zip codes, you could implement an application update that would disallow the entry unless a full five digit Zip was entered. While it sounds good in theory, the reality is that it could cause unintended consequences. Harried data-entry clerks (for example) could circumvent the rules by entering in 00000 as a Zip code, or put in some other nonsense 5-digit number, to make it easier on themselves. Data-entry standards should certainly play a part, but they should be carefully designed — and they're no substitute for a back-end data-quality process.

Data Models

After the source data has been analyzed, categorized, and profiled, it's time to move on to designing the BI target database. The first step in the construction of any database is choosing a *data model*: the set of rules and constraints for how information will be organized and filed away in a database. We're talking about logical storage here, not physical storage — the database-management system handles most of that without you having to worry about it.

A model helps us understand the real world by presenting a fat-free version of it. The model represents the data — which in turn represents the business entities and relationships that populate the real world. But since the real world is a complicated place, the data can sometimes be exceptionally complicated. To be effective, your model must share enough characteristics with the real thing to acts as an accurate representation while at the same time boil down its essential qualities so steam doesn't come out of your ears when you think about it.

The data model will guide how your target database will store and arrange information. That means it's a good idea to put the model through the paces during design so that it can handle all the information needs that could arise.

In designing your data model — and therefore your data itself — you're constantly making trade-offs between reality and usability. If you make the data model too simple, you may be hiding important complexities of the real business operations. But if you make the data model too complex, your users won't understand it, and as a result won't be able to use the front-end applications to their fullest extent — and then you can wave bye-bye to all those great business insights you dreamed of.

Dimensional data model

A *dimensional* data model represents business processes and events, such as sales, or shipments, or factory output.

Fact tables and dimensions

Most data warehouses use the dimensional model in the preceding railroad example, where information orbits around measurable facts like sales numbers. Those important facts occupy the central position in the database, occupying a table from which the rest of the information radiates.

The database stores those central facts in a table known (curiously enough) as a *fact table*. Each row in a fact table is a basic, atomic unit in the database. Database designers are charged with deciding not only what the key facts are, but also with deciding how granular they want to make the fact table. For example, if you're measuring financial performance, make some measure of sales serve as your fact. The designers will then decide whether each row in the table represents a single line-item from a transaction, a single transaction, a daily total of transactions for each store location, or some other aggregation of sales information.

The second key pillar of a dimensional model is how dimensions (particular aspects of a fact) are chosen, categorized, and stored. Dimensions are the different ways you can filter facts, such as sales *by sales person*, sales *by product type*, or sales *by time period*. If sales are the core measures in the fact table, a dimension would tell you something *about* that dollar amount. For example, you might run the following query:

```
Show total sales by state
```

Here geography is the dimension, since you've queried the system to break the sales down by state. If you queried the system to show you total sales by zip code, you would *still* be querying along the geographical dimension, but you'd be slicing the same sales data along slightly different lines. The core facts would be the same, but the dimensional model allows you to break it into pieces in whatever way is useful to you.

Benefits of the dimensional model

The great thing about the dimensional model is that data is stored the way people think. The fact tables are the key measurement of the company's performance that we're trying to measure — whether it's sales, seat-miles, or minutes on hold. And the dimensions are all possible influences on those measures.

Normalized data, on the other hand, is not arranged in a way that reflects how people usually think. That's what makes dimensional data so useful; it doesn't have to be stored in some arcane, secret, programmers-only code. Regular people can query the database and feel comfortable that the results will be just what they asked for in the first place. That's not a trivial benefit; it boosts user satisfaction with the front-end tools, and it brings workers closer to those all-important BI insights.

There are other benefits as well:

- Not only is the data more intuitive for users who will create queries and reports, but it also makes the data warehouse easy to understand for developers. That's good for the construction time and helps with maintenance as well.

- Intuitive dimensional data is important to the BI architect too, because reporting tools and advanced analytics and statistical packages are pre-wired to work in that kind of environment, making new tool integration easier.

✔ Unifying the data from the operational data sources into a single model lends itself to a dimensional model if each system is focused around the same function.

✔ Query speed can be improved. Rather than requiring extremely complex table joins, the dimensional model allows simpler, more direct operations to filter out only the rows required by the requester.

✔ The dimensional model has a flexible schema — although it's not necessarily easy to do, you *can* add more facts and dimensions without having to rebuild the database.

Downside of the dimensional model

Data *normalization* reduces redundancy in databases as a way to improve storage efficiency and reduce the potential for data inconsistency and errors. Those negatives can potentially come into play with the dimensional model. Many of the data-integrity enforcement rules inherent in a relational data model are thrown out the window in a dimensional model. Result: A *whole lot of data* ends up getting stored.

Multidimensional star wars

There are two primary models for storing dimensional data: star schemas and snowflake schemas. Each has its good points and bad points. Data professionals inevitably have a strong opinion as to which is best for the data warehouse they're administering.

Star schema

The star schema is the basic manifestation of the dimensional data model. It has two levels of data and two levels only — facts and dimensions. It's called a star schema because the central fact table has any number of dimensions radiating out from it that offer aspects of the information described in the fact table.

Figure 16-5 is a simple representation of the tables in a star schema. The central event being measured is the sales information stored in the SALE FACT table. The information in the four attached dimension tables is there to describe the most specific sales transactions.

The *star schema* allows analysts to measure facts from a variety of perspectives limited only to the number of dimensions stored along with them. It's a popular way to store data in a data warehouse because it mimics the way users often think of business information.

For example, if analysts are looking for insight on the performance of different retail stores in a given region, they would essentially be asking to see all the individual sales transactions that met the criteria of their query — calculated together. The fact tables in a star schema represent just that — a long list of individual transactions (whatever they might be) that can be filtered and brought together according to the information that describes them.

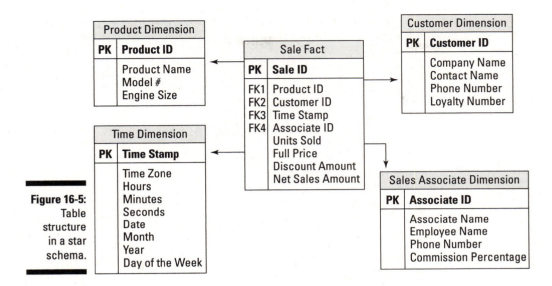

Figure 16-5:
Table
structure
in a star
schema.

This data model is the most popular in use in data warehouses that feed BI applications. It's easy for developers and end-users to comprehend, which makes databases built with a star schema easy to create, maintain, and use.

One dimension you almost always find in a star schema is time; data warehouses are built to provide insight into historical performance of company events. Inevitably, one of the standard ways that analysts look at data is by looking at it across defined time periods. That's important because it shows historical trends, and allows you to make inferences about the past and its effects on the future.

Snowflake schema

The *snowflake schema* is closely related to the star schema in that the data model is centered on a central fact table. But it handles dimensions a little bit differently; some dimensions are normalized to save space and reduce redundancy.

The snowflake schema has become popular because it is said to use the best of both worlds. The core information is dimensional, making the data model easier to understand and access; but rather than storing certain detail information over and over again, it takes advantage of normalized tables in some parts of the database.

What the snowflake schema gains in data redundancy and flexibility, it loses in terms of complexity. That means it's harder for data analysts and administrators to maintain and tune than a snowflake structure.

Figure 16-6 shows the table structure of a snowflake schema. Like a star schema, it's organized around a central fact table that contains some essential piece of information about the company. And it's also surrounded by dimensions. The difference is that the dimensions of a star schema are broken into normalized hierarchies to save space and reduce redundancy.

Other kinds of data models

In data warehouses, dimensional models are the name of the game. But there are approaches other than the star and snowflake schema.

Normalized schema

Relational databases use *normalized* schema, where every effort is made to store information once only.

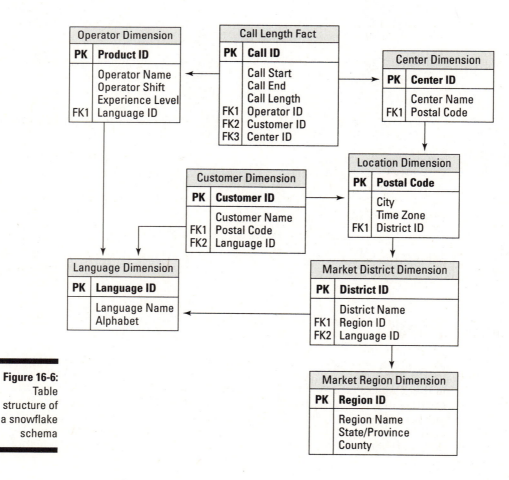

Figure 16-6:
Table structure of a snowflake schema

This makes good sense when you're trying to maintain tight data integrity and use minimum storage space. It's also the right way to go for transactional systems where programs need quick response times when accessing, modifying, and writing records.

Hybrid models

Although data-storage systems usually go one way or the other, sometimes it makes sense to use a blended approach — a normalized schema for one domain of data, and a dimensional model for another domain.

Whether this approach works depends on the nature of the queries you plan to run against the data warehouse. A combination of normalized and dimensional constructs must be perfectly compatible with the kinds of queries you plan to run for your schema to work well. Most experts agree that's a rare occurrence. You have to ask the questions a certain way, and the data must be related in the real world just so. Let your data architects guide you in this decision; just make sure you supply them with enough information to think it through. In addition to determining the structure of the data and the queries you're planning to run, ask these questions:

- ✔ What's more important — system performance or ease of use and maintenance?
- ✔ How flexible does the system need to be?
- ✔ Can the software to be connected to the data warehouse support a hybrid data model?
- ✔ Is anything changing in the future that might force us to run different queries than we anticipated?

There's no sure-fire right answer with data models. Don't squeeze your data into a dimensional model if it's a square peg in a round hole. If the data you're modeling is too complex (whether from the source system, the processes, or a combination of the two), it may be impossible to apply a dimensional model to the business objects and measures. Start with what you have and work out which model works best. Don't start with a model in mind and work backward.

Data Marts

Imagine your company implemented a data warehouse that collected customer and sale transaction information from every division and subsidiary in the business. That should be very useful; throughout the entire enterprise, the data warehouse offers a unified, integrated view of information. But say the market research department wants to access that data and run a specific kind of predictive-analytics application against the information stored in the data warehouse. The company might institute a *data mart* for the marketing team. Several definitions for data marts exist in the BI landscape, but the most commonly accepted one is a single-domain data aggregation used for reporting, analysis, or decision-support. Data marts vary in their architecture; they may receive data from data warehouses, or directly from transactional systems. They may perform transformations and calculations on the data similar to data warehouses. But data marts are always limited in their scope and business purpose.

For example, you might have a data mart that services the point-of-sale system in your business. The fact tables in your data mart that you'd want to query and report from would be sales transaction information, such as the amount of each sale, the line items (such as SKU number), and if any discount was applied to the sale. Those basic facts could be connected to a number of dimensions stored along with the transaction data. The dimensions for transaction data might be time information, store information, and which cashier completed the sale.

Data marts can be great for more casual users without the same level of expertise as a regular or power user of advanced tools. Merge high-level information on a single functional topic into a data mart environment and leave out the detail that you might offer to more experienced users. For example, the CEO might want high-level views of sales information without having to operate a complicated reporting tool or write complex queries.

One danger of modeling every business process/event is that you could end up with many disparate, unrelated data marts. Each data mart will function effectively and answer specific business questions in its domain. Each data mart's value to the organization, however, will be restricted; questions can't be answered across different functions of the business.

Operational Data Stores

This may surprise you, but an *operational data store* (ODS) is designed to integrate and store . . . wait for it . . . operational data for reporting and analysis purposes. Your organization may have need to take snapshots of current operational data that can be made available and examined to support tactical functions such as decision-support processes or reporting of some kind. Because data warehouses are designed as keepers of the historical record, they may not be able to respond fast enough to meet tactical needs. If that's the case, an ODS may be for you.

Business intelligence is about delivering insights that are, among other things, timely. An ODS can help ensure that insights are delivered in time to act on them by delivering up-to-the second views of operational data.

An ODS functions like a data warehouse: different systems around the company feed it operational information which it processes into a homogenous form so analysts and report-writers can get one single view of the information.

Unlike a data warehouse, however, the ODS is not meant to maintain a vast historical record of information. The information in an ODS is meant to be a current (or at least very recent) view of the company's operations. That gives businesses a chance to do instant analysis to react to a given situation.

Many companies use the ODS as a staging area for the data warehouse. The integration logic and processes reside on the operational data store. That way the incoming data is transformed properly for smooth integration. Then, on a regular basis, the data warehouse takes the current batch of data from the ODS and adds it to the existing historical data already in the system.

Chapter 17

BI Products and Vendors

*F*or project managers and BI project sponsors planning a new business intelligence initiative, selecting the software to power the environment is one of the biggest choices of the implementation.

The good news is the industry has matured; a host of powerful, capable choices await the application evaluator. There are general-purpose applications, specialty applications, all-in-one packages, and cafeteria-style plans. The software industry has risen to the demand for good BI tools that can dig up those business insights that are (you know the mantra) accurate, timely, high-value, and actionable.

All those choices can be a little overwhelming, so this chapter surveys the current state of the software industry as it relates to business intelligence. That state is always changing, and not always easy to define.

This book is accurate as of the completion of the manuscript. But if the past is any indication, several major acquisitions will take place the moment the book goes to print, and the entire industry landscape will change overnight.

The BI software market is notoriously dynamic. There are niche players who pop into existence and make a name for themselves in one specialty. *Pure-play* vendors specialize in creating products for a single business purpose — in this case, BI. Then there are the large software vendors who made their mark outside of BI. As they try to get in on the lucrative business intelligence software market, they often buy up smaller players to complete their BI product portfolio. Complicating it all is the shifting landscape of product features and corporate needs. Important functionality currently packaged in a larger application suite may be spun off tomorrow as a standalone product. What I'm saying is *caveat lector* — reader beware!

Overview of BI Software

Everyone defines the boundaries of the marketplace a little bit differently. For the purposes of this book, we define the BI market as an aspect of everything in the technology stack — from the operational data to the user-facing tools that spit out those valuable insights:

- ✔ Database-management systems (DBMS)
- ✔ Data-integration tools
  - • ETL (extract, transform, load) tools
  - • Data warehouse tools
- ✔ Querying, Reporting-and-analysis tools
  - • Ad-hoc queries
  - • Enterprise report management
  - • Notification and messenger services
  - • OLAP and other analysis
- ✔ Other front-end tools
  - • Data-mining and analytics
  - • Visualization tools (dashboards, scorecards, graphics)
- ✔ Access tools (portals, mobile access)

It's been said many times many ways in this book, but it's worth saying again: There is no such thing as a one-size-fits-all solution in BI software. Some companies try to touch every space, but there is no one company whose product does everything *well*.

Don't become too enamored with these labels. Ask different BI experts and they'll give you a different family tree for business intelligence-related software. But you have to start somewhere, right?

The dimensional model

Among every main BI group, the software BI software can be thought of along five major qualitative (or semi-qualitative) dimensions. I haven't included price because it's a given that you must evaluate every resource for your project along the lines of how the dollars and cents fit into the project budget.

✔ **Feature set:** Can this application do precisely what I need it to do when installed in my environment? Different software vendors focus on different functionality, so just because you're looking at two different OLAP tools doesn't mean you're getting exactly the same thing.

✔ **Compatibility:** Will this application work with others? BI tools up and down the technology stack by their very nature must interact well with the other kids who already live on the block. But that doesn't mean they're all best friends. This is extremely important because most companies already have a data environment of some kind that their BI tools must conform to.

✔ **Packaging:** What does the software vendor put into a single release of their BI software? You might get everything you need with one set of licenses; then again, you may be purchasing off the *á la carte* menu.

✔ **Performance:** How fast can it handle the volumes of data I'll be throwing at it? And if that number goes up dramatically in the future, will the software be able to grow with it?

✔ **Ease of use:** Closely related to how much training and support you'll get from the software vendor. Some companies are out to make money on their software licenses, others on their support. Make sure you account for both when you select your software.

What makes choosing software a little bit easier for most folks involved in BI projects is the fact that they often don't have a lot of choices. It's not that there aren't a wide range of products on the market; quite the contrary in fact. The problem, or rather the reality, of most projects and companies is that they dictate a certain set of features by their very nature.

Working together

The compatibility dimension is the first thing that BI professionals think of when considering a new installation or an upgrade; the software you install must work with the data currently *in* the system, and it must speak *to* the system.

The last ten years have seen a lot of progress in standards, which has opened up the market. Almost all products can speak some form of the standard known as *Open Database Connectivity (ODBC)*, which translates requests and responses to a database system into a kind of lingua franca available to all. Vendors are publishing *application programming interfaces* (APIs) that allow developers to access a product's functions in code. The Extensible Markup Language (XML) standard has been important — and the continued proliferation of the World Wide Web itself (along with the advent of the browser as a productivity tool) has spurred this process along.

Even though these standards are established, nothing is universally compatible. And the concept of compatibility is far from attaining the checklist-like simplicity that we all wish for it. In practice (for example), applications that store data in XML may not work with another XML-based system.

Mixing vendors to get just the right set of features — or to create an overall solution that's in the right price range for your budget — is a good plan. But you'd better have the experts on hand to make all those supposedly-compatible components work together.

Even when you find the right product or vendor that sits at the perfect intersection of price and your required qualitative dimensions, you may have to narrow down the field still more. Companies often mandate certain standards, or may have pre-existing relationships with certain vendors; if yours does, then there's another set of restrictions that your project team has to adhere to.

The BI Software Marketplace

The BI software marketplace is populated by companies of all shapes and sizes. Among the market leaders are familiar names such as Microsoft and Oracle, but also smaller pure-play BI companies such as Business Objects. Additionally, there are niche players who perform a single function very well, along with vertical specialists: companies that focus on BI for a particular industry.

A little history

The origins of today's multibillion-dollar business intelligence software market are humble and scattered. The disciplines that came, went, metamorphosed, changed names, and came back again almost always began with niches of innovators inside companies looking to squeeze some knowledge from all that data. No wonder the companies that formed the early BI marketplace were, like their adopters and champions, niche players.

The early days of BI — in its various forms — evolved with smaller companies creating islands of technology; their number-one concern was winning in a competitive niche. That meant offering high-performance and feature-rich products (as defined by their market) rather than being flexible. Instead of offering universal compatibility, the small BI vendors would build their packages to work well with one core database system.

That all changed as client-server networks grew in popularity, and eventually gave way to the Internet and World Wide Web. Software became more modular. As companies began to mix-and-match their BI components, interactivity and compatibility became more important.

Mergers and acquisitions

The BI software marketplace is like a shark tank, with small fish swimming for their lives and eventually *doing one thing well enough* (ironically) to get them eaten by a larger fish. That larger fish then gets eaten by an even larger fish, and so on until there are fewer competitors in the market.

Big fish, small fish

In recent years, the shape of the market has been set by the acquisitive nature of the big business software vendors: Microsoft, Oracle, IBM, and SAP. At the same time, the pure-play BI vendors have not rested on their laurels; they continue to buy up competitors and complementary players to improve their standing in the market.

The acquisitions cascade upward. In the BI arena, often the mid-sized companies (such as Hyperion, Cognos, and Business Objects) have been the market leaders up and down the BI technology stack. With the exception of the database arena, the major software companies have played only a minor, but increasing, role in the marketplace. The mid-market companies have taken aim at the other medium-size and small players in the market, buying them up to round out their BI portfolios. In recent years the software giants have gotten into the game, entering the BI market in one fell swoop with the acquisition of a mid-size player.

Build versus buy

The generic decision for any company, in any domain, is *build versus buy*. If the company recognizes a feature or function that it needs for one of its products, or for use internally, it has a choice to make: either take the time to write the code, or purchase an existing product from another company. There are pros and cons to each:

- ✔ **Build:** If a vendor creates a homegrown solution, you can rest easy knowing that the new feature will usually be perfectly compatible with its existing portfolio of products and solutions. The downside, of course, is that the solution you get won't be as evolved as a mature BI product. That's because it takes time to gain the expertise and experience required to produce a great product. It takes years of hard work, innovation, multiple releases, and (sometimes) costly mistakes for software to evolve and improve before it's acceptable to the market.

- ✔ **Buy:** If a vendor spots a hole in its portfolio, or if its people believe their own product is at a disadvantage in the market, they can just buy an existing player to catch up quickly. A perfect example came in 2003 when Business Objects bought Crystal Decisions, then a leading provider of reporting applications (something B.O. didn't do at the time). The downside to this approach is that you can't automatically assume that your company's products will work well together with those of the acquired company. Oracle (for example) has gone through ravenous phases in its BI growth — but all that gobbling-up has sometimes left the company with a confusing set of products with overlapping functionality.

✔ **Kill:** Oops, there's always this *third* option available to software vendors: Buy your competitor and then shutter the company, leaving your own product to dominate the market. Often a competitor's product has a few redeeming features worth cannibalizing. Oracle has used this approach multiple times in the enterprise resource-planning (ERP) realm — buying competitors, absorbing their products' features, and then slowly transitioning their customer base to Oracle products. From the perspective of a BI software purchaser, you have to be aware that this is always a possibility for the product you buy.

As an interim solution, many vendors will *partner* with a complementary vendor as a way to please their customer base. Microsoft, lacking an analytics package of its own, did this for years with Comshare and a few other vendors of powerful analytical reporting packages. Partnering can mean a simple marketing relationship where the two companies cooperate on acquiring customers, or building a technical relationship to ensure that code from each application is well integrated, or some form of co-operation between those two extremes.

You shouldn't have to do it, but it's a reality of the BI marketplace: When you decide to go with a particular BI vendor, it's a good idea to do both a product analysis *and* a market analysis. Make sure no red flags are flapping in the breeze on either front. Is the company trying to sell you products it recently acquired? (If so, how well does it know its new products?) Is the company a candidate for a takeover? (If so, are they in a position to guarantee ongoing support for their product?)

Sure, you should do this with all major purchases . . . heck, before you buy that vacuum cleaner, you might as well check the company history. But the BI market is especially quixotic, so keep the eyes peeled for warning signs. Just a taste of recent acquisitions in and around the BI world in the past few years:

✔ Hyperion bought Brio

✔ Oracle bought Hyperion

✔ Oracle bought IRI

✔ Business Objects bought Crystal Decisions

✔ Business Objects bought Cartesis

✔ Microsoft bought ProClarity

✔ Actuate bought EII

- ✔ Ascential bought Mercator
- ✔ IBM bought Alphablox
- ✔ SAP bought Pilot
- ✔ SAP bought Outlooksoft

Figure 17-1 shows how the BI software market breaks down. Nobody does everything well, not even Microsoft and Oracle.

Major Software Companies in BI

As business intelligence and its related disciplines have become more engrained in the processes of corporations, major software companies that already supply productivity and data tools have reacted by offering BI tools of their own.

The result is that platform vendors like Microsoft and SAP have become major players on the BI scene. In some cases, their applications have been organically grown — planned and produced by the company's own development team. In other cases, the major company fills out its toolbox by buying the company that created the product it needs.

Figure 17-1: Overview of the BI software marketplace (valid for today only!)

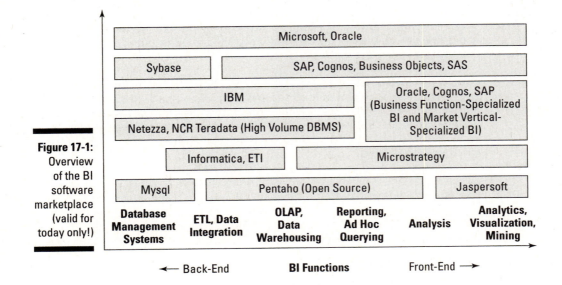

Bundles of joy

Major software companies operate a bit differently in how they deliver BI to the marketplace than do the pure-play vendors.

A company like Microsoft or Oracle has a gigantic existing install base of customers using other pieces of its business software. The two companies, along with a handful of others, dominate the enterprise database market. That gives them leverage when it comes to markets they are not traditionally strong in. And that was the case with BI just a few years ago.

BI vendors strategically bundle components of their software together depending on how they see the needs of the marketplace. That's good news for many project owners because it means they often have software licenses already in-house. For example, if your IT department owns Microsoft SQL Server licenses, some of the most important BI tools are included with that product. No need to buy anything extra; you have it already.

The only downside is that this approach can make it difficult to evaluate products side by side. And if the budget winds are blowing just so, it means you might end up having to use a product simply because it's already in-house, instead of purchasing a different product that has the capabilities you actually need.

Oracle

Oracle, already a heavy player in the core database and enterprise resource planning (ERP) space, is a formidable presence on the BI market landscape. Oracle offers integrated BI with its transactional and ERP applications — for example, the balanced scorecards and analytics built into its Supply Chain package.

Oracle, like Microsoft, has a presence up and down the BI technology stack. Oracle CEO Larry Ellison follows the same philosophy with BI as with other software niches: convince customers that integration is a headache and that getting a unified, single-vendor platform (and perhaps sacrificing a little in some areas) is superior to taking a best-of-breed approach that might require extensive integration.

Oracle's dedicated data-warehouse solutions include Warehouse Builder and the Oracle BI Enterprise Edition (essentially the old Siebel analytics platform, swallowed in an acquisition), plus platforms for building and integrating customer BI solutions. Then there's the PeopleSoft performance-management application and Hyperion's Essbase OLAP solutions that have been integrated.

If that sounds like a lot of moving parts, it is. One of the chief complaints about Oracle's approach to BI is that they've been so acquisitive over the years — and have so many parallel and specialty offerings — that it's difficult to navigate through their entire menu of offers without losing your way. Each new acquisition means the software giant has to undertake an integration effort that can take years.

Oracle plans to join all these moving parts together in 2008 in a product suite called Oracle Fusion, which will merge the enterprise applications, database technology, BI features, and other goodies underneath an umbrella of unified middleware.

The Business Intelligence Suite will feature the following sub-products in various states of bundling:

- ✔ Dashboard
- ✔ Answers (querying, reporting, analysis)
- ✔ Delivers (messaging and alerts)
- ✔ Publisher (reporting distribution and routing)
- ✔ Essbase Analytics (universal OLAP)
- ✔ Disconnected Analytics
- ✔ Warehouse Builder (ETL, data quality, metadata management)

Oracle products are expensive, and their BI wares are no exception. The BI Suite Enterprise Edition costs $1,500 per named user or $225,000 per server processor. The good news is that it works with other data sources; if you don't have enough scratch left over to build your solution over an Oracle database, you can use something cheaper and still expect it to work.

The next generation of Oracle's products will be called 11g, will feature a more event-driven architecture, and will be out in late 2008. BI professionals will be keeping an eye on it for further integration of the multiple platforms — and clarity on some of the dueling technology tracks (for example, there are two OLAP platforms and two data-warehouse approaches). In addition, Oracle will be making a major upgrade to its scorecard application. Of course, all of that is subject to change.

Microsoft

Bill Gates's little Washington-based outfit has a habit of being disruptive when it enters a new market. At first Microsoft plays nice with the competition as it builds its comfort level; then it stretches out on the couch and starts making itself at home.

Gates's vision includes managing information better (whether starting with too much or too little) — and that's just what his company is doing. After starting slowly, Microsoft is now one of the biggest players in the BI marketplace, thanks to its popular enterprise database product, SQL Server.

Microsoft Office

Office sits on most business personal computers in the world — providing a natural environment for front-end BI. Specifically, Microsoft has built Excel into a powerful BI tool; in particular, these features are very BI-friendly:

- ✔ Excel acts as a query-and-analysis engine through advanced pivot table features.

- ✔ Excel offers an attractive reporting and visualization engine for nearly any kind of data environment.

- ✔ Worksheet functionality can now be embedded in other places outside Excel, through the increasingly important SharePoint middleware package.

 Pivot tables have been helping knowledge workers perform BI functions for years, and they're better than ever in Office 2007. Even Microsoft's new conditional formatting options can add significant value to BI activities: when pivot tables are more easily understood, they're more likely to produce business insights.

SQL Server

Microsoft is scheduled to unveil its next-generation database product SQL Server 2008, sometime in mid-to-late (well, yeah) 2008. Microsoft's flagship DBMS has been under intense development to improve business intelligence capabilities in some key areas:

- ✔ **Unstructured data management:** This is one of the many "next frontiers" of information integration and exploitation. It's easy to add up sales figures and make the most use of them, but how can companies gain key insights from non-numerical data?

- ✔ **Visualization:** Microsoft enhanced visualization capabilities in its reporting package by licensing code from a reporting-visualization specialty firm (Dundas Data Visualization), which contributes mapping and charting capabilities to the next generation.

Those features are in addition to the standard SQL Server BI fare:

- ✔ **Integration Services:** Known for years as Data Transformation Services (DTS), this is Microsoft's ETL tool.

- ✔ **Analysis Services:** Offering OLAP and data mining services, taking advantage of Microsoft's so-called Unified Data Model.

- ✔ **Reporting Services:** A robust reporting creation and communication tool offered for the first time with SQL Server 2005

- ✔ **Presentation Tools:** Microsoft's use of ProClarity dashboard and visualization software give Bill Gates & Co. an enterprise-class front-end toolkit for the first time.

Did Mr. Gates mention he wanted to be your one-stop business intelligence vendor? If he didn't yet, he will soon.

SAP

SAP is the world's leading Enterprise Resource Platform (ERP) vendor, and because of that it takes a bit of a different perspective on BI.

SAP offers its Business Warehouse and other BI-related tools as part of larger technology bundles, rather than as stand-alone products. The only companies using SAP BI tools are the ones already using their ERP software.

IBM

Unlike Oracle and Microsoft, Big Blue is more into the partner game than anything else, focusing on its core DB2 database management platform and Websphere application server as the platform from which to stack BI offerings. Rather than taking competitors on in head-on collisions like the other big vendors occasionally do, IBM has nurtured relationships with software companies in better position to immediately help their customers.

DB2 is IBM's core DBMS. It can be purchased in a data-warehouse setup called DB2 Warehouse Edition (9.1 is the most recent version). This offers developers tools for creating integrated data flows, data mining, and analytics — all through its Alphablox and Cubeviews packages (both products of former acquisitions).

IBM had a long-standing relationship with Hyperion and its Essbase OLAP product, giving it a solid partner in the multidimensional analytics market space. But that partnership petered out in 2005, which left IBM seeming a little rudderless. Since then, they've taken more aggressive moves in the middle of the BI stack, including the purchase of data-integration vendor DataMirror Technology in mid-2007.

Pure-Play BI Vendors

In the business intelligence kingdom, specialist companies, who built only BI products, were sovereign for a long time. Although their reign is giving way to the major powers, it's also true that pure-play vendors still have a major part to play in the evolution of BI. They continue to be at the edge of innovation, being more nimble and less risk-averse.

In terms of investment protection, going with a pure-play vendor can offer some comfort, provided the company is in good shape financially. If it's not, you run the risk of your vendor going bankrupt. On the other hand, if the company is marginally healthy, and the product is a good match for your needs, you're probably safe. If the company is acquired by a competitor or a platform vendor, chances are your favorite application will survive in some form.

Indispensable qualities

The goal of integrating a pure-play vendor is to have it behave as if it's a perfectly molded part of your system; as powerful as it needs to be to handle whatever your volume of data, but giving a richness of features that's often not available from larger packaged software. Here's a checklist to start with:

- ✔ **Compatibility with major databases:** This above all: to thy database be true. And for that matter, the pure-play application should be able to speak with OLAP services, major applications, and Web services.

- ✔ **Platform flexibility:** Does it work in a Windows, Linux, or Unix environment?

- ✔ **Output options:** Do their products take advantage of common browsers? Or do they function best as desktop applications for a data-rich, interactive experience?

- ✔ **Application scalability:** To play in the mid-sized and enterprise market, the niche players have to be able to handle reams of data, and do so with speed and grace.

- ✔ **Support:** The vendor should be prepared to support the application with training hours, consulting hours, classes, certification, and/or a body of literature if necessary. If not, it had better be *very* easy to install and maintain.

So before buying, ask yourself these questions:

- ✔ Start with the product above all — is it superior to the competition? Don't limit yourself to the big boys.

- ✔ What is the industry whispering about it in trade magazines and at conferences?

- ✔ Is the product an essential part of their technology stack? Or is it duplicated somewhere along the way, making it potentially unnecessary?

- ✔ Do the vendor's sales team talk about the product at length? Are they knowledgeable and willing to answer your questions? Or do they nudge you onto some other topic?

- ✔ Is the vendor financially healthy?

✔ Are you comfortable with the vendor's BI roadmap over the next 18 months to two years?

This is a big decision. Get help as you need it, both inside and outside the team. A bad decision now could cascade for years and years . . . like a water-fall of shame.

Vendors by strong suit

The following pure-play BI vendors are described according to each one's strongest play in the three main subject areas moving from back to front: database, ETL, and all front-end players lumped together.

Other database and data-warehouse players

Some of the smaller vendors have come up with some impressive database and data-warehouse products. Here's a taste of what they offer.

NCR Teradata

NCR Teradata — Teradata actually has a fairly comprehensive BI stack and could be squeezed in anywhere, but it's placed in the database players list because of its reputation as a handler of gigantic amounts — terabytes and petabytes and femtobytes (nah . . . that doesn't sound right) — of data.

This is offered through its Enterprise Data Warehouse product, and it is used primarily by companies that have massive amounts of transactional data flow daily through their networks — such as large banks, telecommunications, or travel-services firms. Teradata's competitive advantage is that it can offer warehousing, querying, reporting, analysis, and in-situ data mining, as well as predictive analytics on a large scale.

Teradata has partnerships with DBMS and BI providers of all kinds.

Netezza

Database-software providers are making another attempt at pushing the "appliance" concept — essentially the database software comes preconfig-ured atop a stripped-down operating system and other support software, and the whole shebang is loaded onto a purpose-built server. The idea is that you can plug your analytics appliance or reporting appliance into your network with minimal fuss.

Oracle tried this in 2000 with its 9i database appliance, but the product never sold well. Still the idea lives on; one of the new names to pop up in this market is Netezza. This company offers high-end data appliances: dedicated data-warehouse servers that use ready-made hardware and software compo-nents tuned and scaled for installation in an enterprise system.

Even IBM is now dabbling in the BI data-warehouse appliance under the moniker of Balanced Configuration Unit — no small validation of that business model. IBM also competes directly with Teradata in solutions tailored to high-volume transactional data warehouses — a market that grew at a healthy clip last year, despite some skepticism that it hasn't much room for more players.

MySQL

Sure, it's a product rather than a vendor, but there's nothing wrong with selecting a product you know you *like* rather than starting from scratch with a vendor.

Free or not, MySQL is a powerful and robust database platform, and because it adheres to most data standards, it's a player in the BI market.

ETL Products

Extract, Transform, and Load (ETL) tools are at the heart of any BI system. They are increasingly involved in other data-transformation tasks, regardless of where the actual code exists and executes. Think of the ETL module as a data-retrieval-and-management system. Its job is to communicate with every source of operational data, extract the right pieces of information, transform all that data into the right format, and then load it into the target system.

For example, you might be building a data warehouse that includes a field in which you want all entries to be in all capital letters with no spaces. Your ETL developers would build scripts to speak to the varying source databases in

---

The growing open-source BI movement

As was the case for operating systems (such as Linux and Unix) and software infrastructure (MySQL database), the open-source phenomenon has come to the BI world as well.

Pentaho (it's supposed to be pronounced as if you've put a thumbtack into a map of northwestern Nevada: "Pin Tahoe") brings together several different open-source BI projects — notably an ETL tool and a reporting tool. Jaspersoft is another open-source BI player, specializing in reporting. And they aren't the only ones.

The models these two companies are using follow in the footsteps of Red Hat Linux before it became a power in the operating-system market. The company's value in the equation is packaging the software with other key components and support of all kinds — from installation help to troubleshooting to training.

The approach is to deliver a capable product at a low cost of ownership, which is possible because of the negligible cost for developing the software. What buyers are paying for — and what the vendors are angling to sell more of — are the so called 'value-added' services (such as training and consulting hours).

a way that they understand. Then the scripts would run a transformation process that would remove all spaces and capitalize all letters. That process would ensure a certain level of uniformity in the data before it's loaded into a central data repository such as a data warehouse.

In the real world, of course, the extractions and transformations can be quite complex and can involve billions of rows of data.

In the late 1990s and early 2000s, the ETL market was like the Soviet Union in the late 1980s: large and fragmented. A number of specialty ETL vendors served the BI marketplace; vendors offering database products (such as Microsoft, Oracle, and IBM) had versions of ETL — of varying abilities.

In recent years, the ETL marketplace has consolidated, impinged upon from both sides of the BI information stream:

- The primary database vendors have made more inroads into the market, bundling an ETL product in with their DBMS offering, as was the case when Sybase purchased a pure-play ETL product called Solande.

- In some cases the makers of BI end-user tools have spread themselves into the ETL market, as well, to become more "vertically integrated" in the BI market. Following is a list of the main ETL vendors along with a few words about the product they offer.

Many BI project managers focus on ETL but lose sight of data quality. Although you certainly have to get the data into place and get it normalized, if it's not cleaned up, you won't get good-quality insights. A good question to ask any ETL vendor is whether their product includes a data-quality module that includes tools to recognize "unclean" data and whip it into shape.

Informatica

Mention ETL and Informatica is the name that inevitably is the first to roll off the tongues of BI experts. They are the leading pure-play ETL vendor in the market, and have been for several years by remaining neutral in the software wars.

The Informatica data-integration tool is called Power Center; its success can be credited to its quality and interoperability with every kind of platform. That's the key to successful ETL, for obvious reasons: Transactional data can come from any type of system — an SAP supply-chain application, an Oracle HR package, several SQL Server or DB2 databases, and who knows what else. Informatica can speak to them all, and doesn't rely only on open standards to do it.

IBM

IBM made a big splash in the ETL market by purchasing Ascential, a leading provider of ETL and one of Informatica's main competitors. There are questions about how well Ascential can be integrated into IBM's software ecosystem, but the move was popular with many analysts, who saw it as strengthening IBM's data-integration capabilities.

Oracle

As is the case with IBM, Oracle offers a comprehensive suite of BI products. And like IBM, Oracle didn't stick with its own integration product; in late 2006 Oracle announced it was buying Sunopsis, another leading pure-play in the ETL space. Until that product is fully integrated, Oracle's ETL tools reside in its Warehouse Builder package; there are also embedded ETL features in the core Oracle database. The problem with Warehouse Builder is that it can only put integrated data into an Oracle data warehouse.

Business Objects

BO made a name for itself originally with a suite of analysis and reporting tools. But the company has expanded into the ETL market with a product called DataIntegrator.

Microsoft

Formerly packaged with its SQL Server database offering as DTS (Data Transformation Services), Microsoft's ETL tool changed its name to Integration Services in 2005 (it's also known as SSIS). This tool is more robust and powerful than the old DTS application, and it comes pre-bundled with most SQL Server 2005 versions.

Other players

The preceding vendors own the lion's share of the ETL market, but there are several other notable players worth mentioning, including SAS, a leader in analytics tools. SAS has an ETL offering suited for companies that need complex transformations.

There are also other pure-play vendors such as Ab Initio, iWAY, and Kalindo, each with its own niche in the ETL world.

If you have strong developers, enough time, and the right kind of project needs, you may end up doing what many companies have chosen to do: building your own ETL software. This allows you to customize your data integration routines more precisely to fit your environment. A potential benefit is the immediate cost savings of not having to drop a large chunk of change on third-party software licenses. Just make sure you calculate the resource cost of maintaining that homegrown ETL package over time.

Analytics and other front-end vendors

The line between querying, reporting, and analysis is becoming harder to draw as queries become basic reports, which are then massaged to become managed and distributed reports, which can then be analyzed in OLAP tools and other analysis programs.

SAS

SAS is a well-known player for the high-end analytics tools it attaches to its enterprise-class data warehouse, built on top of one or more of the mainstream DBMS platforms.

From a competitive standpoint, no other vendors offer the experience and pedigree of SAS in sending data through the gymnastics of complex statistical analysis. SAS allows its users to generate consolidations and reports on large volumes of data with highly complex statistical functions.

SAS is one of the leading front-end vendors because its products cover so much real estate — including reporting, scorecards, metrics, and data mining that feeds tools for predictive-modeling and decision-support.

Cognos

This key pure-play vendor offers a large, robust set of BI products. Cognos was always known for Impromptu and Powerplay, its querying and reporting tools. But these days Cognos emphasizes an architecture based on Web services.

Business Objects

By some standards, Business Objects is the number-one overall BI vendor, but to make that case you'd have to include an awful lot of caveats about Microsoft. To be sure, BO is a pure-play vendor that's still standing after all these years — no mean feat.

BO is based in France and offers its products and services under the umbrella BI tool called Web Intelligence. The company has recently inked a partnership agreement with IBM.

Business Objects solidified its position at or near the top of the BI market by its acquisition of Crystal Decisions, an already-profitable company with a large population of existing customers for its BI reporting products. In 2007, BO reintroduced Crystal Reports as a Web service — a hot trend across all software markets.

Microstrategy

Microstrategy is a public company that was once a larger player in the BI world. The company relies on its consulting services as much as on its software licenses these days; it appears to be getting squeezed slowly out of the market by the competition.

Microstrategy is traditionally known as a data-warehouse and data-mart vendor, but in recent years it has placed increased emphasis on a sophisticated dashboard and visualization platform.

BI made simple: Access

It's possible to create a BI environment with the most rudimentary of technology tools. Microsoft Access has shown itself to be a remarkably versatile and powerful database tool. Microsoft Excel can act as a potent alternative to a fistful of expensive querying, reporting, and analytics tools — especially with the new BI functionality built into MS Excel 2007.

You can, in fact, create an entire BI environment with nothing but Office tools. Using VBA and scripts, you can write your own ETL tools that take advantage of ODBC and other common protocols to converse with data sources throughout the company. Then Access can house the data itself, acting as a "warehouse." Access has a built-in reporting tool, or it can

feed data into Excel, which can handle ever-more-complex pivot tables.

Of course, this approach has its limitations. Access is limited in the amount of data it can handle, and the speed with which it can process queries, among other things.

But the lesson is clear: a high-value, timely, actionable insight doesn't care who its mother and father are. Its value is inherent, regardless of whether it came from a fancy million-dollar system or a homegrown program cobbled together with rubber bands and bubblegum. Don't assume that BI has to be your company's version of an Apollo program. Start small and see how it goes before you aim for the moon.

SPSS

This specialty shop has become an important player on the BI scene, offering advanced statistical-analysis packages to go along with its reporting solutions. SPSS is playing catch-up with SAS in the number-crunching space, partly because it was late to the usability game, reluctantly moving away from mainframe formatting.

The sales pitch

The goal of almost every BI vendor is to dazzle your company's marketing department, or some other area that is unable to spot the drawbacks and technical pitfalls in a slick sales pitch. The vendors' solutions are inevitably simple: Buy this one single tool, install it, turn it on, and watch the insights flow.

The reality is far different from what the pitch seems to promise. Usually BI vendors have an entry tool that gets your company hooked on the product line, but to get the most from it you have to buy further add-ons, including other modules and platforms.

Not only that, but the installation is never quite as easy as advertised. It's always a good idea to have a central governance board to vet software-acquisition proposals by various departments and teams in the company. That's especially true when those teams will be turning to the IT team to install — and then support — the BI application.

Part VI
The Part of Tens

The 5th Wave   By Rich Tennant

"Did you know you could be 20 percent more efficient if you store spices in the same cabinet?"

In this part . . .

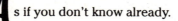s if you don't know already.

This part is a cornucopia of helpful info-gems that will make your life much easier, in one capacity or another, if you get involved with a BI project.

Chapter 18

Ten Keys to BI Success

In This Chapter

▶ Using sound business principles in a technology-centric project

▶ Being ready to adjust the plan and your approach

▶ Having realistic expectations about the project

*N*o book on business intelligence would be complete without a list of the top elements that have to be present in your BI initiative to make it a success. Consultants and pundits make their own lists — just as every vendor, academic, and anyone else who's ever been around a BI implementation makes his or hers. Of course, every situation is different; companies, market conditions, and personalities involved all conspire to make a complicated situation downright confusing. But if you combine the ideas in this list with your own knowledge of your company's unique qualities, you'll be on your way to a successful implementation and a valuable business intelligence program.

Picking Good Key Performance Indicators (KPIs)

How does your organization measure success? It seems an innocuous question — but an astounding number of executives can't answer it.

Measuring and managing key performance indicators (KPIs) is the ultimate goal of any business intelligence solution. KPIs are metrics and measurements that indicate at a glance whether the company is living or dying. The insights gained through BI should lead to better decisions — followed (presumably) by better performance that will show up later in the KPIs. The idea is that if you've picked your KPIs wisely, the business will prosper over the long term.

Choose KPIs that line up with your business goals. If you run a call center (for example), your BI solution should feed on KPIs like Average Hold Time and Average Handling Time. If you're the Chief Operations Officer (COO) of an airline, you know your KPIs will be specialty measurements such as Revenue

Passenger Miles, Available Seat Miles, Available Seat Miles per Employee, and other industry-specific indicators. These metrics may mean little to anyone outside your line of business, but to the executives at your company, they make the world go around.

Adjusting the Recipe

There's plenty of good advice out there, from best practices to full solutions. Every element of the bedrock of technology and business practices on which you build your solution is covered in a manual somewhere. But (here's a familiar mantra) there's no such thing as a one-size-fits-all solution. Companies are too complex for that; two seemingly similar technology and business problems rarely look the same up close.

Look at lots of options and take a combination of the best ideas and answers *that fit your business*. Bottom line is, use what works for you.

Coming to Terms with Complexity

Vendors and consultants make it all sound so easy: install this, configure that and presto, you have a BI solution that will send your business through the stratosphere. If only it were that easy. As straightforward as the diagram may look on paper, when you actually start descending into the details, you'll find a rat warren of complexity.

Planning for complexity is the best way to protect yourself from its negative effects. Assume that problems will take longer to solve in a BI project. Give yourself more time than you might in more familiar. And most of all, adopt and enforce core processes that can be adapted to suit all kinds of problems. That way, if you find that a given challenge is different from the way you initially diagnosed it, your team will be flexible enough to switch gears without coming to a complete stop.

Thinking (and Working) Outside the Box

It's an excruciating cliché but an important point. To find success in your BI project, there are times when you have to throw away the book (metaphorically speaking, of course — and not *this* one) and think about things in a different light. You have to set your ideas free from their cardboard prison.

The complexity of the technology isn't always a bad thing; it gives you alternatives when you've hit an apparent roadblock. Don't assume you have to follow every step of the path laid out by the vendor or the consultant; if you can get your team to think outside the . . . well, *you* know . . . if you can do that, you're likely to build a solution that takes best advantage of the unique strengths of your company and your team.

Picking a Winning Team

Your BI implementation will only be as good as the team of people that design, build and support it. And because business intelligence systems are interwoven into the fabric of the company, you need to have project members that understand both the technology and the business aspects of the task at hand.

And it goes beyond simply finding experts in their fields; you want to find people with the right attitude. Things don't always go perfectly on a BI project; it can be a roller coaster. Will your developers and business analysts and data architects be screaming with their hands in the air and big smiles on their faces? Or will they be turning green with every dip and turn?

Doing Your Homework

Business intelligence is a rapidly evolving discipline (like pretty much everything else in the technology world), and there's lots of knowledge out there — in books, white papers, blogs, marketing material, and a whole lot of other formats.

Never assume that you know enough. It can only work to your benefit if you become a subject-matter expert in the areas of BI most relevant to your implementation — and urge your team to do the same. Professional organizations such as The Data Warehousing Institute (TDWI), and expert trade publications such as *DMReview,* are great places to start.

Remembrance of Things Past (Especially Mistakes)

There are pitfalls and bumps in the road that simply can't be avoided. The trick is to remember what you did, make note of how the mistake could have been avoided in the first place, and figure out the best way to mitigate the situation should it happen again. Incorrigible optimists would tell you to think of every error as an opportunity to learn a little something.

BI project teams succeed because they take full advantage of their experience. And we're not just talking about business intelligence know-how; it's about other core skills such as project management and coding. Company-specific experience also helps seasoned staffers navigate confusing organizational charts, identify helpful resources and potential problems, and take full advantage of the corporate culture.

Considering Corporate Culture Completely

Every organization has a character all its own, and before setting out on your big BI adventure, you should give yours a quick one-question personality test. The way the company operates, how it's organized, where the power is, and how decisions are made, should all be a part of your planning process.

Successful business intelligence projects always include corporate culture in the early information gathering and design phases. At the heart of the corporate culture issue is the question of where the power rests in the company:

- **Centralized:** In centralized enterprises, the subsidiaries and outlying teams are operationally subordinate to a central core of executives.
- **De-Centralized:** A decentralized culture means that decisions made at the top of the organization are merely starting points for negotiation.

Design your BI team, project plan, and the system itself to merit the approbation of those holding the power, wherever they are in the company (up there or all around). That way your project is aligned with the culture; you'll get buy-in and cooperation from the people who hold sway.

Just Going Through a Phase

The possibilities for your BI project are virtually limitless. You could connect every operational data source in the company though data warehouses, and then route it to departmental data marts that would feed an array of querying, reporting, and analytics tools — customized to each department, with sweet visualization technology to boot. And when it's ready to launch (sometime in the next decade), you could have the Rolling Stones play at your stadium launch party.

Right.

It's great that you're dreaming big and in color, but executive leadership rarely has patience for such massive projects. Most companies prefer to move cautiously when money is being spent; they like it when projects can show small-scale successes along the way as opposed to making a big splash. And technology projects are notoriously tightly scrutinized by the boondoggle police, so don't book the Stones just yet.

Take your BI vision and divide it into manageable phases. Each phase should have

- ✔ Well-defined scope
- ✔ Tangible deliverables
- ✔ Benefits that can be demonstrated to one and all
- ✔ Modest time-horizons

If more than one Olympics is scheduled to occur before you're scheduled to deliver anything, you really need to consider breaking your plan into smaller pieces.

Adopting a Bigwig

Every project needs a high-level project sponsor who's wise, well-liked, even-handed, and ready to roll up his or her sleeves and get things done. (When they aren't available, a C-level executive will do just fine, too.)

Business intelligence projects are especially vulnerable to internal skepticism because they're often not well understood. And because the projects can touch so many pieces of an organization — that's the very nature of BI — it's important that you have friends in high places. Whether they are directly involved in the project is not nearly as important as just having their genuine moral support. A person with hire and fire power for huge swathes of the company has an amazing capacity to evangelize to and convert the skeptics, and they're pretty good at knocking down roadblocks too.

Chapter 19

Ten BI Risks (and How to Overcome Them)

In This Chapter

▶ Planning for the worst

▶ Convincing the company to climb on board the BI bandwagon

▶ Dealing with data disasters

▶ Spotting problems before they're problems

Transforming your company into a BI-friendly environment is fraught with peril; it's a task that shouldn't be entered into lightly. Plenty can, and often will, go wrong. Here are some problems to look out for that can strike your business intelligence initiative. Included are some ideas about how to overcome them.

Resistance Movement

A BI initiative can put your organization into a state of flux — and nothing gives people the heebie-jeebies like change. Regardless of the scope of change, it's always likely that you'll encounter some level of resistance to the install, de-install, or upgrade procedures you're trying to do.

Regardless of where and when it strikes, resistance to change must be managed by the BI project team and associated employees, all singing the same song. What starts as minor friction can quickly turn into full-blown negativity, leaving your movement toward BI de-legitimized and in tatters. Adherence to a change-control program is a good start, but the real key is communication.

Building lasting, institutionalized relationships with IT and data-management folks throughout the company is a great way to extend your network of allies. Setting up a central BI Committee or a Center of Excellence (COE) gives you an ideal company organ to exchange ideas, and it creates an umbrella of expertise over ongoing BI projects. Before you alter the company-wide reporting standards, talk it over at a monthly COE meeting. Not only will you get invaluable input, but it's also a step toward buy-in .

Moving Targets

One thing is sure in a large BI implementation: The data source, application, or process you're working on *will change* sometime between the moment you finalize the project requirements and the time you go to implement it.

Companies are in a constant state of flux; so are their data entities. That can create big headaches. For example, if you update a reporting tool to work with the latest customer-data definition, what will happen when you need to look at historical records that follow the *old* data model? Nothing can wreck a BI process faster than failing to account for the volatility of data.

Planning for and maintaining visibility in your master set of data hierarchies and relationships can help mitigate this problem. It's also wise to integrate your project plan with other plans in progress within the company. Is there (say) a planned upgrade to a new version of supporting software? Are changes in the works to make the ERP metadata reflect the latest corporate acquisition? Planning for changes like that ahead of time beats cleaning up messes after the fact.

Tool Letdown

There's enough hot air coming from BI vendors to put a fleet of blimps in the sky. Many a project manager has been burned by an application that fails to live up to its billing.

Putting the right tools in place is critical to the success of most BI implementations. Even with well-known vendors, the software-evaluation cycle is by no means a pro-forma activity, so don't skimp on it. Two principles apply here:

- ✔ You should establish a baseline process so you can give third parties a fair shake during their day in court.
- ✔ The level of scrutiny you give to a tool (or, for that matter, a vendor providing services) should increase along with its level of importance in your system.

After determining the scope and architecture of your BI system, go through the following steps:

1. Research and develop a list of candidate vendors that at least claim to offer a solution for the function in question. Referrals from professional organizations are a good place to start.

2. Pay close attention to the vendor's sales effort. Do they call you when they say they're going to? Are they willing to give you bad news about limitations to their product? An honest and forthright sales effort is a good indicator of a healthy company.

3. Demand a comprehensive demo.

4. Watch the comprehensive demo. But don't get lulled to sleep by the flashing lights and nifty graphics. Ask a lot of questions. For example, you could ask about whether every demonstrated product is included with the standard license scheme. Ask the sales team to explain common problems their customers encounter. A demonstration is not a presentation, it should be the start of a long dialogue between your team and the vendor's sales team.

Don't skimp on the software-evaluation cycle. Use multiple criteria to judge the software; don't just settle for the crowd with the nicest sales people or the slickest demonstration. Dig deep; it'll pay off in spades later on.

Being a User Loser

What if you built the system and nobody showed up to use it? The users are what will make your system a success or failure. There are lots of reasons why users may not flock to the tools you roll out. First and foremost, if the BI environment doesn't add value to their mission, they won't use it; it's as simple as that. Ensure that it does add that value by including end-users early in your process.

Too many techies think they know what the users want, and so they leave the average user out of the concept-and-design process. Get the end-users involved early in the process of gathering requirements; make sure you address those concerns and do your best to fulfill their needs.

Then, when the BI program is launched, support the user community well. Offer training and helpdesk services to pull more folks into the fold. And if the worst case does come to pass, where you build it and they don't come, find out why *quickly*. Don't sit back and wait for complaints and feedback to roll in

To spot problems well ahead of time, monitor usage trends in your BI domains as a standard policy. Whether the problem is simple or complex, the sooner you understand it and address it, the better your chances of righting the ship before it sinks.

Mister Data Needs a Bath

If there were ever a poster child for a Garbage-In-Garbage-Out system, it's the realm of business intelligence tools. If you have questionable source data feeding into your reporting, dashboard, analytics, and other user-facing applications, then their output won't be worth a ream of dot matrix printer paper. Questionable information can turn into bad information — and have an adverse impact on every one of its consumers downstream.

Data quality is an ongoing problem in BI, especially when there's a data warehouse involved. Different source systems have varying layers of controls and business-rule consistency. Include time to audit, analyze, and (if necessary) fix the data at the source if at all possible.

Source data is not a fix-it-and-forget element. Consider: Can you even *recognize* when you're getting bad results? And if you do recognize a problem, can you trace it to its source? Imagine what could happen if one of the operational data sources feeding your data warehouse just went through a business-rule change (which nobody told you about, of course) that allows users to change active account numbers — a field that your ETL process uses as a primary key. (Yikes.) Suddenly there's a chance that historical transaction information may have nothing to do with future transactions for the accounts that have changed. You'll have no way of knowing that this problem is lurking . . . *unless* you've put some careful auditing and data-change-management procedures in place throughout your system.

Dough a No-Go?

If your project suffers a budget reduction of some kind, don't feel bad, you aren't the first and you won't be the last. Whether it makes sense to continue any project depends on the circumstances. But one thing is certain: If the financial resource allocation isn't done honestly, then the project is doomed to fail.

Don't let enthusiasm for a project get in the way of making a rational decision about what can be realistically delivered. A natural tendency exists to say, "Well, I know half the budget's been wiped out, so we can deliver the following limited scope . . . ." Whoa. Slow down — think long and hard before you do that. For openers, try answering these questions:

✔ Are you considering all the transition costs associated with adjusting the direction of the project team to accommodate the smaller scope?

✔ Does the limited release still provide enough business value to make it worth it?

✔ Is there yet *another* budget cut lurking out there, a few months farther down the road?

Be blunt about the financial realities you face. BI implementations can provide tremendous value, but they are expensive. And if the company isn't willing to make the investment in a proper implementation, perhaps it's time to rethink the project altogether.

Scope Creep

Certain elemental forces are at work in a BI environment; there will always be pressure on the budget from unexpected costs or overruns, and of course there will always be pressure to do *just a little more* than you originally set out to do. That phenomenon is known affectionately as *scope creep*.

BI projects have a notoriously high incidence of scope creep because BI crosses into so many departments and often touches many different pre-existing systems. Before you know it, you're getting requests from mid-level managers you've never heard of before, and cleaning up data you hadn't planned on touching.

Avoiding scope creep is an active responsibility for you and the rest of your team. For starters, remember these basic principles:

✔ Don't hurry through the original scope; make sure everything is addressed.

✔ Anticipate change; build flexibility into your project plan. Assume there will be some last-minute tweaks by the Chief Financial Officer (or someone else you can't refuse).

✔ Hire great Business Analysts to deliver excellent business requirements, to put them into flawless documentation, and manage them throughout the life of the implementation.

✔ Respect your processes; remember that detailed change-management process you worked out so carefully back in the planning stages of your project? It wasn't just for show. Use it.

Scopes naturally creep. It's what they do. Vigilance is the watchword.

Rigidity

Okay, I just finished lecturing you about being too rigid when it comes to scope — but as with all things, there's a flipside: sometimes flexibility is advantageous.

During the development process, there is a tendency to think bottom-up — to make decisions on specific details (such as report layouts) without taking the broader context of the BI environment into consideration. That can lock you in to key decisions too early in the process.

Don't assume you know what the users are going to want and need. Here are some ways to prepare for their changing wants:

✏ Build some flexibility into your project plan that allows easy adjustments to front-end elements.

✏ Install self-service tools that allow users (with a little bit of training) to control their own experiences with the tool — running queries, building and formatting reports, whatever fits in with their work and the project's design.

Environmental Crisis

An initial BI initiative might call for different front-end tools to meet the diverse needs of different teams throughout the company. In addition, companies often install and add onto their basic BI infrastructure over time, creating multiple data environments that feed different customers throughout the company. This fragmentation of environments can lead to confusion over how to access certain information.

No wonder some vendors offer portals (or similar integration packages) that bring together multiple information sub-domains in a company's BI constellation. Portals work by presenting a user with a single interface that accesses several different BI environments, such as reporting or analysis tools. Usually two steps are involved:

1. A user enters a query for data.

2. The portal seeks out the system that can speak the same language and then does one of two things:

   • Returns the request

   • Moves the user directly into that specific BI tool

Chapter 20

Ten Keys to Gathering Good BI Requirements

Requirements are the bridge between nebulous ideas of what a business intelligence application or application suite might accomplish, and the completed, fully functional software and processes. They are the blueprint for the technical teams that will assemble the pieces of the BI initiative.

Requirements represent fully formed, clearly demarcated definitions of exactly what a piece of software will and won't do — and how it can accomplish the goals of the program.

Don't lump requirements management in with the project's other preparatory steps. The first priority of the requirements phase is to work out what functionality is *required* of the application(s). Any other design activity that takes place before that step is complete can jeopardize the entire program.

Managing requirements includes eliciting, organizing, communicating, and managing the specifications of the software and processes. Although all of these are important, eliciting requirements is first among equals.

But it's not always as simple as asking a question, and writing down the answer. Most analysts like the term *elicitation* rather than merely *gathering* — possibly because it's fancier, but more likely because it implies making the effort to draw out the requirements and business rules from the minds of the users and stakeholders; they won't just be lying around waiting to be picked up. You must shake the tree a little bit to get them to fall. And sometimes you might even have to climb the tree to get at them.

The following ideas are the best ways to make the most of the requirements phase; getting the stakeholders to admit to what they really want — and then distilling what they tell you into a list of what they and the project stakeholders actually *need*.

All the Right People

Constructing a good initial requirements document is only possible if the right people are there to help. And it's not just about being invited; the folks who show up for the meetings have to be ready to participate.

Facilitating a requirements session is as much art as science. Some of the smartest, best-organized technology brains in the world can't stand up in a room full of people and provide direction for a meeting. So the first person on your attendee list should be a skilled meeting facilitator. That may be an experienced business analyst on your team, or it could be a hired gun from outside the project team. Whomever you choose, a good facilitator will turn those meandering, unfocused meetings we all dread into productive requirements sessions.

When you schedule requirements sessions, make sure you plan two things very carefully: the agenda and the attendee list. After you determine the topics to be covered for each session or interview — well beforehand, please — don't just leave it to the representatives of each department to staff your meeting. Ask exactly why each person needs to be there.

For a BI solution, consider inviting attendees with these three distinct perspectives:

- ✔ Representatives of the user base for the business area you're covering.

- ✔ Subject-matter experts (people who know the business area, but who may not actually be prospective end-users for your BI applications).

- ✔ Technology representatives who can provide guidance for the conversation in terms of what's feasible and what isn't for the solution being discussed.

Techies also benefit from requirements meetings by gleaning key facts from of the negotiations that may not be addressed as agenda items, or even said out loud. The user-interface team (in particular) can get a jump start by absorbing what's said about the user community's usability tastes. As an added benefit, the meetings will steep the data analysts in the importance of certain data elements, possibly generating some early ideas about the logical design of the database.

Don't expect all the salient points of the meeting to be absorbed by osmosis into all the attendees' heads. You need someone there who can (and will) take excellent notes. It sounds mundane, but a good scribe can help deliver great results from a requirements-elicitation meeting — following the arc of deliberations, recording why one alternative was chosen over another, and tracking the action items that come out of the meeting.

The Vision Thing

Before holding a requirements session to dig into the specifics of a project, a good BI project manager puts every stakeholder on the same page in terms of the product's overall direction, vision, and calendar.

Doing so puts the details of the project into their proper context — something that's often overlooked. How can you possibly make a decision about (say) which graphical tools will display your data if you don't know the larger business purpose of the application? Sure, you can take a stab at such details, but usually the solution you get won't be congruent with the grand strategy of the BI implementation.

Don't just have a frank discussion with the stakeholders about the overall project goals and vision. Tie it directly into the requirements-gathering process. Explain how the activities undertaken during the requirements discussions aren't just idle chatter; they quite literally fill in the blanks for the application design.

When it's time to host a design session with your internal clients, remind them of where the BI application is headed, what problems it must solve, and what the important constraints are. Keep that vision at the forefront throughout the requirements-gathering phase — and throughout the entire project.

Connecting BI to the Business Themes

Every business has themes: What's the company trying to do? How are its people trying to do that job? Such themes represent the major imperatives of the organization. Here are some typical examples:

- ✔ Provide excellent customer service
- ✔ Grow revenues without giving up profit
- ✔ Offer products that are perfect for the marketplace
- ✔ Seek innovative ways to reduce costs while maintaining service levels

More often than not, these themes drive every major initiative undertaken by the company, either directly or indirectly — including its BI projects.

During the early phases of eliciting requirements, be sure you talk not just about the overall BI strategy for the company, but also about tying that strategy back to those same themes; your stakeholders should already be familiar with them.

Make Sure the Insights Are Within Sight

For a business intelligence project, be sure to define all requirements within the context of a specific insight you're trying to achieve or discover.

Each insight should fit into one of the major themes of the business.

As an example of how this works, imagine a large networking gear manufacturer that offers several different product lines. Their consultants sell solutions that involve a mix of components, all manufactured by their different divisions. Some components are even built by ex-competitors who were acquired and now operate as subsidiaries. Because sales and accounting systems vary across so many organizations, and because the terms negotiated vary from client to client, it's hard to get a profitability snapshot of any single client or solution.

Knowing the contribution of each division's profitability would be an insight of enormous value to the company. It would allow the sales management team to improve the company's performance by tightly managing the product mix for all future deals.

The BI project team should approach gathering requirements with that insight planted firmly in their mind. What data do they need to gather to achieve that insight? How does it need to be manipulated? What tools will the sales management team require to use to best take advantage of this particular insight? You may not know all the problems you're trying to solve, but it always helps to start with a handful of business challenges that everyone agrees desperately need solutions — that list becomes a central rallying point for the requirements process.

Business analysts are often tempted to gather requirements in a vacuum, keeping a tight focus on the agenda, and therefore the business processes that must be defined. Although filtering out noise of larger discussions allows the team to concentrate on each step in the process, don't filter *everything* out. As long as the insights you're after are well-defined and the stakeholders perceive them as immutable, they can catalyze the requirements process and keep it aligned with the broader business goals.

Greatest Hits from Yesterday and Today

Part of eliciting requirements is understanding the terrain on which the company is currently standing. That way, when you decide where to go, it helps you draw a line on the map to get there.

The requirements-elicitation phase is a good opportunity to talk to the stakeholders and prospective users of the application about how they're wrestling with the business problems now — *before* the first piece of the BI solution is up and running.

It's just possible that the way problems are being approached today can offer clues to how the developers should approach the BI solution. Seeing step-by-step examples of how a team currently uses information to achieve a certain insight is often more useful than merely cataloging information needs without any context.

In many cases, the user groups and stakeholders clamor for a change (or at least an upgrade of some kind) — but not always. When you go through the ways your departments are handling data and harvesting insights, you may decide that some of those steps — or even an end-to-end process — should be preserved. It could happen. Even though the software on the market now is more powerful and flexible than ever before, you shouldn't feel obligated to make a change where none is needed. Think long and hard before you rock the boat.

Consequences of Going Without

During the requirements-definition phase, it's useful to talk about the real business value of the insights you're seeking. It's not always easy to define, but a good starting point is asking the user community a simple question: If the project didn't go forward and you were unable to get these insights, how would it affect the company?

This is an important road to travel; it helps the project team prioritize the requirements in a way you can't always get by simply asking, "What priority should this effort take?" Asking what would happen *without* the solution also gets the group talking about qualities of the solution — such as response time, usability, scalability, and other similar specific factors that give the design team insight into what's lacking from the current solution.

In addition, does the pursuit of multiple business insights result in one process working at cross-purposes to another? In those situations, you have to do more than simply decide which one wins; it's just as important to think about why. All this discussion and discovery helps frame the project priorities, and makes gathering requirements more fruitful.

What's the Big Idea?

Gathering requirements is an exercise in understanding your company's information needs at the conceptual level. The best approach is to postpone all those high-detail discussions such as how the tables will be formatted, which data fields are required for each interface, and other specifics. Review the main themes of your business, and answer general questions first — these, for example:

- What information do you need and why do you need it?
- What (in general) are you going to do with the information once you have it?
- How will the information be processed or transformed?
- What insights will come from it?
- What preliminary steps are needed to derive the insights you're seeking?
- What information domains must be covered?

Such broad interrogation also helps the requirements discussions move along. It's easy to bog down in detail and bring the session to a screeching halt as two or three parties argue about which font to use in the standard report, or whether a display should include a pie graph or a bar chart. Such details can be hashed out later. *Get the big ideas first.*

Going Straight to the Source

After the general information needs are outlined, you must dive deeply into the source data. This task may require meetings with an entirely different set of experts, but it's still part of the broader requirements process. Initial questions at this stage include these:

- Where is the data housed?
- How can you get to the data?
- What state is the data in?
- What are the ramifications of manipulating the data?

Things aren't always as they seem. Different departments may have different definitions and thresholds for data quality. Standards and definitions vary from one team to the next; use the process of eliciting requirements to flush out any differences.

During this step, your analysts may locate multiple potential sources for the information you're trying to harvest. For example, the same data on daily sales could be held in different systems. The core information is the same, but there may be subtle differences in accessibility or format. As you evaluate data sources, decide which one is the best for the needs of your BI project.

Understanding regulatory and compliance issues is part of what this phase is about. For example, if your system is taking custody of personal-contact information, you may have to follow certain rules for storage and access, meet security standards laid down by a central data-stewardship body inside your company, or even toe the line with an external regulatory agency.

Adjunct Benefits

As important as focus is, peripheral vision can be equally valuable.

Building an application that takes advantage of and utilizes so much information opens up possibilities. With all this data, what else can the users do? Does the application add unforeseen value to other preexisting processes? The requirements sessions must meet their intended goals of flushing out business rules and requirements, but you should also use it as a discovery session, to get the stakeholders thinking about the possibilities before them.

The risk, of course, is *scope creep* — where your project gets weighed down by extra requirements. A good requirements-gathering process — run by well-trained and experienced business analysts — will be your best bulwark against the scope-creep scourge. . Ideally you can protect the boundaries of your project without stifling ideas and discussion. Stay on target but take note of the possibilities that open up by introducing your BI application.

The BI requirements session is a little different from that of more common IT applications: The solutions often cross organizational boundaries, bringing together lots of different teams that normally only interface with each other as necessary to perform their own specific tasks. A BI application must serve the needs of several groups at once. Teams may not be used to doing things for the common good.

If you have the data and you're joining it together, stay aware of all the possibilities. You might just discover a pathway to insights you never thought possible.

What's First and Why

Prioritizing requirements is just as important as listing them completely and attaching complete definitions to them. But it can be a painful process for the stakeholders who might feel they are being forced to choose between features.

Nevertheless, a good requirements session includes defining how important each major feature of the application is. And, in turn, good requirements documentation includes some kind of explanation of where the user and business stakeholders' priorities lie.

You have a number of possible ways to work out priorities for features and functionality; an experienced business analyst can run the requirements session through a number of exercises (such as weighted voting and cohesion analysis) to open the discussion.

While your BI project is still in the planning process, define in advance how prioritization disputes will be resolved. Coming up with a method on the fly could come across as biased one way or another. So devise a scheme that suits both the project and the client, get the blessing of the project sponsor, and then — most important of all — tell the stakeholders about it *before* the requirements session begins.

Chapter 21

Ten Secrets to a Successful BI Deployment

....

In This Chapter

▶ Designing a solid solution

▶ Resolving issues today rather than tomorrow

▶ Keeping the team focused on what's important

▶ Getting ready for liftoff (*before* launch day)

....

The first installation of BI tools is the trickiest, because not only are there the common technology hurdles facing you, but there are cultural hurdles and engrained habits that must be dealt with as well.

Because the environment is full of moving parts, it's easy to lose focus on what really matters. And this is no time to lose focus! When the curtain rises on your BI applications, the company will form a lasting judgment about your team's ability to perform, and about the usefulness of a business intelligence solution. In short, the first release will presage things to come, so it's vitally important to get it right the first time.

Start Early!

A BI project is like a big operations management problem, where the timing and quantity of raw materials deliveries affect how quickly and efficiently the factory can manufacture its products. BI requires specific decisions early on that affect the overall process down the road.

Among the first lists a BI project manager should make is of any critical *deliverables* (that's project-speak for discrete items that somebody has to complete or present to the project team, like a document, a project task, or a chunk of application code.) It's important to stay on top of all delivery deadlines — especially those where the lead time could balloon out of control. For example, if the process of procuring and installing extra network hardware in your company's data center is long and involved, *start now*. If your company requires a lengthy evaluation process for vendors before a purchase order can be issued for your core analytics software, *start now*. If there is a shortage of professionals with a particular skill you'll need, start the recruiting process *sooner* rather than later.

The more potential chokepoints you can identify early on for the assembly of the BI solution, the less likely they are to choke your project down the road.

Get What You Paid For

After you write a big check to your vendors, they should be on the hook for supporting you throughout the process. (You *did* negotiate that up front, right?)

Because a BI solution often involves multiple applications working seamlessly together, you'll need to get full support from your vendors. Good project managers know what was negotiated in the contract so they can demand the service and support promised. That means knowing and enforcing the vendor's *service-level agreement* (*SLA*) — the level of service, response time, and performance they've agreed (in writing) to deliver. If the software you bought is not performing as promised — or if anything you paid for isn't up to snuff — call the vendor on it and demand a remedy. Most BI implementations don't have the luxury of time, so if there's any doubt about the SLA, solve the problem as early as you can.

Software deals sometimes include such added value as training and support hours built in to the standard seat licenses. Take advantage of them early on in the build process. Demand exactly the service and support you were promised. Hold vendors to their SLAs. Don't save up vendor goodwill until release 2.0; there may not *be* a release 2.0 if your 1.0 version fails.

Only Losers Ignore Users

Users give context to the project; they help you fit the tools and processes into the specific business situation. They help define the problems you're solving, and they give you essential clues to how those problems will be solved. So get the user community involved early on. Earn their respect, ask for their help, and get their support throughout the life of the BI project.

Users will help guide the requirements process, but user representatives should provide consultation every step of the way — including during tool evaluation, testing, data analysis, and governance.

For example, during the coding process, an ambiguous requirement might prompt the development team to make assumptions about how the system *should* work. Stop right there. Your team actually doesn't know the requirements better than the users, so they shouldn't act as if they do. A healthy project team has regular interaction with the users, and can call on them for input from the real world as needed.

Name-Dropping

You'd think everyone would understand how wonderful and important the BI initiative is to the company, right? Well, even if they don't, it still affects them.

Your BI solution will likely spread across several teams and even business units, affecting a variety of different people. It's hard to keep them all on the same page because there's such a flock of them, and they have different needs and priorities. Even your own team-members can lose sight of the project's goals.

That's why it's a good idea to send notes periodically to everyone, giving them updates on the project's status, reinforcing the importance of the initiative, and reviewing the benefits of completing the mission on time. Hold rah-rah meetings if you must. And when you communicate with the outlying corporate units, if you mention the names of the executive sponsors, you're all but guaranteed to maintain your audience's attention.

People can ignore the wants and needs of a project manager or a database administrator, but drop the CEO's name into the e-mail as someone who's closely watching the outcome of the project, and they tend to take heed.

Testing 1-2-3 . . . 4-5-6 . . . and So On

Don't skimp on testing. No matter what.

The quality-assurance process has always gotten short shrift in IT projects; testing times get squeezed to accommodate the launch date in the face of project changes or delays. Unfortunately the same phenomenon occurs in the BI realm; testing gets cut where the projects can least afford it.

By the time you get to the testing phase the broad questions have been answered. You should have a good understanding of whether the array of applications you've designed suits the general needs of the users. But well-designed systems can still fail if they've been executed poorly.

If the system takes forever to respond to simple requests, or if the data warehouse in unstable, the users will avoid your system like quicksand. And it's only during the quality assurance process that you can identify problems with the implementation.

Testing shines a light on any problems with your original design. They could be issues with the database schema, connectivity, or even hardware. Or it could be a matter of usability. The more comprehensive the testing phase is, the more likely your first roll-out will be a success.

Go to Battle from a War Room

Every army needs a headquarters. And the best HQs are far enough away from the battlefield that upcoming movements can be planned and objectives assigned without interruption — but close enough to the action that communication with field commanders is easy, and there are clear sight lines to what's happening at the front.

Many BI managers advocate a "war room" for the first BI release. It's a great way to focus all project command-and-control functions and activities for the final important phases leading up to the release.

A "war room" is pretty much what it sounds like: putting all the key managers and architects in the same room during the final coding and testing steps. It saves time and heartache by simplifying the communication of changes, problem resolution, and testing issues. The war room means problems aren't solved in isolation (a phenomenon that can spawn other problems such as duplication of effort or confusion about deadlines). It also provides a rallying point for the team, creating a bonding atmosphere and unifying the sense of purpose among the group.

A cohesive team is usually an effective team. And since BI initiatives usually involve a complicated technology environment, getting the IT and business talent as close together as possible can boost performance in the final, critical phases of any project.

Project Management Management

Project management often involves a good deal of administrative activities, such as maintaining and communicating the project plan. For larger projects, it often makes sense to designate a *project controller* or *project administrator* who does nothing but manage the project plan and work through administrative tasks in the war room.

If you're well into a BI implementation that you're overseeing, the latest iteration of the project plan may have very little resemblance to the original version. That's not a sign of poor planning; it's a reality of building a complex technology solution. When you first create a project plan, it's a best guess about how things will go and what will be important to the project's success; after you get down to work, however, the project evolves rapidly from its original form. Some tasks you thought would be easy turn out to take much more time and energy; some tasks you expected to consume a ton of resources get done in a snap, or turn out to be unnecessary altogether. It's a natural process; don't let it break your stride.

Deal with Any Foot-dragging Immediately!

The environment — heck, the build itself — is a massive amalgam of moving parts, many of them critical to the function of the entire program. That's why you absolutely, positively *must* take nothing for granted when it comes to cooperation from external sources — whether it's a team within your company, a consultant, a vendor, or someone in-between. If somebody has what you need for your project to succeed, you'd better stay on them until they deliver.

The number-one source of delays for BI initiatives is in getting cooperation from the owners of the data sources which will feed your system. BI environments typically draw operational data from many different sources throughout an organization. Getting that data flowing for the first time can be a major headache. After all, you're the one getting the immediate benefit from the data movement — it makes your application(s) work! — so the folks who own the data don't always have a huge incentive to work with you.

If you sense any hesitation where it concerns access to data, tread carefully but decisively. At the first missed deadline, go immediately to the source and makes sure all loose ends are tied up. Make sure there are no security concerns or other hidden reasons why the flow hasn't begun. Have things changed since you first negotiated the file transfer? Has the political landscape morphed? Has the leadership changed?

You never can be sure of the data's exact structure and quality until you actually see it. Sure, you could design an ETL process based on a set of specs, but if anything is certain in the world, it's that data storage can be uncertain. For openers, different groups have different definitions and different standards. You just won't know what you're dealing with until you get your hands on those files for the first time.

Prove That Concept!

There's nothing worse than the curtain being raised on the big day and finding that your cast and crew needed one more dress-rehearsal.

A *proof-of-concept* (POC) is a great way to model the difficulties involved in a full-scale implementation, to flush out uncertainties, and to prepare your team for what's ahead. A POC is a subset of the total solution you have in mind. The scope is narrowed down to a few of the most important elements and functions. At its core, a business intelligence POC usually consists of a limited data-harvesting solution combined with a stripped-down version of one or more user tools. In most cases, a POC sets aside the detailed work of getting the user interfaces just right at the outset, and may even use more rudimentary tools and protocols than would be used in the full solution.

What you're interested in here is *whether* it works.

The POC system isn't meant to be the core of what will become the full system. It's usually made of pieces that can be quickly mashed together to demonstrate that the basic assumptions of the BI initiative are valid — for example, that it *is* possible to retrieve sales-transaction data from the regional branches, that an ETL process *could* be built to normalize the information, that it *could* be warehoused and used for end-user applications to gain business insights. The goal here is not to check off every system goal on the list, it's just to work through enough of the major obstacles to facilitate a go/no-go decision.

The Devil Is in the Details

Or perhaps he's hiding in that box you're always trying to think outside of. Sure, the glory is in finding the stunning business insights, or rolling out the graphical renderings, but don't lose sight of the day-to-day elements that make your system truly valuable to your enterprise.

Your initial roll-out should be easy to use — and fast. It should be accessible, intuitive, and reliable. When users mix the BI system with other applications they're already using, it should happen seamlessly. Those qualities are the foundation of a good overall solution. So whatever the scope of the initial roll-out, the system should be infused with quality; it should do its job well. If you don't think you'll have time to do that, you should consider reducing the scope of the project.

A business intelligence solution is often a patchwork of varying applications and a palimpsest (remember that word for your next Scrabble game) of IT solutions built in bygone eras. Some components will work better than others. Some pieces will be released before they're fully baked. Communicate those

shortcomings — even minor ones — to your user community and stakeholders before they appear in an error report or an email from an annoyed analyst.
Those folks are more likely be patient with a weakness here and there if they
know you're aware of the need for improvements.

We've Got a Live One

For BI applications, the flow of data irrigates the applications, allowing them
to spring to life. While you're building the front end, you'll probably use
dummy data just to make sure the software is working properly.

But while the front end may change, in both appearance and in functionality,
the data flow must be rock solid. If that doesn't work, nothing will work.
Because of its importance, it's a good idea to graduate from mocked-up data
to the real thing as soon as possible.

"Going live" isn't about whether the user-facing applications work (after all
that testing, they'd better); it really means getting actual operational data in
from all the outlying feeder systems. Getting the data feeds fully up and running is a huge milestone; throw a party and celebrate.

You always have to be careful in a project where you're altering source data.
Fortunately, BI systems usually only read data from external sources; that
means there's little risk of damaging source data. That's good news for your
project team because it means you should be able to start taking delivery on
the data regardless of whether your system is working correctly yet.

Going live also means receiving that operational data in the actual timeframe
you've designed the BI system for — in the same format you expect to see
when the applications are operational. Sure, you'll start by getting it in batches
as you test. But the sooner you can shift to full-speed-ahead, the easier you
can judge whether your toolset is up to snuff.

Work back-to-front; turn on the data sources as early as possible, *then* perfect
the front end. Once the core data-handling components of your application
are functional, then you can turn on the data spigot for the final stages of
development. That will simulate the way the system will actually operate
when you go live, allowing your developers to complete the full system using
real-world data conditions. If you're forced to wait until the very end before
turning on the full data-flow, your application may behave in surprising ways.

Chapter 22

Ten Secrets to a Healthy BI Environment

. . . .

In This Chapter

▶ Watching carefully

▶ Listening to users

▶ Evolving with the business itself

. . . .

*Y*ou flipped the switch, turned on your BI applications, and everything worked like a charm. I hope you didn't overdo it at the launch party because there's still a lot of work to be done. (But you knew that.)

Building on the initial success of your business intelligence deployment requires planning and resource consumption that will rival the initial implementation. That's because BI is ultimately there to offer a glimpse into the inner workings of the company — and some of those insights will provoke changes that you'll have to help implement.

As the company changes its approach over time, BI must be prepared to evolve with it.

The following basic habits will mean the difference between a BI system that's fully utilized, and one that withers and dies on the vine. These ten ideas will help keep your BI environment healthy.

Data TLC

A comprehensive business intelligence environment often involves data that goes through an extensive and confusing chain of virtual custody and transformations.

Pay careful attention to every link in that chain. You never know when a change could occur elsewhere in the company that renders a formerly reliable stream of information completely unrecognizable.

Data is the lifeblood of BI. When it gets lost, transposed, or transformed to the point where it no longer adequately represents the operational reality of the company, the system can no longer deliver valuable insights. Think of data along these lines:

- **Data quality:** Is the data usable and complete?

  Imagine you're trying to do a geographical analysis of customers and you find a large percentage of customer records are missing Zip codes. In a similar situation, customer-service representatives at your company may be entering phone numbers into the CRM system in a variety of formats — some with parentheses, some with dashes, and some with just digits. Part of caring for your data is being prepared to clean it up and ensure that it's all in a uniform, usable format.

- **Data integrity:** Is the information *correct*? Does it represent what everyone believes it does?

  For example, data quality degrades when one company entity measures things one way, and another entity measures it another way. Two divisions may be sending you sales data, but if one is sending you a daily summary and the other is sending you a mass of individual transactions, you'd better be prepared to do some work on that data before you combine it.

Hitting Budget Targets

The only thing worse than spending a *lot* of money on a BI initiative is spending a whole lot *more* than you promised the project's executive sponsors you'd spend. The significant cash outlays aren't restricted to the beginning of the project; there will be maintenance costs for the BI systems too. So you'll need to take great care in estimating them at the outset.

Data may be the lifeblood of BI, but money is the fuel that makes the project go. And your ability to secure funding in the future will depend largely on your ability to be a responsible steward of the company's greenbacks the first time around and after the system is switched on.

The final product may be different from the original design. So the maintenance costs may be quite different from what you'd originally estimated.

The best bulwark against blown budgets is a comprehensive and accurate scoping process. You need to understand all the major system components (that is, budget items) before you promise the bigwigs that it's going to cost a certain amount. Consider the following possible domains during the scope phase:

- **The number and nature of the functions performed by the system.** Did you implement more functions than you had planned?

✔ **The number of third-party software vendors involved.** If it's more than you anticipated, you might have different license payment structures than you had originally planned for. And if you ended up building some tools yourself, don't think that's all free when it comes to maintenance. Your team's time will have to be accounted for to keep your homegrown tools humming along.

✔ **The number of different data sources and the quantity of data to be processed within a given time period.** Are you handling the amount of data originally estimated? If it's more, you might be on the hook for more storage, connectivity, and security fees.

Your budget can only be as accurate as your initial scope estimates.

Sometimes, in addition to missing budget targets, you get the all-too-common budget *surprise*. If disaster is a possibility on the project, seriously consider sending up a red flag well in advance. Hey, it happens sometimes: Vendors fail to deliver, one aspect of the environment turns out way more complicated than you figured, or the solution — for many reasons — just doesn't come together the way you expected. You might buy yourself some time by delaying the bad news, but doing so reflects poorly on your approach to the project; it indicates — justifiably or not — a fundamental lack of concern for the company's investment.

Hitting Schedule Targets

The project schedule is another constraint that has to be managed carefully. Because BI projects are often a jigsaw puzzle of events and resources, when you miss one deadline, the effect can cascade across other milestones and throwing your project off the rails permanently.

Hit your schedule targets for upgrades and enhancements. After you power up the BI environment and evangelize its uses, you'll find that folks start counting on you.

But it's not just the software calendar that you should adhere to. Provide adequate room on your planner for training, reviews, governance meetings, and humdrum maintenance tasks.

Rinse and Repeat

Insert one or two of those standard clichés here: Don't reinvent the wheel as you're building a better mousetrap. If you had a process or a technology that worked brilliantly the first time through, use it again.

You probably learned a lot from your initial implementation about any range of topics. Maybe it's as simple as the way you structured the project team, or the person who taught the training class to the employees. Or maybe it's some large aspect of how the technology works.

Regardless of the scope of the success story from the first round, try to relive it as you maintain the environment. There are no points for originality in the BI world, only for success. So go with what you know works well . . . until it's no longer working well. Then, and only then, you should find an alternate plan.

Rinse and Don't Repeat

You've undoubtedly collected some bumps and bruises along the way in developing your BI environment. With any luck there's no permanent damage. But you can turn all those mistakes into valuable lessons that will help refine your process going forward. After all, life is for learning, right?

Business intelligence will provide insights into critical processes and functions in your organization, and the net result will be that the company changes the way it operates. It's the same with the BI implementation team itself. The experience of building the system will provide many valuable lessons that can be employed in the next go-round.

The key to learning from your mistakes is to have a process for tracking and disseminating the lessons. Maybe it's as simple as doing regular reviews and post-mortems, or you may want a more formal tracking system. No matter what you decide, just make sure that you go beyond identifying mistakes and missteps to creating resolutions. "Lessons learned" don't count for much unless you adjust your process accordingly the next time.

Maintain Team Knowledge

Repeating what works and avoiding past mistakes are part of an overall knowledge-preservation effort on your team. To make business intelligence part of a long-term movement in the company, the more expertise you can preserve inside the project team, the better you can serve the organization.

Some of the ways you can capture and maintain a continuum of team knowledge include these:

✔ **Write down what you do.** Create comprehensive process documentation including descriptions and flow diagrams for every aspect of the system including all data sources, the entire ETL process, the data repository, and all the user applications.

✔ **Document your code.** Have developers comment their code so that if one programmer leaves, others can understand the work he or she's left behind.

✔ **Develop and enforce a mentoring system.** See to it that the junior members of the team work hand-in-hand with the old salts, so all the secrets get passed down.

Remember What You Forgot the First Time

It's inevitable that the initial rollout will only include a subset of all of those features and items that you actually wanted to put into place. On top of that there will be suggestions and needs from the user community and stakeholder groups; they may be new functionality, or perhaps tweaks to the user interface or some other aspect of the BI environment.

Just because you can't do them all at once doesn't mean you shouldn't endeavor to do them all eventually.

Track those items that got squeezed out of your initial implementation so they can be added during the maintenance and upgrade process. It gives the users what they want and need in a very straightforward way, and helps the BI team portray itself in a positive light, by appearing responsive and organized.

Regular Updates

A business intelligence environment is like an infant: It can't operate unattended for very long without starting to smell funny.

If you let your system go for too long without monitoring and upgrading its components, it will spiral out of control. Your tech guys will be the first ones to tell you that the systems in a BI environment need regular bug-fixes, upgrades, patches, and all kinds of general attention to keep everything ship-shape. Believe them; they know what they're talking about.

It's normal for software companies to release upgrades for their applications; the makers of end-user applications in a BI environment are no exception. The upgrades and patches take care of minor problems, inefficiencies, and security problems, some of which may affect you directly, some of which may not. The same regular patches exist for all the supporting infrastructure such as the database tools, the ETL applications, and other middleware in your system.

In addition to responding to updates from vendors, there may be changes within your company (at the source-data level, for example) that require attention from your tech team.

With so many moving parts, a good BI environment schedules time and resources for the simple act of maintaining the systems.

Staying in Touch and in Tune

Monitoring how your application suite is behaving will help identify problem mountains when they're still mere molehills.

To maintain a healthy environment, you'll need to invest in good diagnostic applications and devise a process for monitoring application health — and quickly reacting to any problems that appear. That means more than simply tracking whether software is running. You need to monitor performance — how *well* it's running — to truly measure the health of the system.

Usage statistics tell you whether your targeted user community is adopting the BI programs. In your research you should have a baseline idea of what usage stats might look like. Compare those over time and follow the trends.

Communicating Changes

Your system is only a success if people are actually using it to achieve business goals and to seek and locate business insights. They can only do that if they know what functions are available and how to use them. So as a practice, your team should let users know when you've made upgrades and changes that may affect how they use the system. Did you add a server that's going to cut response time in half for queries? Send a note to the user community and tell them about the upgrade.

If there's a new application or function available, you'll want folks using it as soon as possible. Communicating in general lets the organization know that your team is active and that the system is evolving to meet their needs. It also spurs feedback from the company, which can never hurt.

Don't just talk to your user base; your communications reach should extend throughout the organization. A comprehensive communications plan means keeping the executive team informed of the latest enhancements to the system. The wider your communication reach is, the better.

Stay on the Train

When you buy software licenses, they'll normally come with a training package, or a set number of classes that your developers and other resources can attend in order to learn how best to install and utilize the software. But what's in the package is rarely enough training for the level of expertise you really need.

BI vendors usually *understate* the amount of training required to successfully utilize their products. They want to make you believe that you just plug in the new application, flip the switch, and watch it go. But it never works that way; you have to maintain an appropriate level of expertise on your team to get the most out of the systems you've bought and built.

Make ongoing training a regular component of the maintenance process as a way to keep the experience and expertise on the team at healthy levels. As an adjunct benefit, professional development keeps the BI team satisfied and lowers the likelihood of their departure for greener pastures.

Maintenance as a Process

In a typical application implementation, the maintenance phase begins after the software has been launched successfully. Unfortunately, a BI environment is different than a traditional IT implementation for a number of reasons.

Sure, there are standard software updates and tuning that have to happen on a regular basis. New people must be trained on how to use and administer the system. But the larger difference is that the very nature of business intelligence projects demands that the system is not really meant to be stable. It's actually supposed to evolve over time. Your team should be set up and prepared to deal with an evolving system.

BI is about transformation. Think about what business intelligence really means to the business: the BI environment, once installed and activated, should begin to produce insights about the business for its users. Those insights will (slowly but surely) make their way into the strategic planning process. They will put pressure on those original processes to change — which will in turn lead to new and expanded needs for the BI system.

For example, if a user community is suddenly given access to detailed client-profitability data, they may identify better business processes for (say) structuring contracts. But it's also likely they'll identify new dimensions of customer and profitability information that could be used to discover even more business insights. In this case, BI is not merely a catalyst for business change; the business intelligence system actually feeds the demand for its own evolution. Once users have access to BI insights, they'll get a taste for the power of information, and they'll demand more data and more dimensions of that data. It's a cycle of change that never really ends.

Maintaining a healthy BI environment means being ready to react to the changes BI produces in the business as best as possible. It's not always easy to anticipate those changes, but if the team and the maintenance philosophy are structured right, it's at least *possible* to respond appropriately.

Chapter 23

Ten Signs That Your BI Environment Is at Risk

Let's hope all that planning pays off and your BI systems work flawlessly. I wish you nothing but green lights and happy users in your future. But the bad news is, if it's not all smiles and handshakes in the user community, you won't always know it. It's not always obvious to the project team when systems aren't doing their job, or when people are dissatisfied.

Here are some symptoms you should keep a watchful eye for that may indicate your BI environment is at risk of failure.

If these things happen it doesn't mean all that planning — or your whole BI initiative — was for naught. It just means it's time to shore up the technology, the support, and the company processes.

The Spreadsheets Just Won't Die

If a report gets generated automatically, but nobody sees that report, does it really exist?

Your BI initiative may have taken shape exactly as you specified; it could be perfect in its conception and implementation. But if people aren't using it, all of that counts for nada.

One of the easiest ways to tell whether people are getting the most from your BI system is to monitor the transition between the old-style reporting-and-analysis tools and the new BI approach to the same problem. If folks still show up at meetings with the same old spreadsheets and the same old reports they used before the BI implementation, it might indicate that you still have a ways to go to make your product more useful and user-friendly.

Don't take it personally. Ask why people haven't migrated, and listen to the reasons. It's possible they haven't been trained adequately, or it's sometimes the case that the manager hasn't mandated the switch. Those hurdles can easily be overcome. But if the truth is that the spreadsheet is just better, you may need to revisit your project and find where you got off track.

Everybody Asks for Help

Right after your initial implementation, you should receive a torrent of requests for assistance with using the applications. But after the initial transition, folks should begin to get used to the new systems; the calls to the helpdesk should begin to trail off.

Of course, there's a big difference in the kind of calls you're getting, so you should always monitor the problems being encountered. If the systems are breaking, or if response times are unacceptable, those are problems you'll have to fix yourself. But if everything is functioning as expected, the calls will be questions about how to *do* something, or about where a feature can now be found.

First impressions can be valuable. Track the usability complaints from your end-users and incorporate fixes for the major flaws in subsequent releases.

Nobody Asks for Help

As Oscar Wilde famously quipped, "the only thing worse than being talked about is *not* being talked about." And so it goes with your BI environment. The only thing worse than getting a bunch of helpdesk calls is getting almost no helpdesk calls.

If you kick off your program and you hear nothing but crickets at your helpdesk phone bank, get out among the user community and find out what's happening. Maybe you put together a lucky one-in-a-million application with no flaws, but more than likely a more sinister force is at work.

The first question to ask is, do people know about the new BI environment? And if so, are they using it? If they're using it and not encountering any problems, are they using all its functions, and are they using each function to its fullest capabilities? On another tangent, if you don't get much feedback, maybe users aren't sure where to go for help.

Water-Cooler Grumbles About Usability

The best software in the world exists at the intersection of Useful and Usable streets. If you find one without the other, you're nowhere.

The two qualities are equally important, and yet so much more effort goes into the former characteristic relative to the latter. More often than not, developers and architects focus all their energy on making the products functional, worrying little about whether the user can easily get done what they need to get done.

For these problems, you won't necessarily get calls into the helpdesk. They will manifest themselves in the banter around the water cooler, and at the company picnic, and in low-level team meetings.

Never underestimate the role of usability in software. Make usability a priority during the design process.

And we're not just talking about user interfaces. Sure it's important that the tab order is correct, that the buttons are big enough, and that the font is readable. But the *process* has to be usable as well. A great interface is worthless if the database round-trip supporting it takes 5 minutes. Usability encompasses a lot of areas; and it must be on your mind when you design every element of your BI environment.

Good-Old-Day Syndrome

A relative of the water-cooler grumbling about usability is the chatter you'll occasionally hear about the way things *used to be* at the company. Maybe it concerns discomfort over a new process, or maybe it's a specific application that's being fondly remembered.

But if people are talking about it, it means the current BI suite isn't doing its job as well as it should.

Separate out transition talk from meaningful opinion on the quality and utility of the BI environment. Introducing a new application produces instant good-old-days syndrome. The indication of the problem occurs when that syndrome never seems to go away.

Usage Numbers Decline Over Time

Your usage statistics should steadily rise as more and more people turn on to the usefulness of the BI application suite.

Don't worry about occasional dips in usage numbers; there will be inevitable fluctuations as user teams get up to speed. But if you notice a steady decline in usage statistics, beware of some underlying problems in your environment:

- **The most obvious source of the problem is that people aren't yet comfortable with the new reporting or analytics tool.**

  That's hard to diagnose because those complaints often stay hidden. But it's easy to fix; give some enhanced training classes, or have your executive sponsors remind the team of the new standards.

- **Maybe your application is simply not delivering value to the user community. The insights that you promised aren't being produced.**

  That problem's easier to diagnose, but harder to fix. You'll need to check back in with all your stakeholders and do an assessment of where the shortcomings are, then make some tough choices about whether to tweak the environment, or (in the worst case) to pull the plug entirely.

BI Tools Aren't Part of Strategy Discussions

In a healthy BI environment, particularly as it concerns IT, the data-collection and aggregation tools should become part of the strategic landscape of the company.

Business intelligence is as much an ongoing management philosophy as it is a set of tools and processes. BI, if done right, should produce changes in the way things are done at your company. If it's successful in delivering insights about the profit margins of each product line, the corporate bigwigs will want to transplant the successful approach to other data-heavy areas of the business.

If you find that's not happening, there may be a problem with what you've delivered. A BI-centric approach to strategy will spread only as far as your existing environment is successful.

The same holds true no matter the size of your BI environment. If you have a low-level implementation that only serves a department or two, then the planning process for that limited area should include BI. Moving up the ladder, if

BI is used in one functional silo of the business, BI should begin creeping into the long-range business strategy discussions for that area.

Executive Sponsors Lose Enthusiasm

Nothing stays the same in business. While you are reading this sentence, some factor has probably changed dramatically without your even knowing it. So watch your step in the BI arena; the Big Kahuna championing your project today could be badmouthing it tomorrow.

Don't take the support of your executive sponsors for granted. Their situation may change, or the circumstances surrounding the business can easily evolve out from under you. Stay in close touch with the sponsor's needs; be as responsive as possible to his or her concerns.

One of your priorities is to make sponsors look good. It might feel like it's your project, but their name is on it. So you need to create a workable product in a way that suits your executive sponsor's wishes.

Executive Sponsors Lose their Jobs

There's always the possibility that your corner-office champions change jobs or leave the company. That leaves any pet projects they left behind at risk; often the replacement exec starts by evaluating his or her portfolio for weak links.

Even if the project is sound and the business utility is high, it's always possible the new executive won't see it or understand. So be prepared to make your case early. Don't wait till he or she contacts you; make a pre-emptive strike before any hint of negativity has had a chance to take root. The sales pitch you made to the original sponsor was successful, so why not deliver an encore performance? Just make sure you recognize what the factors were in your original sponsor's departure; if they had anything to do with your project or with BI in general, be prepared to address them head-on. A great way to do that is to demonstrate examples of your early successes. And if there are any manager-level folks who've benefited from your project, have them put in a good word for you as well.

From a political perspective, it's important to be aware of the circumstances surrounding the departure of your project's benefactor. If that executive left under a cloud of controversy, you might change your approach in a way that minimizes your connection to the previous regime.

If your pitch fails and the new executive doesn't take the bait, look elsewhere for a champion. Perhaps the progress you've made has changed some minds in other areas of the company, or in other corner offices.

Resistance to Upgrades and Expansion

Money talks when it comes to IT projects. Projects that have the faith of the company and the confidence of the executives are the ones that appear on next year's budget.

After the initial implementation, you probably have lots of plans about upgrades and expansion features. You may want to build on to current applications or add brand new ones — say, add capacity to the database or put some cutting-edge protocols in place.

But if you're having trouble getting budget approval for such ventures, you should probably take a hard look at the environment you're currently operating. Is it doing what you promised it would do? You'll need to establish a track record before going to the well again — and if that's not possible with the technology and tools you have in place now, you'd better find a way to justify pouring more money into the project.

Index

• C •

• *D* •

BUSINESS, CAREERS & PERSONAL FINANCE

0-7645-9847-3   0-7645-2431-3

Also available:
- Business Plans Kit For Dummies
  0-7645-9794-9
- Economics For Dummies
  0-7645-5726-2
- Grant Writing For Dummies
  0-7645-8416-2
- Home Buying For Dummies
  0-7645-5331-3
- Managing For Dummies
  0-7645-1771-6
- Marketing For Dummies
  0-7645-5600-2
- Personal Finance For Dummies
  0-7645-2590-5*
- Resumes For Dummies
  0-7645-5471-9
- Selling For Dummies
  0-7645-5363-1
- Six Sigma For Dummies
  0-7645-6798-5
- Small Business Kit For Dummies
  0-7645-5984-2
- Starting an eBay Business For Dummies
  0-7645-6924-4
- Your Dream Career For Dummies
  0-7645-9795-7

HOME & BUSINESS COMPUTER BASICS

0-470-05432-8   0-471-75421-8

Also available:
- Cleaning Windows Vista For Dummies
  0-471-78293-9
- Excel 2007 For Dummies
  0-470-03737-7
- Mac OS X Tiger For Dummies
  0-7645-7675-5
- MacBook For Dummies
  0-470-04859-X
- Macs For Dummies
  0-470-04849-2
- Office 2007 For Dummies
  0-470-00923-3
- Outlook 2007 For Dummies
  0-470-03830-6
- PCs For Dummies
  0-7645-8958-X
- Salesforce.com For Dummies
  0-470-04893-X
- Upgrading & Fixing Laptops For Dummies
  0-7645-8959-8
- Word 2007 For Dummies
  0-470-03658-3
- Quicken 2007 For Dummies
  0-470-04600-7

FOOD, HOME, GARDEN, HOBBIES, MUSIC & PETS

0-7645-8404-9   0-7645-9904-6

Also available:
- Candy Making For Dummies
  0-7645-9734-5
- Card Games For Dummies
  0-7645-9910-0
- Crocheting For Dummies
  0-7645-4151-X
- Dog Training For Dummies
  0-7645-8418-9
- Healthy Carb Cookbook For Dummies
  0-7645-8476-6
- Home Maintenance For Dummies
  0-7645-5215-5
- Horses For Dummies
  0-7645-9797-3
- Jewelry Making & Beading For Dummies
  0-7645-2571-9
- Orchids For Dummies
  0-7645-6759-4
- Puppies For Dummies
  0-7645-5255-4
- Rock Guitar For Dummies
  0-7645-5356-9
- Sewing For Dummies
  0-7645-6847-7
- Singing For Dummies
  0-7645-2475-5

INTERNET & DIGITAL MEDIA

0-470-04529-9   0-470-04894-8

Also available:
- Blogging For Dummies
  0-471-77084-1
- Digital Photography For Dummies
  0-7645-9802-3
- Digital Photography All-in-One Desk Reference For Dummies
  0-470-03743-1
- Digital SLR Cameras and Photography For Dummies
  0-7645-9803-1
- eBay Business All-in-One Desk Reference For Dummies
  0-7645-8438-3
- HDTV For Dummies
  0-470-09673-X
- Home Entertainment PCs For Dummies
  0-470-05523-5
- MySpace For Dummies
  0-470-09529-6
- Search Engine Optimization For Dummies
  0-471-97998-8
- Skype For Dummies
  0-470-04891-3
- The Internet For Dummies
  0-7645-8996-2
- Wiring Your Digital Home For Dummies
  0-471-91830-X

* Separate Canadian edition also available
† Separate U.K. edition also available

Available wherever books are sold. For more information or to order direct: U.S. customers visit www.dummies.com or call 1-877-762-2974.
U.K. customers visit www.wileyeurope.com or call 0800 243407. Canadian customers visit www.wiley.ca or call 1-800-567-4797.

SPORTS, FITNESS, PARENTING, RELIGION & SPIRITUALITY

0-471-76871-5

0-7645-7841-3

Also available:
- Catholicism For Dummies
  0-7645-5391-7
- Exercise Balls For Dummies
  0-7645-5623-1
- Fitness For Dummies
  0-7645-7851-0
- Football For Dummies
  0-7645-3936-1
- Judaism For Dummies
  0-7645-5299-6
- Potty Training For Dummies
  0-7645-5417-4
- Buddhism For Dummies
  0-7645-5359-3

- Pregnancy For Dummies
  0-7645-4483-7 †
- Ten Minute Tone-Ups For Dummies
  0-7645-7207-5
- NASCAR For Dummies
  0-7645-7681-X
- Religion For Dummies
  0-7645-5264-3
- Soccer For Dummies
  0-7645-5229-5
- Women in the Bible For Dummies
  0-7645-8475-8

TRAVEL

0-7645-7749-2

0-7645-6945-7

Also available:
- Alaska For Dummies
  0-7645-7746-8
- Cruise Vacations For Dummies
  0-7645-6941-4
- England For Dummies
  0-7645-4276-1
- Europe For Dummies
  0-7645-7529-5
- Germany For Dummies
  0-7645-7823-5
- Hawaii For Dummies
  0-7645-7402-7

- Italy For Dummies
  0-7645-7386-1
- Las Vegas For Dummies
  0-7645-7382-9
- London For Dummies
  0-7645-4277-X
- Paris For Dummies
  0-7645-7630-5
- RV Vacations For Dummies
  0-7645-4442-X
- Walt Disney World & Orlando
  For Dummies
  0-7645-9660-8

GRAPHICS, DESIGN & WEB DEVELOPMENT

0-7645-8815-X

0-7645-9571-7

Also available:
- 3D Game Animation For Dummies
  0-7645-8789-7
- AutoCAD 2006 For Dummies
  0-7645-8925-3
- Building a Web Site For Dummies
  0-7645-7144-3
- Creating Web Pages For Dummies
  0-470-08030-2
- Creating Web Pages All-in-One Desk
  Reference For Dummies
  0-7645-4345-8
- Dreamweaver 8 For Dummies
  0-7645-9649-7

- InDesign CS2 For Dummies
  0-7645-9572-5
- Macromedia Flash 8 For Dummies
  0-7645-9691-8
- Photoshop CS2 and Digital
  Photography For Dummies
  0-7645-9580-6
- Photoshop Elements 4 For Dummies
  0-471-77483-9
- Syndicating Web Sites with RSS Feeds
  For Dummies
  0-7645-8848-6
- Yahoo! SiteBuilder For Dummies
  0-7645-9800-7

NETWORKING, SECURITY, PROGRAMMING & DATABASES

0-7645-7728-X

0-471-74940-0

Also available:
- Access 2007 For Dummies
  0-470-04612-0
- ASP.NET 2 For Dummies
  0-7645-7907-X
- C# 2005 For Dummies
  0-7645-9704-3
- Hacking For Dummies
  0-470-05235-X
- Hacking Wireless Networks
  For Dummies
  0-7645-9730-2
- Java For Dummies
  0-470-08716-1

- Microsoft SQL Server 2005 For Dummies
  0-7645-7755-7
- Networking All-in-One Desk Reference
  For Dummies
  0-7645-9939-9
- Preventing Identity Theft For Dummies
  0-7645-7336-5
- Telecom For Dummies
  0-471-77085-X
- Visual Studio 2005 All-in-One Desk
  Reference For Dummies
  0-7645-9775-2
- XML For Dummies
  0-7645-8845-1

HEALTH & SELF-HELP

0-7645-8450-2

0-7645-4149-8

Also available:
- Bipolar Disorder For Dummies
  0-7645-8451-0
- Chemotherapy and Radiation
  For Dummies
  0-7645-7832-4
- Controlling Cholesterol For Dummies
  0-7645-5440-9
- Diabetes For Dummies
  0-7645-6820-5* †
- Divorce For Dummies
  0-7645-8417-0 †

- Fibromyalgia For Dummies
  0-7645-5441-7
- Low-Calorie Dieting For Dummies
  0-7645-9905-4
- Meditation For Dummies
  0-471-77774-9
- Osteoporosis For Dummies
  0-7645-7621-6
- Overcoming Anxiety For Dummies
  0-7645-5447-6
- Reiki For Dummies
  0-7645-9907-0
- Stress Management For Dummies
  0-7645-5144-2

EDUCATION, HISTORY, REFERENCE & TEST PREPARATION

0-7645-8381-6

0-7645-9554-7

Also available:
- The ACT For Dummies
  0-7645-9652-7
- Algebra For Dummies
  0-7645-5325-9
- Algebra Workbook For Dummies
  0-7645-8467-7
- Astronomy For Dummies
  0-7645-8465-0
- Calculus For Dummies
  0-7645-2498-4
- Chemistry For Dummies
  0-7645-5430-1
- Forensics For Dummies
  0-7645-5580-4

- Freemasons For Dummies
  0-7645-9796-5
- French For Dummies
  0-7645-5193-0
- Geometry For Dummies
  0-7645-5324-0
- Organic Chemistry I For Dummies
  0-7645-6902-3
- The SAT I For Dummies
  0-7645-7193-1
- Spanish For Dummies
  0-7645-5194-9
- Statistics For Dummies
  0-7645-5423-9

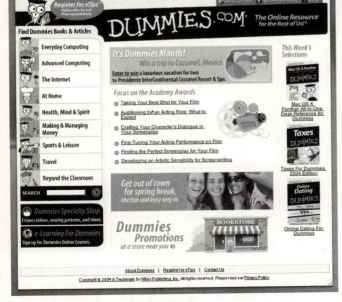

Get smart @ dummies.com®

- **Find a full list of Dummies titles**
- **Look into loads of FREE on-site articles**
- **Sign up for FREE eTips e-mailed to you weekly**
- **See what other products carry the Dummies name**
- **Shop directly from the Dummies bookstore**
- **Enter to win new prizes every month!**

* Separate Canadian edition also available
† Separate U.K. edition also available

Available wherever books are sold. For more information or to order direct: U.S. customers visit www.dummies.com or call 1-877-762-2974.
U.K. customers visit www.wileyeurope.com or call 0800 243407. Canadian customers visit www.wiley.ca or call 1-800-567-4797.